THE AMERICAN SPIRITUAL CULTURE

The
American
Spiritual Culture

And the Invention of
Jazz, Football, and the Movies

WILLIAM DEAN

Continuum
New York London

2002
The Continuum International Publishing Group Inc
370 Lexington Avenue, New York, NY 10017

The Continuum International Publishing Group Ltd
The Tower Building, 11 York Road, London SE1 7NX

Printed in the United States of America

Excerpt from "East Coker" in FOUR QUARTETS, copyright 1940 by T.S. Eliot and renewed 1968 by Esme Valerie Eliot, reprinted by permission of Harcourt, Inc., and outside the United States by permission of Faber & Faber Ltd, London.

Library of Congress Cataloging-in-Publication Data

Dean, William D.
    The American spiritual culture : and the invention of jazz, football, and the movies / William Dean.
        p.   cm.
    Includes bibliographical references and index.
    ISBN 0-8264-1440-0
    1. Religion and culture—United States. 2. Popular culture—Religious aspects. 3. Popular culture—United States. 4. United States—Religion. I. Title.
BL2525 .D425 2002
291.1'7'0973—dc21

                                                    2002010910

Contents

109482

$\mathscr{A}$cknowledgments

A T THE COLLEGE OF ST. TERESA IN WINONA, MINNESOTA, in the fall of 1960, a student rose to ask writer Flannery O'Connor whether, in the course of her career, she had received any crank letters. O'Conner answered, "Some old lady said that my book left a bad taste in her mouth. I wrote back and said, 'You weren't supposed to eat it.'"[1]

I am profoundly grateful to those many friends and critics who chose not to chew up raw drafts of this book, when it was tempting to do so, but instead taught me to cook.

Though having seen only the book's recipe, the Lilly Theological Research Grant Program (administered by the American Theological Society) and the Iliff School of Theology generously supported the research and provided the sabbatical time, without which this volume would never have materialized.

Added to their support were the labors of five consecutive graduate research assistants: Constance Wise, Carter Turner, Heather Calloway, Todd Kissam, and John Gray. On the chance that this book would be tried by fire, they provided the insulation—and my department's talented secretary, Maggi Mahan, wrapped everything together. In addition, parts of the book's interior were skillfully inspected by Andrea Dean, Roland Delattre, Mark Flory, Emmanuel Goldsmith, Vincent Harding, Anne Kleinkopf, Jeffrey Mahan, David Petersen, Mike Schmidt, Gene Tucker, Jim Wall, and especially Henk Pietersie and Jerome Stone. I received helpful technical advice from Janet Carlson and invaluable copyediting and typesetting from Maurya Horgan and Paul Kobelski. This disturbing truth must be added: while these people subtracted errors, I alone added them, at what I hope was not the same rate.

Editor Frank Oveis of Continuum International Publishing Group had the imagination to see in the penultimate stage of this book what others might have missed. Several fellow intellectual travelers pushed against this book vigorously: any more, I sometimes felt, and it would go off a cliff; any less, and it would have collapsed into a heap of untested assertions. It is Patricia Dean—among other things, my wife, shrewd companion, and lifelong editor—who deserves the credit for what clarity this book gradually acquired. She was the magician who gently placed a dark cloth over this book's cavernous hat, performed secret rites, slowly pulled back the cloth . . . and out jumped clean young rabbits.

These were ordinary people doing decent things. And yet their total contribution was far more than what the sum of their independent effects can explain. Say Amen, somebody.

$\mathcal{J}$ntroduction

$\mathcal{J}$ UST AS I WAS COMPLETING THIS BOOK, I READ FROM A biography of Abraham Lincoln a few lines that illustrated quickly what I had teased out slowly in the many pages that follow. In those many pages, I describe an America that harbors its own distinctive spiritual culture. This culture has guided America for one simple reason: Americans have believed that it speaks for a truth, even a reality, greater than America. It follows that, if the spiritual culture and the belief on which it is founded were to die—and there are signs that they will—then so, in most important respects, will the American nation.

Then, as I have said, I came upon the simple illustration of my hard-won argument. It was a brief account of the Lincoln–Douglas debates, which lasted from August 21 to October 15, 1858, and became the high point in the senatorial contest between Abraham Lincoln and Stephen A. Douglas, attracting the sort of national attention that allowed Lincoln and Douglas to become presidential candidates two years later. Partway through the series of debates, Lincoln had begun to inject the slavery issue. These lines describe Douglas's reactions and include his own words:

> Douglas was aghast at Lincoln's proposal to turn a debate on public policy into a forum on morality. Citizens and communities, in Douglas' lexicon, were simply individuals possessing the right to do as they pleased with what property they pleased as a matter of choice, and questions of whether their choices were moral or not were not the business of anyone outside those communities. . . . Douglas did not see why he couldn't simply "look forward to the time when each State shall be allowed to do as it pleases." Questions of morality were purely personal and had no place on the public square of

9

debate. If a state "chooses to keep slavery forever, it is its business, and not ours. If it chooses to abolish, very good, it is its business and not mine. I care more for the great principle of self-government—the right of the people to rule themselves—than I do for all the niggers in Christendom."[1]

After reading this, I realized that few Americans today could seriously adopt Douglas's once-popular stance. Consciously or unconsciously, most (even if not all[2]) Americans now believe that, over the long run, nothing can be trusted "to do as it pleases"—not a person, not a state, and not even a clear, democratic majority of the people. Even if a majority does favor slavery, that peculiar institution is simply wrong, morally wrong. Americans now accept this as a fact, one based on something greater than their own choice, greater even than the choices of all the people in Christendom.

That fact is based on a spiritual culture, but also on a truth underlying that culture. But what is that "truth"? Is it a principle? Is it a historically tried and tested law or tradition? Is it a God or something that functions like a God? Or is it, finally, a mystery? Unless these questions are answered, the American public will not understand itself, because it will not understand the grounds for its own moral and spiritual life. The following pages are devoted to one answer to these questions.

Admittedly, to invoke religious grounds for national self-understanding is extremely dangerous business. Have the modern West and Middle East not learned well enough that God and Nation should never be mixed? How could this not be clear, after the European religious wars of the sixteenth and seventeenth centuries; after the religion-sponsored maltreatment of women, Indians, and African immigrants in America; after the recent, overtly religious wars in Northern Ireland, the Middle East, Chechnya, and Afghanistan; and after the bloody campaigns of the Nazis, Stalinists, and Maoists, all based on worldviews so grand they are covertly religious? Can we afford ever again seriously to introduce any transcendent reality into a consideration of national affairs?

But this is too innocent. Essentially religious justifications *will be introduced*—whether explicitly through the faiths of world religions or implicitly through the metaphysical ideologies of secular leaders. The problem has been not that religious reasons were introduced, but that they were insufficiently examined and criticized. We live in the dark shadows cast by the misuse of religion to justify national action, but those shadows cover the earth. It seems impossible, then, to deny the presence of moral and implicitly religious grounds for public action—for they are there, for good or ill, like it or not.

A second illustration of the relevance of religious grounds: in the 1980s, New York's controversial mayor, Ed Koch, would regularly remind his New York constituents of the need for judgment and, implicitly, of the need for a standard in terms of which that judgment might be rendered. Alighting from his car, he would survey the suddenly crowded sidewalks and yell out to his constituents, "How'm I doin'?" It may seem odd for a politician positively to invite critical appraisal, particularly one that might begin with various items of city management but that, especially in New York, might lead anywhere. Nevertheless, in America, Koch's question is not at all unusual, for it has been asked thousands of times, beginning with the American Puritans, who addressed it not to noisy bystanders on a sidewalk but to a silent audience of One. "How'm I doin'?" they asked in so many words. This question has always presumed the existence of a higher standard by which to test how we're "doin'"—just the sort of moral and, finally, spiritual standard Senator Douglas wanted to keep out of the realm of public policy.

The rule of self-judgment before a divine standard is invoked also by American presidents. With slavery in mind, Thomas Jefferson would say, "I tremble for my country when I reflect that God is just: that his justice cannot sleep forever." Abraham Lincoln would warn that "the Almighty has his own purposes," and that even then the Almighty was judging America in its Civil War. Over a century later, Richard Nixon, having learned something from his public experiences, would caution his fellow Americans not to be foolishly caught off guard by the power that "moves the world for good or ill."[3]

In Mayor Koch's New York City the self-judgment was not so straightforward, primarily because the ultimate grounds for such judgment were hardly intelligible, let alone believable. That religious confusion has become our twenty-first century problem. But some lesser religious confusion has always been an American condition, and for good reason. Puritans, New Yorkers, and most Americans were, and still are, relatively recent immigrants, removed from the cultural influences of some Old World. Uprooted as they were, they could not judge themselves by any mother country's standards, now no longer available in bloodlines, ancient landmarks, or given artistic, intellectual, and religious traditions. America was not tracing paper; it could not copy the standard line from an indelible past.

Knowing this, Americans had to do the only thing possible: they had to look not backward but forward, testing their performance in terms of its future consequences. Hence, they became eminently pragmatic and made pragmatism eminently American. But they were not stupidly pragmatic, believing that any consequences whatsoever were equally good. They wanted to know whether a consequence was successful, and that required some standard of success that transcended the world of ordinary consequences. Thus, the question of a transcendent principle for pragmatic judgment was endemic to America.

If Americans were out of sync with Old Worlds, they could not simply appropriate Old World standards but had somehow to find their own standards or, as was usually the case, to warp Old World standards until they fit their own unique contours and circumstances. This shook Americans to their foundations and caused them, consciously or unconsciously, to rebuild their world from the bottom up. So, it is not surprising that today the Americans are the most openly and energetically religious, even theological, of all peoples among the economically "developed nations."

These standards were shaped to fit the dimensions of a nation rather than of a person. Americans have been religious in all the obvious ways— belonging to churches, synagogues, and mosques; nurturing a private spirituality; and believing in science-violating miracles. But they were religious also in public ways, for, as a whole people, they aimed to find standards large enough to frame their common life and to judge them and their country. As a people, they were always testing themselves, seeing their corporate life as the great "American experiment," making their own performance the object of that experiment, and invoking standards.

If this was implicitly religious work, it involved a public religiousness that, in principle, did not violate the separation of church and state. Rather than outlaw such public religiousness, the First Amendment *guaranteed* it, making it, perhaps, *the* form of "free exercise," and keeping it free by making sure it was never "established." This was a religiousness inevitably buried in any serious political philosophy or in any public activity that addressed the whole gamut of American affairs. This was a religiousness that was to test society's deepest assumptions and to keep them warm and limber by the fire of free and unrelenting disputation.

But, despite its obvious importance, public religious disputation has also been curtailed. It was curtailed partly because serious religious criticism was seldom practiced, and such criticism was scarce because serious religious critics were scarce. Nevertheless, just as there are economic, political, social, and aesthetic cultures in America, there is also a spiritual culture. Just as there are social critics and culture critics, there are also religious critics. In fact, the spiritual culture is the foundation of America's common culture, and its religious critics, however hard to find, are the most basic thinkers among American public intellectuals. Today, however, the American spiritual culture stands largely impervious to serious theological analysis, and America's religious critics are losing their voice. Given the growing confusion and division in America— notwithstanding the so-called "coming together" that followed the terrorist attack of September 11, 2001—the need for ongoing appraisal of America's spiritual culture, as this might be conducted by religious critics, is urgent. It is particularly urgent, it should be added, because that terrorist attack was born of partial misconceptions of American cultural and spiritual values, all too easily acquired when America has become so unaccountably reticent.

The paucity of religious criticism can be illustrated by Richard Posner's recent *Public Intellectuals*. There he lists the 546 American public intellectuals most cited in the period 1995–2000, of which I count only six as religious critics—that is, public intellectuals whose basic analysis is religious. Assuming Posner's count is accurate, this low count, so disproportionate to its need, can be attributed to religious thinkers as much as to their potential audience. With only a few exceptions, academic religious thinkers are unresponsive to today's much-touted "spiritual hunger," and nonacademic religious thinkers are unresponsive to the intellectual challenges of postmodernism—its pluralism and relativism, in particular. Academic liberals are, to put it gently, too vulnerable to cultural and academic fashions; and nonacademic conservatives, including the religious right, are not vulnerable enough to the cultural and intellectual demands of the age. If no dramatic changes occur, in the twenty-first century no erstwhile religious critics will be able to justify their inclusion on any new list of leading public intellectuals.

The key to the religious critics' dysfunctionality may be that they have little comprehension of America and its specific cultural, intellectual, and religious history. They may be, in short, poorly equipped to recast religious thinking in molds that fit the emotions and meanings of most Americans. Even though they know that the American situation calls for the reconception of their religious thinking and criticism, they continue to pour that thinking and criticism into molds provided by other times and places—primarily, ancient Jerusalem, medieval and Reformation Europe, or nineteenth-century revivalist America—or in molds with no place for spiritual values.

What is needed, in short, are religious thinkers grounded in the emerging American story and a concept of God or of "the Ultimate" that is ger-

mane to that story. Finally, to be persuasive, their proposals must be veri-
fied in and validated by contemporary American culture, even popular
culture.

Lively disputation between religious reasons and public decisions has,
however, also been curtailed partly through the erection of a high wall separating church and state and by the digging of a deep moat between public and religious standards of truth. Together, these have sometimes abused
the First Amendment, making it the enemy rather than the protector of the
free and anti-establishment exercise of religious criticism. Of course, given
the terrible previous associations between religion and public life, some
separation and much intellectual skepticism are in order. However, there
are signs that the lessons of the past have been overlearned and that skepticism about the public exercise of religious analysis has gone too far. It
appears that during the recent cultural night, the linchpin for the American experiment and, with it, America's *raison d'être*, was quietly slipped off
and thrown away.

Nevertheless, Mayor Ed Koch was unwilling simply to do as he pleased.
When he asked "How'm I doin'?" he sought confirmation through asking a real and a religious question, one that could have painful answers.
And, in this, he was more representative of America than was Senator
Stephen A. Douglas, who—for at least one moment in his famous debates
with Lincoln—wanted a state and, apparently, a country that would "do as
it pleases," and let the chips fall where they may. Both Koch and Douglas
were coping with an elusive American spiritual culture.

In the pages that follow, I will attempt to respond strategically to the
elusiveness of the American spiritual culture. I will come at the nation
obliquely, as you would at a friend who has intentions she or he would pre-
fer not to reveal. I will use metaphors rather than measuring sticks, historical illustrations rather than social-scientific inductions.

After defining in a preliminary way the idea of a spiritual culture (introduction to part 1), I back into the question of the specifically American
spiritual culture, identifying first an emerging American skepticism that
seems antithetical to any spiritual culture (chapter 1). Next, I approach the
spiritual culture frontally, telling a version of the American story (chapter
2). I call the American people a displaced people and show how their displacement urges that they acquire not only a spiritual culture within their
corporate life, but the faith that this spiritual culture is supported by something greater than itself. Their displacement is analogous to that of the
ancient Israelites, who survived because they had a spiritual culture and

something greater than themselves who worked within that culture. I first approach that "something greater," that God, by calling it a sacred social convention, known and justified by its pragmatic consequences for the people (chapter 3). Second, I argue that this American and pragmatic way of speaking can eventuate in a kind of atheism; when this happens, Americans will have trimmed their sails to catch a sacred reality, but will have caught little more than their own breath. Nevertheless, there is in this an irony: the dawning acceptance of their own atheism has opened them to a new theism, which is best described as a mystery (chapter 4). Ironically, when the opaqueness of God is accepted, the presence of God can be better felt; I call this "the irony of atheism."

Apart from corroboration, this theory of America's invisible spiritual culture is just that, a theory. Partly to confirm that theory and partly to understand America as a quite visible country, I conduct three brief forays into three American popular arts, each time seeking evidence that the country is, in fact, animated by the kind of spiritual culture and God that I have attributed to America. I briefly examine jazz, football, and the movies (chapters 5, 6, and 7) and dwell on the large assumptions with which they are burdened. I ask why each of them was invented in America, peeling each art back like an onion, attempting to discover how it presupposes implicitly religious values.

I do not argue that the American spiritual culture was, itself, somehow responsible for the invention of these popular arts, but only that, had the American spiritual culture not been as it was, it is unlikely that jazz, football, and the movies would have been invented in America. Each of these arts requires for its existence a particular kind of culture, just as much as a panda requires for its existence a particular kind of bamboo forest. If America was a nation of displaced, dispossessed people, then that nation was built around a cultural void—specifically, the absence of a rich, ancient cultural heritage. If this void was to be filled, Americans had to learn to improvise on traditions of their remote motherlands and to make them their own. That cultural need for impromptu improvisation provided just the environment fit for the birth of jazz, itself based on improvisation. But where improvised identities could not fill the void, Americans needed to go further, to imagine a quite new identity. That need for imagination, even fantasy, made America an ideal place for the birth of the movies, themselves based on fantasy. Additionally—I would say, darkly—the American cultural void has, at times, felt like a cultural wilderness; and in that wilderness rough and ready tactics often seemed necessary for survival. It is no accident that football, with its ritualized violence, arose in a nation so deeply marked by the wilderness experience. In each case, these popular arts presupposed and then took on real but seldom acknowledged religious meaning. Perhaps, jazz, the movies, and football, even with their religious significance, could have been invented in cultures conscious of a rich, ancient, and indigenous cultural heritage, but it seems unlikely.

Finally and more importantly, I attempt to demonstrate that the quite visible popular arts of jazz, football, and the movies, as well as the cultural values that support them, issue in what I am calling the irony of atheism. Eventually, the deeper, religious meaning of each of these arts is undermined and comes to a kind of atheism. But precisely this atheism gives rise to a religious mystery.

PART 1

God the Opaque

Introduction to Part 1

The Spiritual Culture

O N AUGUST 8, 1974, RICHARD MILHOUS NIXON RESIGNED THE presidency because he knew he had already been impeached unofficially and that, for this reason, he would be impeached officially. But how had Nixon been impeached unofficially?

He was impeached by the country's moral culture. The judgment to impeach was not a judgment arising from economic, political, or military considerations; Nixon would have been impeached even if in these areas his leadership had been beyond reproach. The impeachment was a legal judgment, but it was more than a legal judgment. People reacted with personal indignation or sadness, as though Nixon had violated an unspoken national agreement. Judge Richard Posner argues that "Nixon was forced from office not because it was widely believed that, even though his wrongdoing had been exposed and his associates packed off to jail, he could and would still do serious harm to constitutional government, but because people were outraged by his conduct . . . ."[1]

However, Nixon was impeached for more than moral reasons and the outrage was more than moral outrage. Most important, Nixon's agony was more than moral agony, as was evident in the talk he gave to his staff on the morning his helicopter lifted him for the last time from the White House lawn. In a shaking voice, Nixon reminisced about his parents; he spoke of the deepest valley and the highest mountains, of the self-destructiveness of hatred, and of prayers to different gods that were prayers to the same God. Finally, he was seeking not moral exoneration but something closer to religious forgiveness.

Nixon was impeached by what can be called the nation's spiritual culture. That culture had risen already to a high pitch because of (to use Jefferson's language) "a long train of abuses and usurpations," involving civil rights, the war in Vietnam, and the 1960s countercultural revolution, each of which elicited reactions that were more than moral reactions. Americans had been stunned with the realization that the African-American

19

struggle for civil rights was actually a chapter in the unfinished story of slavery; that the Vietnam War could be fairly described as "the horror" (to use Marlon Brando's words in *Apocalypse Now*); and that the cultural revolution was ridiculing some aspects of America's deepest spiritual traditions. The Oval Office tapes that so effectively indicted Nixon became more than legal evidence; they became symbols of spiritual disintegration. When Gerald Ford pardoned Nixon, he did this because he detected that the nation was in more than legal and moral turmoil and that it was too dangerous to intensify that turmoil through a public criminal trial of Nixon—even if the pardon meant that he (Ford) would not be elected.

To say that Nixon was impeached by the American moral culture is to say that Nixon was impeached for the nation's own "good." To say that Nixon was impeached by the American spiritual culture is to say that he was impeached for a good greater than the nation's good.

What Is a Spiritual Culture?

In at least one respect a country resembles a person: it is informed by a heritage of past events that it continually reshapes for present purposes. Like a person, a country is coherent for a number of reasons; among these is the reason that arises from its picture of the world, which orients its impulses, giving them a purpose and a direction. English philosopher Julian Huxley knew that a person is made coherent by the correlation of itself "as a whole to its experience of the Universe as a whole."[2] Referring not to a person but to a society, philosopher John Dewey argued that a society is made coherent by its "sense of an extensive and underlying whole." Dewey argued that, in any particular instance, no society truly knows how to react to its local environment unless it has a vision of its total environment (its "universe"). This vision of the totality enables a society to interpret its particular environment—much as, say, a parent's theory of the whole family enables him or her to discipline a particular child.[3] A spiritual culture provides that vision for a country, just as a spiritual faith provides that vision for a person. Further, just as a personal faith need not be *explicitly* religious to orient the person, a spiritual culture need not be *explicitly* religious to orient a country. And just as a person's spiritual faith can be unconscious, noncognitive, and emotional, so also a country's spiritual culture can be unconscious, noncognitive, and emotional.

To understand *how* the spiritual culture affects the country, one more term must be added: the nation, the living community within the country. The nation is informed by the spiritual culture's sense of the whole as the nation makes the decisions that determine a country's course in the world. It follows inevitably that, without an active spiritual culture, a nation drifts, flounders, and eventually disintegrates.

I have argued that a spiritual culture was at play in the impeachment of Richard Nixon. But the nation, not the spiritual culture, reached the conclusion that Nixon should be impeached. In this process the spiritual culture provided the purposes and ideals that led the nation to decide to impeach Nixon. Nixon saw visible signs of the nation's decision to impeach him, and he acted on those signs. Thus, a spiritual culture has a public function.

The American spiritual culture is not simply Christian, nor is America simply a Christian nation, for the spiritual culture contains many elements that are non-Christian. (However, it is still predominantly Christian and biblical, with between 75 and 85 percent of the people calling themselves Christian and only 3 to 4 percent identifying themselves as religious but non-Christian.)[4] Nor can the spiritual culture be equated with a country's organized religion (the life of its churches, synagogues, and mosques), for the spiritual culture need not be overtly religious, institutionalized, or based on creeds or dogmas.

Further, the American spiritual culture can be perceived as singular, so that it can be treated as one culture, more or less continuous throughout a country's history, but taking different shapes in different historical periods. Here I may depart from two recent, excellent commentators, each of whom seems implicitly to posit four, historically consecutive and different spiritual cultures in the life of America. Economist Robert Fogel argues that there have been four "great awakenings" in American history, and political scientist Eldon Eisenach holds that there have been four "religious establishments" in American history.[5] Even they, however, seem to point to something like a single spiritual culture when they choose to name these as episodes of what can be commonly classified as great awakenings or religious establishments.

Although the spiritual culture provides what works as the dominant ideal for a country, not everyone in a country accepts the spiritual culture. As I attempt to define an American spiritual culture, I do not pretend that all Americans would accept this definition for themselves. Many groups reject the dominant spiritual culture, however it is defined. In fact, the self-definition of some Native Americans, Wiccas (witches), Black Muslims, or participants in non-Western religions requires an explicit disavowal of the American spiritual culture and any definition given it.

My definition of the American spiritual culture resembles what others have said about similar dimensions of American culture. It resembles what

American religious historian Sidney Mead called "the religion of the Republic" (although Mead gives a metaphysical structure to his religion of the Republic that need not be present in the American spiritual culture). My definition of the spiritual culture also resembles what Robert Bellah called "civil religion" (although civil religion accentuates the social and political aspects of the spiritual culture). Both Mead and Bellah make highly instructive observations about (rather than endorsements of) typically American ceremonies, speeches, and gestures as they pertain to what I am calling the spiritual culture.

For Mead, the religion of the Republic was espoused by leaders as varied as Benjamin Franklin, Thomas Jefferson, Abraham Lincoln, William O. Douglas, and Dwight Eisenhower. They made the religion of the Republic neither organized nor denominational, and certainly not the worship of the state. They sought "not to create a syncretistic common-core, but to plumb for the universal which is dressed and insofar disguised in the particularities of doctrine and practice which distinguish one sect from another. This conception enabled . . . [them] to distinguish between the substance of religion and its forms exemplified in sectarian tenets and observances."[6] Extending this imagery, Mead quoted Paul Tillich's dictum that "religion as ultimate concern is the meaning-giving substance of culture, and culture is the totality of forms in which the basic concern of religion espouses itself," so that "religion is the substance of culture, culture is the form of religion."[7] The religion of the Republic not only made the freedom and equality underlying American democracy sacred but grounded them in the deity.[8]

Robert Bellah, calling Mead "my closest predecessor,"[9] borrowed a term from Rousseau's *Social Contract* and named the religion of the Republic "civil religion." For Bellah, civil religion had its own institutions, standing alongside Christian and other religious institutions. He mined great public speeches and events to reach conclusions more far-reaching than, but similar to, Mead's (even to the point of finding within civil religion an essence, so that the forms of civil religion provided "a genuine apprehension of universal and transcendent religious reality").[10] Bellah argued that American civil religion, at its best, adopted what Paul Tillich called "the Protestant Principle" (according to which the finite, historical expression of religion might convey infinite meaning even while denying that it embodied that meaning).[11]

But what I am calling the spiritual culture is not equivalent to Mead's or Bellah's concepts or to analogous concepts advanced by others;[12] neither is it equivalent to the civil society or public philosophy advocated by John

Dewey in *The Public and Its Problems* and by Walter Lippmann in *The Public Philosophy*.[13] Although these latter and other secular versions of the religion of the Republic have implicit theological dimensions, their civic virtues are oriented primarily by nonreligious traditions and beliefs. Those theorists who discuss public philosophy today tend to ignore the possibility that it has theological resources.[14] Most philosophers and social scientists are leery of the very idea of a public philosophy, finding it awkward or dangerous even to describe, let alone defend, any national consensus at work in American culture.

My commentary on the spiritual culture is close to the public theology discussed recently, for example, by Victor Anderson and Linell Cady.[15] My commentary, however, differs from theirs because it assumes: (1) that the spiritual culture is only implicitly political, (2) that it includes common and distinctively American elements, and (3) that it is so inchoate that it is barely susceptible to discussion in formal theological and philosophical categories.

I do not suggest that a spiritual culture is necessarily good. My descriptions of the spiritual culture are just that, descriptive and not normative. When I do speak normatively, I will sometimes defend the goodness of a spiritual culture, but I will also assume that the actual function of a spiritual culture can be morally ambiguous, about as capable of causing good as of causing evil. After all, it was partly because it had an active spiritual culture that Nazi Germany was capable of the havoc it wreaked. My only consistent defense of an American spiritual culture is that, without an active spiritual culture, America cannot for long be viable, coherently organized or, in any significant sense, good.

This is true partly because in America the governing sector of the country, set beside the for-profit and the voluntary (non-profit) sectors, relies on the spiritual culture for the norms that inform its laws. The question is not whether the state will adopt norms (for it will, sooner or later), but what norms it accepts. Some ideals from the spiritual culture shape the law, so that the state's best protection is to do what it can to help refine the spiritual culture that provides these ideals.

It is precisely for this reason that the First Amendment to the Constitution is so valuable to America, for that amendment encourages the process that refines the spiritual culture. Among other things, the spiritual culture should be the site of open and critical debate about the truth of the ultimate values that inform American laws. If this disputation is to include an open, free expression of all voices, it must be protected. The "free exercise" clause of the First Amendment allows the spiritual culture to freely test and criticize its ideas without interference. Also, if this debate is to include as wide a range of alternatives as possible, no one voice can arbitrarily be given authority over the others, and the "anti-establishment" clause of the First Amendment prevents just such arbitrary authority. Thus, the state must be neutral about debate in the spiritual culture, because that neutrality, both in protecting free exercise and in preventing arbitrary dominance of one alternative, provides the minimal conditions for the healthy conduct of that debate. Ideally, neutrality should arise because the state recognizes its genuine dependence on the spiritual culture, not its independence from it.

Thus, the state must be separated from religion because the state is so dependent on religion, for religion comprises much of what operates in the spiritual culture. In being separated from the spiritual culture, including the religion at work in the spiritual culture, the state is betting that free, as against restricted, debate will yield the best advice, giving good ideas the playing field on which to defeat bad ideas. To be maximally effective, this debate should be public as well as private. Those who would stifle *public* debate on issues related to the spiritual culture are not protecting the state but endangering it. Ironically, the now-vaunted wall of separation that would keep religious debate entirely out of public arenas reduces rather than enlarges the freedom of the state, if freedom, as John Stuart Mill asserted, is made possible by the free testing of ideas against their rivals.[16]

Finally, the spiritual culture is distinguished by its claim to speak for a good greater than the country's good, so that it is capable of judging the country with an authority that is or is said to be more than the country's own authority. Although this higher good is sometimes called "God," it is sometimes called, for example, "Reason" or the "Patriotic Spirit" or "the Law" or "Human Decency." In any case, most Americans implicitly invoked this higher good when they judged Nixon.

However, despite the vitality of the American spiritual culture even as late as 1974, there have been signs of its significant decline in subsequent decades.

Evidence and Implications
of the Spiritual Culture's Decline

In recent decades, many of the social thinkers who have commanded the most popular respect have pointed to one aspect of the decline of the American spiritual culture, the growth of individualism. Among them are Robert Bellah, Christopher Lasch, and Martin Seymour Lipset. Their work is being extended by people such as political scientist Michael Sandel, economist Robert Reich, sociologist Francis Fukuyama, philosopher Richard Rorty, political scientist Jean Bethke Elshtain, and many others.[17]

Admittedly, these many testimonies to the waning of the American spiritual culture can be dismissed by dropping them into what historian David Hollinger has called "the American canon of lonely prophets of darkness."[18] It can be said that they only perpetuate an American tendency toward what literary critic Alfred Kazin has called the "endless whimpering of 'feeling religious' without inner content."[19] However, I find in them a powerful embodiment of the mood that historian Perry Miller discovered at the end of the Second World War, when he said that America's "smiling aspects largely ceased to smile."[20]

In *The Real American Dream,* culture critic Andrew Delbanco said of America:

> Something died, or at least fell dormant, between the late 1960s, when the reform impulse subsided into solipsism, and the 1980s—two phases of our history that may seem far apart in political tone and personal style, but that finally cooperated in installing instant gratification as the hallmark of the good life, and in repudiating the interventionist state as a source of hope. What was lost in the unholy alliance between an insouciant New Left and an insufferably smug New Right was any conception of a common destiny worth tears, sacrifice, and maybe even death.

This transition from reformism, to hedonistic solipsism, to the repudiation of the state represents a decline in what I am calling the nation's spiritual culture. On the one hand, the American spiritual culture persists. "The deposited ideas of Christianity and civil religion are still the bedrock of our culture, whatever intellectuals may think," Delbanco wrote. In fact, "the most striking feature of contemporary culture is the unslaked craving for transcendence." On the other hand, the ideas and the craving are eroding. Admittedly, this goes back as far as the middle of the nineteenth century, when Ralph Waldo Emerson ranted that people act "as if God were dead," and as if the Christian story were as dead as the poetic teaching of Greece and Egypt. "History," Emerson said, "gave no intimation of any society in which despondency came so readily to heart as we see it & feel it in ours. . . . Every man [is] for himself . . . there is a universal resistance to ties and ligaments once supposed essential to civil society." In recent decades this erosion has become an avalanche. Today, Delbanco argues, American culture is "in trouble in a way it has never been before."[21]

In his Prologue, Delbanco promises to close the book by offering a new hope, "a few thoughts about what new idea, if any, may be gathering form and strength." But, as one critic was soon to note, "it is hard to find these

thoughts in his final pages."[22] Instead, Delbanco comments on spiritual
musings of Graham Greene and Walker Percy and suggests that only a new
spiritual culture will do, but he never delivers on his promise to describe
the "new idea"—and, thereby, he inadvertently supports his own generally
pessimistic assessment by his own mute witness.

There is much in recent history to corroborate Delbanco's pessimism.
For example, Canadian philosopher Charles Taylor has recently noted that
the archetypal American philosopher William James simply dismissed
Catholicism's God-enchanted world, as well as Protestantism's later belief
in a religiously interpreted natural order and social polity, and replaced
both with a world of private individuals having private experiences. For
Taylor, James's *Varieties of Religious Experience* as much as says, "individual experience good, churches not so good." Taylor argues that James was
ahead of his time, for in the last fifty years most Americans have openly
concluded that religion, right or wrong, is for individuals, until today "99
percent of contemporary observers" find Americans identifying religion
with individuality.[23] (Thus, today we say, "I'm not religious, but I am spiritual," and mean "individual spirituality good, institutional religion not so
good.") George Marsden, America's foremost historian of American religious conservatism, has noted that the American Bible believer "stood
alone before God" and believed that "the church, while important as a sup-
portive community, was made up of free individuals."[24] Wallace Stevens
wrote in "Sunday Morning" of the archetypal American woman, clad in a
peignoir, vaguely haunted by "the dark / Encroachment of that old catastrophe," with coffee and oranges beside her, seated in splendid isolation,
detached from society.

Yet all such extreme individualism argues for, not against, the need to
concentrate on the public and its spiritual culture, particularly given
America's religious heritage. In America the great majority of people base
their faith on Abrahamic scriptures, which told the story of a nation and
had very little interest in the solitary person; and also on the New Testament, which warned against self-love and argued that "the body of Christ"
and the kingdom of God were the great things. Yet Americans continue to
use scriptures about communities to gain salvation for themselves as individuals. When Americans were personally offended by the criminal antics
of Richard Nixon, they felt and acted as public members of a nation,
rooted in a common spiritual culture, itself ostensibly rooted in a person-
and nation-transcending good. But that spiritual culture seems to be
retreating, unacknowledged and uncriticized, into the dark recesses of the
public unconsciousness.

1

Skepticism

When Zarathustra was alone, however, he said to his heart: "Could it be possible! This old saint in the forest hath not yet heard of it, *that God is dead!*"
—Friedrich Nietzsche, *Thus Spoke Zarathustra*

FOUR OUT OF THE LAST FIVE AMERICAN PRESIDENTS HAVE UNDERSTOOD that the American spiritual culture was in decline. In July 1979 Jimmy Carter gave his famous "malaise speech," referring not only to America's "crisis of confidence" but to the need for "a rebirth of the American spirit."[1] Ronald Reagan may or may not have recognized the weak state of America's spiritual culture when in 1981 he told biographer Lou Canon, "What I'd really like to do is to go down in history as the president who made Americans believe in themselves again."[2] Whether or not he was speaking of the spiritual culture depends on what he meant by "believe in themselves again." Nobel Prize–winning economist James Buchanan has suggested that Reagan was speaking of the spiritual culture, rather than of simple national pride. He detected in Reagan an effort to tap "into a part of the American soul." Reagan, said Buchanan, recognized and responded to the average person's "yearning to become a participant in the imagined community" and to be guided by "a supraexistent ideal," "a comprehensive vision of what might be," or "an animating principle," or to peer through a "window on reality." For Buchanan, this is exactly what Reagan's immediate successor, George Bush, lacked—made evident, for example, in his disparagement of "that vision thing."[3] Clinton began what may have been the most rhetorically effective speech of his first term—given without a text before the eighty-sixth convocation of the Church of God in Christ—by

27

referring to the "great crisis of the spirit that is gripping America today." He acknowledged that "the fabric of society" had to be repaired, but added that "unless we say, 'Some of this cannot be done by government because we have to reach deep inside to the values, the spirit, the soul, and the truth of human nature,' none of the other things we seek to do will ever take us where we need to go." He added, "We will somehow, by God's grace, turn this around."[4] Finally, it can be argued that George W. Bush's initial effectiveness in responding to the terrorist crisis of September 11, 2001, lay in his recognition that not only the stability of the state, but the viability of America's spiritual culture had been shaken. Perhaps these presidents were merely playing to a gullible, pious public. Nevertheless, even if that were the case, each of these presidents earned his office by accurately reading the public and, once in office, assumed that most Americans believed that the spiritual culture was important.

Many American foreign policy analysts, freer than politicians from the temptation to curry favor with the electorate, speak in a similar way about spiritual cultures. When foreign policy analysts are good at doing what they do, they may be the closest America comes to having big-picture public thinkers or national metaphysicians. Their highest calling is to picture the whole world accurately, so that in its practical affairs America knows what it is relating to. Included in this picture are the various nations' particular spiritual cultures. Foreign policy analysts should be especially concerned when they detect the weakening of a country's spiritual culture, and many are detecting such a weakening of America's spiritual culture and express such concerns.

Richard Nixon, in his post-presidential role as a foreign policy analyst, wrote about America's spiritual life with an unexpected urgency. In *Beyond Peace*, his last book, he briefly overcame his Quaker reticence about talking about religion. "What many commentators now join in calling a crisis of the spirit," he said, "has affected all classes in American society." He crossed political lines and commended Hilary Clinton for her willingness to speak out on this matter, referring no doubt to her speech in Austin, Texas, in 1993, on the "politics of meaning," where she referred to America's "sleeping sickness of the soul."[5] Nixon said, "With the Cold War over, our first order of business here at home, more fundamental by far than jobs or health care or the fiscal deficit, is the spiritual and cultural deficit. This is at the root of what ails America." In the last paragraph of this valedictory and posthumously published book, he said, "We should reach into the soul of this nation and recover the spirit and mission that first set us apart."[6] This critical assessment stands in marked contrast to his presidential boasts that America was number one and that "America's record in this century has been unparalleled in the world's history for its responsibility, for its generosity, for its creativity and for its progress."[7]

Zbigniew Brzezinski's *Out of Control* decries America's role in spreading around the world its consumerist, cornucopia mentality. He makes the "global crisis of the spirit" the key to the descent of the world's great nations, among which America seems to be the principal example:

> It is a striking paradox that the greatest victory for the proposition that 'God is dead' has occurred not in the Marxist-dominated states, which politically propagated atheism, but in Western liberal democratic societies, which have culturally nurtured moral apathy. In the latter, the fact is that religion has ceased to be a major social force. But this condition arose not because officially propagated atheism had won the day over religion, but because of the corrosive effects of cultural indifference to anything but the immediately and materially satisfying dimensions of life.[8]

David Gress, in *From Plato to NATO*, based his case for a restoration of spiritual culture on a distinctive theory of the origin of the West. The Western intelligentsia's "Grand Narrative" of the rise of the West tells of a steady progression from the democracy and philosophy of ancient Greece, to the law of classical Rome, to the individualism of the Renaissance and the Enlightenment, to the science and technology of the modern Atlantic states. As a story about the course of abstract ideals, it moves like a stone skipping over the surface of history, from one moment in Greece, to another moment in Rome, to a series of modern moments in Western Europe. While this story includes valid elements, Gress finds it incomplete and "dangerously wrong," causing enthusiasts to be groundlessly optimistic and brooders to be groundlessly pessimistic. The Grand Narrative is naïve in assuming that Western ideals have floated above the complications of concrete history and that these ideals are so appealing and effective that they will become global. That narrative is parochial in assuming that the coalescence of the modern mind occurred in modern secular Western Europe. And the narrative is historically false in neglecting the dense and complex ways in which the Western mind was constructed. The less grand but more accurate narrative, he says, should emphasize the idea of freedom introduced by the Germans as they settled into the ruins of the Roman Empire and especially the view of life thrust on the West by the Christians. "Because it was deaf to religion, the standard story presented both classical religion and Christianity as peripheral, derivative, and largely irrelevant, except as providers of ideas whose true role was to function as stepping-stones in the great secular drama of Western ascendancy from Plato to NATO." Lacking a "rich and specific" awareness of the central and ambiguous influence of "religion and theology as cultural forces in their own right," Gress argues, the power of the West could well dissipate in the twenty-first century.[9]

Foreign affairs theorist Samuel Huntington argues in a variety of writings that the source of today's global conflict is not primarily political or economic but cultural, and that the most important single factor in cultural conflict is the religious factor. The world has moved from clashes between princes, to clashes between nations (after the French Revolution), to clashes between political ideologies (after World War I), and now to clashes between cultures (after the Cold War). A culture is defined today most fundamentally by its "civilization." Huntington names seven current civilizations: Chinese (or Sinic), Japanese, Hindu, Islamic, Western, South American, and African. Within the civilization itself, the most important element "is religion, as the Athenians emphasized."[10] Huntington's point is that, as they approach the hour of their greatest conflict, civilizations must nurture and protect their religions if they are to have any hope of retaining their identity as civilizations. Particularly, he argues, the West's deepest values—such as social equality, personal freedom, and political democracy—are at risk, and if those values are to be protected the religions of the West must be protected. Equally, civilizations must do better than they are now at understanding "the basic religious and philosophical assumptions underlying other civilizations."[11]

Religion, the Missing Dimension of Statecraft is an anthology arguing that religion has been and will remain crucial to the resolution of interstate conflicts. The book's principal editor, Douglas Johnston, then CEO of the Center for Strategic and International Studies (CSIS), suggests that Americans, especially American diplomats, schooled as they are in the separation of church and state, have become blind to the crucial role religious commitments play in international relations. Particularly since the end of the Cold War, issues of emotional and communal identity, and the religious interests that underlie them, are overlooked by diplomats trained to understand only political power and material self-interest. In this same anthology, military historian Edward Luttwak argues that most foreign policy experts not only overlook but actually forbid analysis of the religious dimension in international affairs. Referring to these experts, he says that they may have "wielded none of the torture instruments of the Catholic inquisitions, nor did they burn dissenters under some Protestant dispensation. But when it came to religion in all its aspects, they strangled free inquiry just as effectively. . . ."[12] Diplomatic missions, he says, should have "religion attachés" and should find ways to eradicate their own economism (their "dogmatic secular reductivism" driven by "a crude materialistic determinism," where all reasons boil down to economic reasons). The thesis pervading this entire volume is that diplomats will founder unless they recognize that national peoples act partly for religious and spiritual reasons.

Each of these American presidents and foreign policy experts is concerned about the political consequences of America's, as well as other nations', deteriorating spiritual culture, and each hopes for the creation of a more adequate American spiritual culture. None of them speaks primarily of the private religious lives of individual American citizens. All of them speak of national identity and, implicitly, of national spiritual cultures, and find both crippled.

The Decline of
the Russian Spiritual Culture

Russia is in trouble partly because most Russians today experience a weak spiritual culture and suspect that the remains of their spiritual culture reflect little more than the mandates of the civil authorities who shape it. Russia once possessed a distinct spiritual culture. During most of the modern era, most Russians found a way to live without Western values (despite the fact that, since Peter the Great, some Russians have enthusiastically allied themselves with Enlightenment reason, Western individualism, science, and technology). The majority of Russians were sustained by the belief that Russia had a unique heritage and destiny, and that it stood for something beyond itself. They were animated with an egalitarianism so fierce that the aristocracy was automatically suspect, with a communalism so fervent that individualism seemed morally crude, with a trust in leaders so strong that the democratic process seemed vulgar and compromising, and with a faith in Slavic nobility and Russian Orthodoxy so passionate that Western alternatives were unappealing. Sociologist Tim McDaniel collapses these beliefs into what he calls "the Russian idea," which was important not by and in itself, but as a representation of great realities, including the will of God.[13] Those realities lent some legitimacy to the Tsars and to the Communist leaders, particularly as they claimed to speak for "the truth" and as they called on people to forget their poverty and remember the moral and spiritual ideals for which the Russian people stood. Because the Russian idea was thought to refer to a venerable reality, it was able to shape a spiritual culture that, in turn, was able to shape the Russian nation and the Russian country. I do not argue that this spiritual culture was particularly good (in fact, as a Westerner, I believe it was not), but only that it was real and that its influence was important.

But as time passed the Russian idea was undermined in at least two ways. First, it was challenged by an emerging modernist yearning for the economic efficiency and the democratic rights burgeoning in Western Europe. Second, the incompetence and corruption of the Russian bureaucracy began to undermine the trust that it stood for something beyond itself and to replace it with the belief that that bureaucracy stood for nothing but itself. The spiritual culture began to look like an instrument of state rulers, whether Tsars or Communist leaders, so that the real authority seemed to reside in them rather than in the tradition or the God that the leaders and the spiritual culture were meant to serve. This distrust crippled not only the Russian spiritual culture, but the entire Russian society.

The economic and political causes of Russian demoralization notwithstanding, McDaniel is right in tracing Russia's current agony partly to the loss of "the moral and ideological underpinnings" of Russian society. He cites a commentator writing in *Moscow News* in 1993 who laments the loss of Russian spirituality. A vital spirituality (*dukyovnost*), the commentator argues, engenders a healthy dissatisfaction for present conditions and a hope for a better future, primarily because it holds up to the society something that transcends the present condition.[14] More recently, former ambassador to the Soviet Union Jack Matlock Jr. has noted that "the Communists' pursuit of a utopian goal by force, dictatorship and terror destroyed the incipient basis for a civil society by eliminating all institutions independent of the Communist Party and thereby atomizing society."[15] Some of those institutions, like the church and the arts, had referred to a reality beyond the will and imagination of the national leaders. In short, Russians in the twentieth century endured perhaps the modern world's starkest schooling in skepticism, which replaced belief in its spiritual culture with suspicion of all social forces.

This demoralization was more than a temporary reaction to the collapse of the Soviet Union. Reporting to the *New York Times* in January 2002, Alison Smale wrote:

> Russians appear disillusioned and cynical. Surveys conducted by the New Siberian University in Siberia since 1992 found at the end of 2001 that only 6 percent of respondents had any faith in political parties, only 10 to 12 percent believe the media, and just 18 percent trust the Russian Orthodox

Church, which enjoyed the trust of 60 percent of respondents just five years ago.[16]

Admittedly, the word "heroic" remains part of the official Russian nomenclature and many Russians still nurse a fierce pride in the Russians' capacity to fight, to suffer, and to survive—evident, for example, in the convincing World War II museum at Moscow's Victory Park. In addition, as individuals, the Russians sustain close interpersonal relations, making them on a one-to-one basis among the world's warmest and most welcoming people. However, in public these same Russians seem lost amid alien powers. In Moscow, people typically avert their eyes when meeting a stranger on the sidewalk, are eerily silent on buses and subways, and trudge anonymously over dusty roads to and from their crowded apartments in huge apartment blocks. Pedestrians in Moscow, even when they have the walk light, typically scramble across intersections as though they believed that the waiting drivers, gunning their engines, were anxious to prove their indifference.

To attribute such skepticism to the failings of the spiritual culture does not impress most social scientists, who tend to confine their explanation to economic and political causes. To take a single example, three recent books on contemporary Russia all attributed Russian economic failure in the 1990s to two causes. First, they blamed Harvard economic advisors and the International Monetary Fund, which in the early 1990s prescribed a "tight-fisted monetarism" that sent a fledgling Russian capitalism into a tailspin. Second, they blamed the so-called Russian oligarchs, who used their loans to the government to gain control of government industries, which they proceeded to dismantle and sell rather than revive in a way that would benefit the Russian economy. With remarkable effectiveness, a *Foreign Affairs* book reviewer undermines each of these explanations, calling them "simple-minded morality tales of good and evil." Instead, the reviewer blames Russian deterioration "on corruption"; and "the sad truth is that nobody knows how to build an honest, effective state machine in a country where a dishonest, corrupt state already exists." Asking how this corruption might be overcome, the book reviewer concludes that his three authors do not know, and that ". . . *The Economist* does not know, the IMF does not know, and this reviewer does not know."[17] But then, as if reverting to an old addiction, the reviewer concludes by casting about only for economic and political explanations for Russian failure.

I am suggesting that the failure of Russian society should be attributed in large part to the failure of its spiritual culture. The corruption and the moral breakdown of the Russian civil society can be traced to a number of causes, but among them is the failure of the Russian spiritual culture.[18]

Reductionism, America's
Reigning Religious Skepticism

In theory, a country's spiritual culture elicits loyalty not to itself but to something greater than itself—specifically, to a reality, such as a God, that transcends that country. In principle, the wisdom and authority of spiritual cultures is not inherent in the spiritual cultures but is to be attributed to a reality beyond the spiritual cultures. The claims of spiritual cultures should work much as sonar impulses work; the claims should fly out through a murky medium and bounce back with outlines of something real. In the West, beginning at least with Augustine's *City of God*, the visible society has been grounded on something like a spiritual culture, which in turn has been grounded on something that transcended the spiritual culture. Now, however, there is talk that the divine grounds have disappeared and the spiritual culture is based on nothing beyond itself. This, I argue, is the key to the current decline of the American spiritual culture.

In the last hundred and fifty years, many sociologists, psychologists, historians, and anthropologists have advanced theories about how religion arises—and these apply to how spiritual cultures arise. For them, religion is the product of certain social or psychological forces and not of something transcending those forces. For these thinkers, the claims of religion are like shouts in an empty canyon—nothing but human voices bouncing back, misinterpreted as divine voices. Religion's pretense that it is guided by a God, by Reason, or by some other transcendent Principle are just that, sheer pretense. Religion reflects only the mundane opinions of those who constructed it, and their constructions are effective, sometimes malignantly effective, because of the social forces they set loose. Those constructions remain powerful because they give societies enough social glue to avert anarchy, individuals enough psychological security to stave off mental illness, or both societies and individuals enough meaning to lend stature to their arbitrary desires. But in a mature and honest society, these social scientists suggest, the constructions should be recognized for what they are: temporary, constructed palliatives or therapies rather than references to a reality that transcends society. In short, the gods, taken literally, are crutches for the immature and the dishonest.

On this conclusion, but in a variety of different ways, converge the arguments of great nineteenth- and early-twentieth-century social thinkers Karl Marx, Ludwig Feuerbach, Friedrich Nietzsche, Emile Durkheim, and Sigmund Freud. After being set aside for decades, their arguments have been taken up by thinkers as different as E. O. Wilson, Anthony Giddens, Jacques Derrida, and Peter Berger (in his role as a sociologist). The ranks of those who propose a thoroughly human source of religion have been recently augmented by social scientists who specialize in the study of religion and religion scholars who have adopted social scientific outlooks— for example, Robert Segal and Stewart Elliott Guthrie.[19]

These thinkers, who contend that religion is entirely about what people have done and thought, not about a God or some other reality greater than persons or societies, can be called "reductionists." Just as chemists who reduce biology to molecular chemistry and physicists who reduce chemistry to atomic physics, some social scientists reduce religion to sociological, psychological, or anthropological processes, leaving to religious practices and beliefs no independent religious validity. In religious studies today, scholars tend openly to reject the theories of the great historians of religion, such as Rudolph Otto and Mircea Eliade, for whom religious practice is *sui generis* (in a class by itself), irreducible, or uniquely real, and therefore largely inaccessible to and incomprehensible by science. Today, scholars sometimes speak of Otto, Eliade, and other earlier historians of religion as, in the last analysis, little more than apologists for their own fallacious faiths.

On university campuses and among the intellectually elite in America, the reductionist explanation of religion is so prevalent that its presence hardly needs corroboration. One measure of the strength of reductionism is the ease with which it has ignored a variety of strong refutations.

First, there are at least four ways of arguing that reductionism, *as a type of explanation*, is a limited explanation:

1. The reductionists' social-scientific mode of explanation is not necessarily the only mode of explanation. For example, a social-scientific explanation of religion does not necessarily obviate a theological explanation of religion. Rather, a social-scientific explanation of religion is an explanation that makes sense in terms of the methods of the social sciences, but not necessarily one that makes sense in terms of the methods of theology or the philosophy of religion. Thus, while reductionism provides one very important explanation of religion, it does not necessarily "explain religion

away," just as the chemist's reduction of biology to chemistry does not explain away, or deny the validity of, biology.

2. The causes to which reductionists point are not the only causes for the phenomena they discuss. If a phenomenon has a variety of causes, to demonstrate one is not necessarily to eliminate others. So a sociologist may prove that religious belief is caused by the desire to cope with social dislocation, but that does not, by itself, prove that religious belief is not also caused by a religious experience.[20]

3. The ulterior motives of those who defend religion do not make those defenses false, for the validity of an argument can but does not always depend on why it is made.[21] Perhaps Otto and Eliade did defend their claims about religious phenomena because they wanted to justify their personal religious faiths. But if that ulterior motive meant that their claims themselves were false, then so are the claims of social scientists, who are just as liable to have ulterior motives for their work—for example, the desire to gain professional status. But would they argue that this made their social science wrong?

4. Reductionism depends on a bottom-up form of explanation and ignores top-down explanations. Bottom-up explanations, when treated as exhaustive, make the whole nothing but the consequence of the parts. But these explanations overlook synergies, where the whole can become greater than the sum of those consequences (and can, in turn, affect the same parts that were said to control the whole). For example, a living being is greater than the sum of its chemical causes, even if the chemical causes contribute to the determination of that being. (And, interestingly, chemical causes alone seem unable to replicate biological phenomena.) Thus, a sovereign human organism occasionally makes decisions that transcend, reign over, and escape explanation by its "subjects," be they organs, muscles, chemistries, or cognitions. Or a community can make decisions that are never entirely reducible to the sum of the decisions made by its constituent members.[22]

Thus, it is possible to say that a reductionist explanation is a fine type of explanation of religion, within the boundaries of its own social-scientific inquiry, but this does not necessarily eclipse other types of explanations carried on outside those boundaries.

Second, *historical precedents* should steer reductionists away from the presumption that their explanations are sufficient. Reductionists often act as though they have found, at last, a sociological, anthropological, psychological, historical, or sociobiological key that will open any lock. This method can reduce to itself any ostensibly distinct reality, making it nothing but the consequence of itself. Reductionists, in short, have given their explanations the same absolute power that philosophers and theologians once gave explanations based on reason or on God. But have we come all this way—having denied, for example, the absolute truth of Plato's and Aristotle's essences or ideas or the absolute truth of God's revelation—only now to elevate another kind of absolute, which would make all things relative to itself? If previous absolute explanations have been toppled with a kind of inexorable regularity, is there reason to trust that reductionism will not also be toppled?

Third, reductionist explanations are implicitly *dualistic*, if not positivistic. Long ago, seventeenth- and eighteenth-century British materialists (such as John Locke and David Hume) believed and their successors still believe that there are facts uninterpreted by values. Reductionists want to return to such a factual world (of, for example, social and psychological events as they function as causes), and they want to explain value-laden religion in its terms. They want to bracket off the subjective values that we attribute to the world and attribute them to physically transmitted influences. They want to explain religion's subjective claims in the terms of its factual environment, as though that physical environment could act alone and independently to determine subjective claims.

For mind-body dualists, including the reductionists, it is the physical and external world that is to be trusted. They remain aligned with David Hume, who believed that matters of fact and cold logic were alone to be trusted and that all matters of value—of art, morality, and religion—were merely what the mind of the believer arbitrarily and, probably, inaccurately imposed on the real world. Equally, social-scientific reductionists hold that the important explanations are provided by the external, material world as it presents social or psychological influences. It is these that are to explain religion.

However, today most physicists doubt that the world is composed, on the one hand, of independent bits of matter located in definite times and spaces and, on the other hand, of nonmaterial observers separable from those bits of matter.[23] For them, nothing from the so-called physical past can affect the present unless it is related to something in the present; and this present to which it is related always interprets the past (mentally, you might say) from its own standpoint. Thus, what exists is always necessarily both past and present, both physical and mental, both factual and interpreted; however, all interpretations depend on standpoints and interests, so that they are always, at least in some slight sense, evaluations and are value-laden. This explanation applies even to nonliving things like photons—which literally become waves or particles depending on whether they are registered (interpreted) by wave-detector devices or particle-detector devices.[24] Everything that affects the present must be interpreted. If one wants to call the past physical and the present observation mental, let that be done; nevertheless, nothing physical gets to be real until it gets into the present and is interpreted and valued by something like a mind.[25] David Hume's factual/logical world, apart from the evaluations given by the mind, simply does not exist. It has been replaced by a world in which facts affect the present only if they are first evaluated.

Now social-scientific reductionists still live in David Hume's world, for they attempt to explain religion in terms of its physical and factual past, as that is known by sociologists, psychologists, or other social scientists. These past facts can explain the present religious mind of the believer as though that mind were utterly passive to past facts and had no capacity to contribute anything to the world—certainly not values that might shape the world and, thereby, be just as true as the past facts. For the reasons I have outlined above, most recent physicists, especially quantum physicists, would respond that past facts have no such determinative powers, and that present minds, or observers, do have some limited powers.

Nevertheless, despite the three foregoing and common or common-sense refutations of reductionism, it has remained popular. In recent decades, the social-scientific reductionists have seemed to provide the ultimate explanation of things, becoming the philosophical theologians of their time. Most humanities scholars not only accurately acknowledge that everything is influenced by its environment but, when driven into a corner, have no way to show that their values are not completely determined by, or reduced to, their environments. Particularly, today's religion scholars are hard-pressed to give evidence of a God that is not completely explained by its social environment, so that it is no great feat for the reductionists to convince them and others that such a God was never there. Certainly, a God explained by its environment could hardly be expected to act independently on that environment or "in the world."

At the same time, reductionism is better resisted by enterprises that can provide evidence that their values have results, or the power to interpret their world. Economists, politicians, lawmakers, and journalists, for example, know they must provide evidence that can be traced to them and that, when they fail to do so, they will no longer be trusted. A business product must create financial valuations (profits, stock value, real estate), or people will doubt the value of the product. A government must achieve some of its objectives, or people will doubt its political efficacy. A law must create order, or people will treat it as though it does not exist or will ignore it with impunity. A newspaper must sooner or later provide real information and reliable predictions, or it will not be read. When businesses, governments, laws, and newspapers provide evidence confirming their interpretations or values, and when they demonstrate that their influence accomplishes more than what their environment could have accomplished without them, they demonstrate that their claims about that world cannot be reduced to their environment.

However, religious thinkers are hard-pressed to produce evidence of their God or God-surrogate, so that they are vulnerable to the reductionists. Where is the evidence that the God to which religious institutions or spiritual cultures refer is real in the sense that it has the power to influence its environment? Without such evidence, the spiritual culture can easily be reduced to its psychological and social causes. For this reason, evidence for God or some equivalent to God remains crucially important to the survival of spiritual cultures today.

The Religious Critic

In early-twenty-first-century America, it is difficult for religious thinkers (especially, religion teachers, religion scholars, and clergy) to revise and defend the theological grounds of America's historic spiritual culture. They could do this if they were to interpret their environment as religious and demonstrate that that religious interpretation had real and needed effects. Those best equipped to do this are "religious critics"—those public intellectuals who are not primarily social critics, not primarily culture critics, but critics who promote a critical interaction between the public and the nation's spiritual culture. They could extend the work of twentieth-century religious critics in the liberal tradition such as Walter Rauschenbusch, Dorothy Day, Shailer Mathews, Henry Nelson Wieman, Paul Tillich, Abraham Joshua Heschel, Harvey Cox, Cornel West, Jean Bethke Elshtain, and, most of all, Reinhold Niebuhr. Or they could carry on the work of neoconservative religious critics, such as Michael Novak and Richard John Neuhaus.

But because future religious critics will live in a society that is increasingly explained as relative to and as a product of personal needs, social context, and cultural situation, such religious critics will be hard-pressed to establish their credibility, and they will receive little help from religion scholars. As process theologian David Griffin has recently said, social-scientific reductionism "is widely accepted among those engaged in religious studies." Religion scholars tend to agree that, when faced with causal explanations, they "cannot, by definition, argue for the truth of religion in the sense of holding that the best explanation for religion arises from a response to something holy in the nature of things."[26]

Neither religious experience nor faith is generally allowed to count as testimony to the existence of the sacred. Today's potential religious critics usually deprive themselves of Augustine's long-accepted dictum, "I believe in order that I may understand."[27] No longer able to begin with their own faith or their own religious experience, let alone the faith or experience of the American public, they often have no way to begin at all. They feel called upon to prove their ideas from scratch, without assumptions—a task impossible for any proponent of any discipline or cause. Without the even temporary validity of such religious entrances to understanding, religious critics cannot plausibly interpret national behaviors as related, in some weak sense at least, to sacred causes. There was, of course, the old language about a "more" (James), "a good not our own" (Wieman), uncanny grounds for a sense of "Peace" (Whitehead), or "the mysterious totality of being the imagination calls the universe" (Dewey). But by the beginning of the twenty-first century, these were generally taken to be the vague musings of forgotten, white elite males.

Today many, if not most, American religion scholars, including many potential religious critics, earn their spurs by demonstrating their high regard for other academic movements—in philosophy, in the sciences, in cultural and literary theory—and for schemes for social change. They tend to adopt the worldviews established by nonreligious inquiries—such as those implicit in process philosophy, in the relational and contingent theories of quantum physics, in Marxist theory, in ecology and environmentalism, and in theories of political and economic injustice (especially for racial, gender, and third-world minorities). These worldviews give religious thinkers the basis for their interpretations of religion or theology and allow them to make God the emblem for the stance defined by those worldviews. These same thinkers often leave the impression that they are bereft of any religious idea independent of, and irreducible to, those worldviews.

Liberal academic scholars of religion, in particular, have been so intent on proving their appreciation for various secular and academic estimates of the world that they have become mere foot soldiers (if not camp followers) in secular movements, whether cultural, educational, or social. They sometimes are given a place at other academic tables and become decent second-rate exponents of other academic disciplines. They will occasionally be called upon, but since they have little that is distinctive to offer, they will seldom be truly heard. They show an appreciation for other groups' interests that is rare in its humility and its capacity to see the moral and spiritual depth in the often naïve approaches of other moral and intellectual movements. They become highly sensitive and thoughtful champions of the unique insights of nonreligious disciplines. Nevertheless, it is not surprising that secular activists and scholars tend not to listen to the person at the table who has nothing independent to add or argue from.

What is left of public religious influence often comes from nonacademics or theological conservatives. For example, it was fundamentalist Billy Graham and neoconservative religion scholars who advised American presidents in the second half of the twentieth century as the liberal scholars of religion and liberal clergy stood helplessly by. Or, for example, it was the culture-rejecting Karl Barth whom novelist John Updike preferred over Paul Tillich, even though Tillich had striven so diligently to show the theological importance of secular artists like Updike.[28]

Ironically and most importantly, by not talking about what difference a God might make to the nation's spiritual culture and to its public life, academic religion scholars often contributed to, rather than diminished, the tendency to reduce God to social and psychological causes. Religion scholars have been genuinely enlightened by the independent insights of their secular intellectual colleagues, and this is demonstrated by their broad sympathies and significant commentaries. However, they have tended not to return the favor of independent insight that they have received—to change secular culture as it had once changed them.

The Task Ahead

American public policy analyst Francis Fukuyama offers a surprising response to these problems. Underplaying the preponderance of Americans who, as individuals, retain a conservative religious belief, he contends that most Americans are now too secular to believe that prayer and ritual "were handed down by God." They can no longer take "religion seriously on its own terms." On the other hand, says Fukuyama, "we have not become so modern and secularized that we can do without religion." For it turns out that without religion there probably cannot be significant social capital (shared values), and without social capital there probably cannot be an American civil society (groups and associations located between the family and the state), and without civil society there probably cannot be a successful American democracy. The current "great disruption" of American social capital cannot be converted to a "great reconstruction" of social capital, he proposes, without the help of religion in some form.[29]

Thus, able to accept the indispensability of religion but unable to accept its truth, Fukuyama's Americans should sustain religious practice as a way of preserving American democracy. Fukuyama proposes that Americans will accept religion in "a more benign, decentralized form, in which religious belief is less an expression of dogma than of the community's existing norms and desire for order." People will practice religion "because they want their children to have the proper values and want to enjoy the comfort of ritual and the sense of shared experience it brings."[30] Religions, that is, will be retained, but for their social therapy rather than for their theological truth.

But, I argue, this therapeutic moment will be brief. Initially, people who know that language about God points to nothing real will act as though it does, hoping that this will bring the moral and social results they sincerely desire. However, groundless institutions cannot be long sustained. As I have said, business people, politicians, lawmakers, or journalists know that if they cannot provide evidence for the independent worth of their interpretations—showing that their economics, politics, laws, or news involve something that has the sort of effects nothing else can have—they will soon be ignored or treated as hucksters. Similarly, discovering that religious therapies stand on no independent evidence, Americans will drop them and turn to whatever other public therapy is more powerful. American democracy may need a spiritual culture, but if that culture can supply no evidence for a God or some other reality that can give that culture what it cannot provide for itself, then that culture will do little to preserve democracy. In short, the skepticism that is setting in forebodes a dangerous future.

There are at least two possible religious responses to the foregoing predicaments. The first is theological and is designed to make practical sense to a secular society. The second is religious, working partly outside secular understandings. Both responses accept reductionistic skepticism as a profound challenge that cannot be dodged or refuted with *ex machina* arguments, which introduce claims contradicting what people commonly know from the sciences and the arts. The first and theological response I outline in chapter 3, building it on the pragmatism of most Americans.

The second and religious approach I will outline in chapter 4, proposing that "God" refers not only to a pragmatically justified social reality but to a mystery.

In both approaches, I will abide by the postmodern dictum that what is claimed to be real must make sense within a particular spatial-temporal context of history. I do not reduce "history" to quantities and facts but see it tied up with values, worldviews, and ways of life. Having accepted such historical limitations and implications, I must abandon universal truths and confine my discussion of the truth of God-language to a particular historical location. I have chosen as my location contemporary America, largely because I find that social location, for good or ill, more important to the attitudes of most contemporary Americans than any other location—more important than, say, regions, ethnicities, classes, jobs, or genders. However, if "America" is to become a meaningful historical place, it must be defined. Accordingly, in chapter 2, I will attempt to define America by telling a story of America and drawing from that story implications that appear to be religiously suggestive.[31]

2

⟁isplaced People

Thus, the belated reveller who landed in the dark at the Desbrosses Street ferry, found his energies exhausted in the effort to see his own length. The new Americans, of whom he was to be one, must, whether they were fit or unfit, create a world of their own, a science, a society, a philosophy, a universe, where they had not yet created a road or even learned to dig their own iron. They had no time for thought; they saw, and could see, nothing beyond their day's work; their attitude to the universe outside them was that of the deep-sea fish. Above all, they naturally and intensely disliked to be told what to do, and how to do it, by men who took their ideas and their methods from the abstract theories of history, philosophy, or theology. They knew enough to know that their world was one of energies quite new.

> —Henry Adams, *The Education of Henry Adams*

HENRY ADAMS WAS A WELL-ESTABLISHED AMERICAN NATIVE, not a new immigrant for the first time setting foot on American soil. He came from the family of Sam Adams—Boston Tea Party firebrand, member of the First and Second Continental Congresses, and governor of Massachusetts. He was the great-grandson of the second president of the United States and the grandson of the sixth. He was also the grandson of a rich Boston merchant. His father, as minister to Great Britain, did more than anyone to keep Britain from entering the Civil War on the side of the South, just as his great grandfather, with Benjamin Franklin, had done more than anyone to keep France from entering the Revolutionary War on the side of England. His father was also a congressman and a leading national politician. Both his brothers were prominent historians and pub-

44

lic servants. One uncle preceded Lincoln to the podium at Gettysburg (after having served as congressman, governor, minister to England, president of Harvard, secretary of state, senator, and candidate for vice president). Another uncle was a nationally recognized liberal Protestant clergyman.[1] Henry Adams himself, for ten years the young secretary to the minister to Great Britain, had been an intimate witness to England's hypocritical flirtation with the American Confederacy and was making his name as a historian and commentator on American affairs. As he walked down the gangplank to the New York pier on his way back from England, he had before him a burgeoning American continent and a personal future as solid as any young American's could have been. Speaking of himself in the third person, Adams called himself the "American of Americans" and confessed, "Probably no child . . . held better cards than he."[2]

It was this munificently secured, deeply educated, richly cosmopolitan young man who mused at the pier in New York at ten o'clock one steaming July night in 1868. Deeply ensconced in what might still be called America's greatest family, and deeply immersed in European culture, his future depended only on maintaining a trajectory from a familial and European past. In many respects he was a classic conservative who secretly venerated the Virgin Mary, openly admired Europe's thirteenth century, and was profoundly alienated from the nation to which, after ten years, he was returning.

Despite this, he would give himself to the hustling nation and to its ambitious future. Against all that might have been predicted of him, he throbbed with the primitive Americans' need to break with the Old World, to defy its theories, to throw themselves blindly into the raw environment and, out of that, to create a new world. He was Establishment if there ever was an American Establishment, and yet he wanted to break out as only a rank immigrant might want to break out. On one side, he began his intellectual life yearning to live in the preceding century and near the end of it wrote perhaps the greatest, most admiring treatise on the Middle Ages ever written by an American, *Mont Saint Michel and Chartres*. Later, he was to compare the dynamo and the Virgin and to choose the Virgin. On his other side, he was the ultra-modern American who, for example, hinted at his secret excitement with American technology by joking that he went every afternoon to the Paris Exposition and "prayed to the dynamos."[3] He whispered political schemes into the ears of national leaders—senators, a secretary of state, and presidents. He brimmed with financial and diplomatic policies to make America the world's preeminent power in the twentieth century—all set in the key of a people who must "create a world of their own." In his last book, *A Letter to American Teachers of History,* he mawk-ishly instructed the teachers that the course of history could be reduced to a physical law, the Second Law of Thermodynamics—and in the process he came close to reducing the great historian he was to just another crackpot, science-enamored American. He was, in part, one of those rugged, self-reliant Americans who, he said, have "the self-respect of a deep-sea fish that carried a lantern on the end of its nose," outraged at "the mere sug-gestion that a sun existed above him."[4]

And yet he had the vision of a glorious European past and was disap-pointed that he, as an American, had no comparable past. To him, all Americans were finally shallow, largely because they were both dispos-sessed of other peoples' cultures and were unfit to "dig their own." In acquitting himself to his fellow Americans in his autobiography, *The Edu-cation of Henry Adams,* he adopted a tone that was singularly irritable, arch, and condescending. Although the book was eventually to be awarded the Pulitzer Prize and to be called one of the great American masterpieces of the twentieth century, he told a friend that it was "drivel" and that he was sending it "out into the world to be whipped."[5] He was a cultural refugee, culturally naked, and secretly bereaved, and so were his fellow Americans. He and they were, in perhaps the deepest sense of the word, displaced per-sons.

Other Americans were similarly haunted by their cultural past, and they described displacement in different terms. Novelist Alice Walker calls it woundedness. In *Possessing the Secret of Joy,* she sets forth two characters who discuss their African origins and the need to abandon particular African practices. One character asks the other, "What does an American look like?" The other claims they all look different and says, "Americans, after all, have come from so many places." The first character responds that, nevertheless, Americans "resembled each other deeply in their hidden histories of fled-from pain." Finally, this character admits to "understand-ing my love of my adopted country perhaps for the first time: an American looks like a wounded person whose wound is hidden from others, and sometimes from herself. An American looks like me."[6]

Plurality and Dissensus

Displacement, even to the extent of woundedness, is related to what now is popularly called diversity—but complexly related. Ethnic and cultural diversity suggests the absence of a strong and shared core tradition, which is one source of Americans' vivid feelings of displacement. On the other hand, if diversity is exaggerated, it can remove all points of commonality among Americans, even their shared feelings of displacement.

This complex relationship is understood by American historian John Higham. He opens his major work on immigration, *Send These to Me*, by noting that, however different the Americans' origins and however much they were marked by those origins, there is yet one "common experience of all Americans": they share, he writes, the "memory of displacement from somewhere else." Higham is far more interested in the facts on the American ground than in the paradox of his language (that people can be united by their disunity). When the "from somewhere else" is remembered, it can foster ethnic justice; it can block the kind of bad assimilation whereby weak ethnic groups are drowned in the values of a dominant ethnic group. However, when the "from somewhere else" becomes the great thing to remember, as he believed it became, it blocks the very idea of common experience or binding values and ushers in "a more and more kaleidoscopic culture."[7] A sense of displacement, when used to preserve ethnic rights and to lift up a common experience, is a social strength; but when it is taken by itself, it can divide people and undermine their commonality of experience.

Higham's conviction that the latter, chaotic option was dangerous could not have been anticipated. As a young historian, he had witnessed the unity of the 1950s and disparaged the "cult of the 'American consensus,'" saying that it hid America's true diversity.[8] By 1975, however, when he wrote *Send These to Me,* he began to worry that, just as commonality once led to a cult of consensus, diversity was beginning to lead to the opposite outcome, which could be named a cult of dissensus. By 1998, as an old man, Higham was referring to "a kind of privatism that excludes and denigrates the public square," and with it "the emergence of a widespread indifference, somewhat flecked with disgust, [which] is the most distinctive phenomenon of the present day." He concluded, "I don't think there's ever been anything like it."[9]

Higham recognized and appreciated the ethnic and regional plurality of America and the strong individuality of most Americans. But he did not appreciate the elevation of those realities into ideals, the conversion of plurality into pluralism, of individuality into individualism, and of honorable multicultural struggles into what political scientist Eldon Eisenach calls "multiculturalism as a principle," in which it becomes something for its own sake.[10]

Higham and Eisenach question multiculturalism as a principle even while appreciating the value of America's multicultural composition. They recognize that the ethnic, racial, and cultural diversity of America exceeds that of any nation in history, and that that has given America an enviable place among nations. When America has honored diversity by extending the rights of people of all ethnic and cultural origins, it has done so properly. Rather than diminishing the American achievement, diversity has been a means to that achievement. For example, if Americans had not been so different, the founders of America would never have guaranteed freedom and equality to the extent that they did. Or today, America's creativity, energy, and prosperity owe much to the mix of cultural experiences and perspectives on which they drew.

But with regard to the common values that will keep the nation viable (and able thus to protect its diversity), for some observers the forces of disintegration seem recently to be outweighing the forces of integration. Ethnologist Ronald Takaki, champion of multiculturalism, began eventually to wonder whether ethnicities will ever "be able to connect themselves to a larger narrative."[11] Michael Walzer, lifelong advocate of pluralism, began to ask how Americans will acquire "framing conditions" and "common interests."[12] Postmodern philosopher Richard Rorty, arch-proponent of private values and celebrated critic of grand reasons for social consensus, now urges his fellow academics to "mobilize what remains of our pride in being Americans."[13] To these, add the concern, noted earlier, over the loss of community and the rise of social dissonance in the writings of Robert Bellah, Christopher Lasch, Martin Seymour Lipset, and Alan Wolfe.[14]

These and other scholars of the American scene imply that Americans, now more than ever, need to develop a distinct and shared American culture—where culture is, as anthropologist Ruth Benedict says, "a unique arrangement and interrelation of the parts that has brought about a new entity."[15] These commentators would never ask Americans to pay for American commonality by selling out American diversity; but they definitely do not want a newly fashionable diversity to destroy what remains of a common culture.

The task is to find in the new appreciation for diversity the unexpected wellspring for a new appreciation of unity, so that what is ostensibly the best argument against unity becomes the best argument for unity. Logically, if not experientially, this makes sense, for the fact of diversity has led to the same sense of displacement that provides America's greatest source of unity. Because appreciation for diversity and for unity are both directly proportional to the same thing—the sense of displacement—they should be directly proportional to each other, so that as one increases, so should the other. As America's cultural patterns change, its ongoing task is to preserve the balance between diversity and unity.

The Americans' singular sense of diversity is derived in large part from their immigrant sensibility, which has endured despite the fact that most Americans are not recent immigrants. Except for downturns during wars, economic panics, and depressions, immigration to America has proceeded steadily throughout America's history. By the mid-1990s, although the ratio of new immigrants to the total U.S. population had been higher, the number of new immigrants, legal and illegal, entering the United States per year was higher than it had been at any time in American history. Also, the cultural diversity of immigrants was greater than it had ever been in American history. The Immigration Acts of 1965 and 1968 abolished all legal preference for immigrants coming from northern Europe, vastly increased quotas for the Eastern Hemisphere, and permitted new immigrants that had become U.S. citizens to bring family members legally into the United States.[16] As it happened, between 1968 and 2000, 85 percent of legal immigrants came from the Third World, with the great majority coming from Latin America and Asia.[17] Naturally, both the fact and the awareness of cultural diversity among Americans has increased. This has only been reinforced in recent decades by an upsurge in ethnic self-consciousness and pride and by postmodern enthusiasm for pluralism and relativism. However, even by the 1770s, St. John de Crèvecoeur recognized America's diversity, claiming that in America "individuals of all nations are melted into a new race of men."[18] This complex amalgamation of diversity and unity remains as elusive as it is important.

Thus, America remains a nation of immigrants with, as Higham says, its "memory of displacement from somewhere else." This memory underlies an archetypal American narrative, what I would call the story of America as a nation of "displaced persons"—to borrow and generalize the term from the 1948 Displaced Persons Act. While this story of America is common to all Americans and, hence, accurate, it points to what cannot be named. It states in a narrative what poet William Carlos Williams, in the long poem *Paterson* and in the volume of essays entitled *The American Grain*, represents through collages of old letters, journals, reports, and newspaper stories: a "flavor of an actual peculiarity," a "strange phosphorus."[19] It recounts what photographers captured in scenes of bedraggled DPs standing helplessly at dockside or huddled in waiting rooms on Ellis Island. I have suggested that the story of America as a nation of displaced persons underlies the image of the supremely acculturated young Henry Adams, standing bewildered one evening on a New York pier in 1868.

When I propose the story of America as a nation of displaced persons, I do not mean several things. First, to propose that the story of displacement is *a* major, if not *the* major, American story does not mean that all Americans will agree that it applies to them. Many ethnic groups, especially those who think of themselves as separatist, feel so much bad historical water has gone over the American dam that they cannot and, even if they could, they would not ever adopt a common American story. In addition, many other people would deny that the story of displacement applies to them; at a conscious level, they feel quite undisplaced, quite well nested in a cultural terrain that feels as though it has existed forever. Second, when I claim that the story of displacement is an American story, I do not mean to imply that it eclipses certain ethnic stories. In fact, the story of displacement is reinforced by the continued power of ethnic stories; if ethnic stories had all faded away, the story of displacement would have lost some of its importance. A common story, especially a common story of displacement, need not suggest the sort of assimilation that demands the abandonment of ethnic and other subcultural identities in favor of a common American identity.

Even so, a national story should call for a kind of assimilation, one that allows commonality to coexist with differences. John Dewey intended this second form of assimilation when he said, "assimilation to *one another*—not to Anglo-Saxondom—seems to be essential to be an American."[20] There will always be a tension between common-culture stories and ethnic stories, but this need not come down to a zero-sum game, so that emphasis on a common culture and its story diminishes ethnic stories, or vice versa. The common story might be understood as a formal reality, a grammar, for which the subcultural stories are specific historical embodiments—as, for certain theologians, the Christian story is a grammar, whereas Methodist, Catholic, and so on are ways in which the Christian grammar works in history.[21] If this analogy from grammar makes the common story seem too formal, then the common story might be understood as one story standing beside all the ethnic stories, with the distinction that the other stories apply to only one ethnic group while the common story applies to all groups. In either case, to say a group of people participates in a common American story should not detract from, for example, that group's African-Americanness.

Admittedly, it will always be difficult for any story to bridge a society as pluralistic as American society. American plurality is a centrifugal force quite capable of overwhelming the centripetal force of commonality, and this places a high demand on any common American story.

An American Story

In 1883, poet Emma Lazarus wrote a prelude to displacement when she wrote the lines now inscribed on the pedestal of the Statue of Liberty:

> Give me your tired, your poor,
> Your huddled masses yearning to breathe free,
> The wretched refuse of your teeming shore.
> Send these, the homeless, tempest-tossed to me,
> I lift my lamp beside the golden door.

Historian Perry Miller approached the story of displacement through his commentary on the American Puritans,[22] exposing what he called their "Puritan minds." Miller argued that these Puritans never quite recovered from one moment in their brief history, the moment when the full meaning of having left home sank in. This was the moment when they realized they were "left alone in America" in what felt like a wilderness.

Most Americans carry the experience of immigration and displacement, but most often in their bones rather than in their conscious minds. These experiences have embedded themselves in emotions, attitudes, and symbolic practices and are transmitted from generation to generation. Just as the Civil War, even today, takes an unacknowledged and unrecognized toll on the daily lives of many Southerners who have virtually forgotten that war, ancestral displacement takes its unacknowledged toll on the daily lives of Americans who may feel comfortable and thoroughly settled. Just as, generations later, the fact that long ago a man was orphaned can give his great-grandchildren unaccountable feelings of insecurity, the immigrant experience can give to most Americans unaccountable feelings of rootlessness.

Homelessness has been felt by European immigrants, many of whom were refugees of persecution, famine, war, concentration camps, or simple unemployment; and by Asians and Hispanics who fled rigidity, strife, poverty, or military defeat. Among African Americans and Native Americans, reasons for a sense of displacement are not only present but incontestable to anyone half-familiar with their histories.

The American story of displacement can be rendered in three episodes. The first episode is the realization that to have left home is to have abandoned an identity. The second episode is the realization that America does not provide a profound, tradition-based identity. The third episode is the realization, both terrifying and exhilarating, that Americans have little choice but to stand at the edge of the void, to lift their own lamp, and to invent a new identity.

This third episode is the one through which most Americans are now living. It has demanded and continues to demand the invention of an American identity, and this requires thousands of other inventions, right down to the invention of distinctively American idioms and popular arts. The third episode is complicated by unforeseen and repeated risks and failures, which make it not the happy resolution it is sometimes claimed to be. From certain ethnic and economic groups, this third episode has called up heroic feats of invention: such as the invention of jazz by African Americans, the invention of the movies by Eastern European immigrant Jews, and the invention of American football by nineteenth-century ivy league college boys and twentieth-century professional players who started at the other end of the economic and social spectrum. The chance to participate in this third episode was for centuries blocked to African Americans, Jews, women, gays, Native Americans, and other "minorities," and it is as though this very blockage has called up from them unparalleled feats of invention—not only jazz, the movies, and football, but new idioms and styles and great works of fiction, music, dance, and religious expression.

This three-episode narrative of displacement may not be unique to America, for similar episodes must mark the experience of several other modern nations, particularly those that have undergone massive immigration from diverse lands and that have overwhelmed native peoples, throwing them into the ranks of the displaced. That is, parallel stories of displacement may be found in Australia, South Africa, and modern Israel.

The dawning experience of loss is what I am calling the first episode, in which people realized they had left home countries marked and identified by long lineages and genealogies; by ancient institutions, rituals, symbols, and landmarks; and by religious and folk traditions. In many of the Old Worlds, special events and places had been windows on an ideal and deeper reality that gave steady meaning to secular history. Sometimes these were windows on a world of eternal being that would endure whatever happened to the world of mere becoming. Transcending all secular history was something eternal; it assured a people that, if through war, pillage, and rape, secular history failed, this people would still be connected to a sacred reality that would give them a lasting meaning. In the deepest ways imaginable, this ideal or sacred world couched, framed, and even blessed peoples of the old countries.

In the New World, the loss of an identity once enjoyed in an ancient or sacred world was felt only gradually. The early American Puritans first believed they could go on living out of European history. It was not until the fall of Oliver Cromwell's Puritan government in 1668 that the New England Puritans realized they were no longer an outpost for England. Then the American Puritans were introduced to the disappointment that was to be registered in different ways down through the American centuries: there was no king in their new Israel; the home office was bankrupt and the frontier franchise was on its own. Later immigrants might live, like the early Puritans, out of the deeper history of their home country, but only for a generation or two. Then the lineages and genealogies and the ancient institutions, rituals, symbols, landmarks, and traditions of the old country would stop working. The loss of an identity-giving Old World was especially acute for African Americans, systematically deprived of most artifacts and practices of their home countries, and to the Native Americans, whose sacred ground was taken from them by alien intruders.

The second episode arose when it was realized that the new land had no clear and established identity to offer, at least none that compared to the identity given them in their former land. Each new immigrant generation found in America little to guide its cultural or moral life. That is, America continued to feel like a moral and cultural wilderness even after America's natural wilderness was largely overcome by the end of the nineteenth century. Unable to retain in its fullest sense the Old World culture and certainly unable to replace it with equally strong American traditions and institutions, Americans were adrift. Even today, scholars can apply to America what Alexis de Toqueville said of America over 150 years ago: "Up to the present, I don't see a trace of what we [Europeans] generally consider faiths, such as customs, ancient traditions, and the power of memories."[23] Historian Page Smith, in his important two-volume biography of John Adams, claims that Adams "understood, however dimly, the terrible vulnerability and nakedness of the human soul" that he as an American had inherited from the American Puritans.

> ... for the Puritan was the first man to stand alone before God and the world without the comfort of ritual, of forms and orders, traditions, customs and formalities, without, above all, any enrichment by the visual arts in the prolonged absence of which the soul withers. Alone, in an alien land, the New England man had to fashion out of nothing but the simple lumber of his faith a coherent, inhabitable world, and endure without respite the almost unbearable strain of that astonishing enterprise.[24]

Smith may exaggerate, but he rightly points to an early form of what might be called a distinctly American form of "tradition deprivation."

In this respect, most Americans are unlike most Europeans. This is neatly captured by Dominique Moïsi, editor of *Politique étrangère* (the French equivalent of *Foreign Affairs*) and deputy director of the Institute Français de Relations Internationales (the French equivalent of the Council on Foreign Relations). Referring to today's Europeans and Americans, Moïse says, "There is a European way to be Western—a product of history, geography, and culture—that is based on the weight of memory. By contrast, America is a culture of will. You are an American because you want to be so. Europeans ask themselves how to regenerate their past; Americans still perceive themselves in terms of the future."[25] To take an example: blue-blooded, St. Louis–born poet T. S. Eliot, innocently generalized in a famous essay that "tradition cannot be inherited, and if you want it you must obtain it by great labour." Poet W. H. Auden found Eliot's axiom to be an unintended admission of his peculiarly American rootlessness. Speaking from the vantage point of one born in England, Auden responded, "I do not think that any European critic would have said just this."[26]

It is the third episode in this story that presented and continues to present the greatest challenge. The American Puritans, said Miller, now had to have "a purpose and an intention sufficient unto itself," and they had "no other place to search but within themselves."[27] If there were to be a sacred errand, it would be found in New World secular action, not in contemplation of a higher world beyond the secular world. Americans, to the extent that they were religious, were inclined to find the divine in their negotiations with nature, within their democratic practice, within—and not beyond—the workings of their art. In the face of emptiness or adversity, Americans usually could not imitate but had to improvise on what sometimes appeared to be raw possibility. Culture critic Albert Murray says of American jazz, "Indeed the improvisation on the break, which is required of blues-idiom musicians and dancers alike, is precisely what epic heroism is based on."[28] It is no accident that a think tank in Minneapolis has taken the name, the Center of the American Experiment, for America and its deepest meanings are understood to have all the shaky uncertainty of an experiment. Americans find their first answers in the contingencies of their own existence rather than in something given by the past or something necessary to their being. William Carlos Williams, in his most popular poem, described a wheelbarrow in the rain beside chickens, and noted that on those simple, secular realities "so much depends." Murray and Williams, like Walt Whitman before them, could find nothing heroic or sacred except in that which stood within secular history.

If there were to be a New World meaning to replace even precariously the Old World meaning, it made sense to locate it within and not beyond history. The earlier two episodes of the American story required most Americans to acknowledge that they had lost the eternal meanings to which the word "being" points and all the support that those meanings provided. Americans, then, are consigned to something less stable even than what European novelist Milan Kundera called "the unbearable lightness of being"; they are consigned to an unbearable lightness of becoming, to the region of continual, unrelenting revision. Americans had only their own changing experiences to rely on. These experiences, in the words of William James, "lean on each other, but the whole of them, if such a whole there be, leans on nothing. All 'homes' are in finite experience; finite experience as such is homeless. Nothing outside of the flux secures the issue of it. It can hope salvation only from its own intrinsic promises and tendencies."[29] When he settled in America, English philosopher Alfred North Whitehead appropriately proclaimed that mathematical verities were temporary and inductive rather than eternal and deductive, and he titled one of his books *Religion in the Making*, acknowledging that even the sense of the sacred is never given, but always only to be made. In short, if there were to be a New World meaning to replace even feebly that of the Old World, it made sense to orient it not toward an eternal world beyond history but to the transitory world of history itself.

Most Americans moved into a relatively flat secular, present history, where there was little beyond immediate processes, knowing they were displaced from all that was stable and permeated with enduring traditional meanings. Americans are one of the most historical of peoples, if to be a truly historical people is to recognize that everything depends on living amid the contingencies of time and place, without reliance on anything beyond history or from an immutable past. Contingent history had to amount to something in America, for at some unconscious level most Americans knew that was all they had. And yet Americans are one of the least historical of peoples, if to live in history means to be immersed in an abiding past. Living in the daylight of the present moment, if Americans listen to anything, they listen to the intermittent crackle of transmissions from the future, and they forget the steady hum of crickets from the previous night. Typically, they are nerved by what is contingent and accidental, temporal and transitory, constructed and experimental. Church historian George Marsden has accurately said, "Substantial elements in the late nineteenth- and early twentieth-century America lacked those assumptions central to modern historical thought and scholarship, including the assumption that history was a natural evolutionary development and the corollary that the present can best be understood as a product of the past."[30] Living with the insecurity of contemporary history, Americans sustained themselves by what Teddy Roosevelt and William James called "the strenuous life" and believed that on themselves everything does, in fact, depend—or, just possibly, on themselves and on a God who was caught in the same battle they fought.

If they had a God, they still could not recover the spiritual security that God had once offered. Because their God lived with them in secular history, they knew that, if through such things as war and social disruption secular history were to fail, everything would fail. If it were to be had at all, spiritual reality would be discovered in or made through real world experiments. Religious truth would be associated with pragmatism, from the pragmatism of Benjamin Franklin to that of Protestant preacher Norman Vincent Peale, from Jonathan Edwards's efforts to test for God's presence within surrounding nature to the Religious Right's effort to find and test for God in the world of politics. Americans' deepest meanings were never to be assumed primarily as an inheritance from the past, as something *already* had, but primarily as something *to be* had.

The need for invention was especially vivid for most African Americans and Native Americans. Cornel West has acknowledged that "New World Africans are deeply modern in the sense of being exiles, banished from their native lands and forced to live lives as perennial 'outsiders,' finding a 'home' only in a dynamic language and mobile music—never in a secure land, safe territory or welcome nation."[31] Indians, as historian Ward Churchill has said, are "like sand in the wind." To argue, he writes, that these Indians are not dislocated because they still live in North America is like "arguing that a Swede displaced to Italy or a Vietnamese refugee in Korea would be at home simply because they remain in Europe or Asia." Although living in "the conditions of diaspora," many of them had little desire to participate in American society, where they had been "othered" by people who themselves felt othered.[32] Even if the Indians were to recover their traditions, in their present context they could not simply replicate those traditions, but would need to improvise them radically to make them intelligible in their new context.

German theologian Paul Tillich migrated from Germany to America in 1934 and captured with his typical insight the peculiarly American burden. Tillich was somewhat blinded by his own history-transcending philosophical idealism from seeing the Americans' confinement in current history and the loss of optimism that accrued from that confinement. Nevertheless, he correctly argued that there is an especially American form of courage having to do with living "in the productive process of history," "as a participant in the creative development of mankind." "There is something astonishing," he said,

> in the American courage for an observer who comes from Europe: although mostly symbolized in the early pioneers it is present today in the large majority of people. A person may have experienced a tragedy, a destructive fate, the breakdown of convictions, even guilt and momentary despair: he feels neither destroyed nor meaningless nor condemned nor without hope. When the Roman experienced the same catastrophes he took them with the courage of resignation. The typical American, after he has lost the foundations of his existence, works for new foundations. This is true of the individual and it is true of the nation as a whole. One can make experiments because an experimental failure does not mean discouragement.[33]

Some Consequences of the Common Story

As actually lived out, the common American story is leading to the development of certain undesirable American traits, and these traits are now causing Americans to damage their hard-won American culture. Described optimistically, the common American story was the story of a people rising up to confront their problems: they would attack their homelessness (episodes 1 and 2) by creating for themselves a new and common home (episode 3). But the traits developed from this common story have encouraged most Americans to turn against the common home and common meanings they have been building. I record three of these traits and their various consequences.

First, Americans tend to be active rather than contemplative, or doers rather than deliberators. Activism can be and often has been a virtue, giving Americans the inventiveness to improvise and to use fantasy to create a new life. But with an alarming regularity, this activism leads them to prize virtually any immediate objective or activity. Thus, today American moralists tend to treat "social change" as a term of commendation, as though change itself, any change, were good. Mobility becomes inherently more valuable than stability. As religious historian Martin Marty's book title suggests, Americans are *A Nation of Behavers*, and in their behaviors it is hard for even Marty to find abiding and common purposes. Americans seem more interested in throwing themselves into the machinery of history than in using it to produce what they actually need. The act itself seems more important than what the act is for. Most problematic, when activism assumes these proportions, it works against any effort methodically, deliberately, and carefully to develop a common American culture.

Second, Americans are populists. Lacking the tradition that gave royalty its divine rights, lawyers their natural law, and the aristocracy its pedigree, Americans tend to be levelers and egalitarians. This populism was perhaps the single most important psychological prerequisite for the world's oldest democracy, which has served as a model for many emerging nations. But again, populism can become uncritical, inciting Americans to draw a line beneath the aggregation of their separate decisions and to sanctify the merely popular total, as though it were a voice of wisdom worthy of judging their activities. Without a tradition beyond history, Americans look understandably for tradition in the history they have themselves largely constructed. But this can become callous and thoughtless, leading them to treasure a merely quantitative democratic majority, and to ignore the deliberative process of an organic republic—which alone has the capacity to build a common culture.

Third, lacking a strong tradition that could encourage a communal sensibility, Americans tend to be individualistic. Individuality can be and has been a great American strength, giving Americans a platform for personal responsibility and for civil rights. But this can lead to individualism, with ambiguous effects, making America, for example, the only major Western nation not to flirt with the one-for-all ideals of socialism and causing America to shun universal medical care, even universal medical insurance. Further, this individualism can lead to a *laissez-faire* capitalism, which would give autonomous individuals unfettered economic freedom, and can foster the belief that competition is an adequate test of personal worth. The nation sometimes is making a moral philosophy out of "looking out for number one" and a political philosophy out of the idea that government is the servant of the self. How, with such an ideology, are Americans to develop a cohesive common story, let alone a common culture?

The combined effects of these and other American developments have been examined recently by many commentators on America, three of whom I cite. In *Democracy's Discontent*, political scientist Michael Sandel has described the emergence of an America for which democratic procedures have become ends in themselves rather than the means toward corporate outcomes. Americans may once have seen liberty as the chance to participate in a self-governing society, but now tend to see liberty as an escape from the constraints of society. According to Sandel, Americans tend not to find fulfillment in social deliberation or virtue in compromise, so that they make joint action for the common good difficult, if not impossible.[34]

In *Twilight of American Dreams*, Todd Gitlin, a former president of the Students for a Democratic Society and hardly a nostalgic conservative, argues that identity politics has begun to undermine the quest for the common good. He opens his book with a long chapter recounting recent battles in California over how public school history textbooks treated race and ethnicity. He goes on to demonstrate that these disputes have led liberal reformers to focus on self-interested ethnic politics and to neglect their historic liberal interest in what might be good for California, especially for its jobs, education, and universal health care. Gitlin's aim is not primarily to describe recent Oakland school board fights, but to describe a nation so fractured by identity politics that the vision of the common good is dimming like the sun at twilight.[35]

Samuel Huntington makes a similar point, but with regard to American foreign policy rather than domestic politics.[36] Simply to have a foreign policy, he notes, a nation must identify its national interests, and to identify its national interests, a nation must have some vision of its common culture. But as multiculturalism has begun to assume the shape of an ideology, the identity of America's common culture—and, consequently, of its national interests and foreign policy—has been obscured. Multiculturalism has been augmented by the growth of a new kind of ethnic community epitomized by the Miami Cubans, who want not so much to join America as to be a diaspora within America, not so much to be a "loyal opposition" as to be a pressure group that changes America's policy toward Cuba. All this undermines Americans' efforts to formulate their national interest and to shape foreign policies that represent that interest, as policies that promote Third World development, protect small nations from aggression, and extend democracy and human rights might.

A Common Spiritual Culture

Earlier I suggested that Americans must find ways to revive the spiritual culture that underlies their common culture. But how might the spiritual culture be sustained in the newly skeptical, even reductivist, society described in chapter 1, and yet be able to address problems like those described immediately above? Most of the remainder of this book attempts to answer these questions. Here I merely allude to the fact that the American spiritual culture need only be revived rather than created *de novo*, for there is a significant and relatively consistent American symbolic, theological, and philosophical tradition on which it can lean.[37]

Admittedly, this is a frail tradition, lacking the gradually built and deeply embedded cultural and intellectual symbols that would lend credibility and authority to distinctively American thought. Americans could not live fully within the terms of an Old World culture, and, with the exception of Native Americans, they had no ancient culture of their own. They had no choice but to work within what I have called the "third episode," constructively improvising a spiritual culture as they went along. But they could incorporate elements of various Old World traditions, even if they had to add a New World framework. Above all, they could utilize a nascent American theological and philosophical tradition.

Historical theologian Joseph Haroutunian pointed in the general direction of that theological and philosophical tradition in a paper read in the fall of 1963 to his colleagues at their annual faculty retreat. In that paper, entitled "Theology and American Experience,"[38] he outlined the particular nature of American experience and argued that American theological reflection on that experience had remained weak. While America had generated a string of theologians,[39] both they and the distinctiveness of the American religious experience they described had never been appreciated, not even within American theological circles. As a result, American theology became, on the whole, "a minor variation of the European." American people had been shaped by America, but their theology had been shaped by Europe. Thus, said Haroutunian, "while professional theologians lived off European theology, the American Christians tried to get along with a minimum of intellectual discipline."[40] Nevertheless, Haroutunian's purpose was to remind his colleagues of what authentically American religious thinking might be.

In his intentions, Haroutunian unwittingly followed a precedent set seventy-six years earlier by Princeton president and philosopher James McCosh, who said, "The time has come, I believe, for America to declare her independence in philosophy. . . . If a genuine American philosophy arises, it must reflect the genius of the people."[41] McCosh, himself was preceded by mid-nineteenth-century theologians Theodore Parker and Horace Bushnell and succeeded by early-twentieth-century philosopher George Santayana—all of whom called for and began constructing religious and philosophical ideas consciously shaped by distinctively American experience.[42]

This tradition of thought must be not only recovered but amplified until it is able to answer the social-scientific skepticism that reduces God to mere talk generated out of American needs and desires. Those who develop this thought must show how they are not doing all over again what religious thinkers tend now to do, which is to create a God that merely fits their own secular standards and is no larger than those standards. How can any God now described be large enough to judge and redeem American aspirations? This is the sort of question that an American spiritual culture must answer if it is to help sustain the nation.

Partly because they lacked such critical thinking, other societies have impaled themselves. Some Afrikaners of South Africa told stories of their Great Trek, tied those stories to their God, and used the religion that resulted to support apartheid. Some Jews told Zionist stories of the origin and loss of the "Jewish homeland" and the need to recover it, implicated their God in that story and began to treat the most recent natives of these homelands, the Palestinians, with a harshness that contradicted much of the Zionists' own Jewish morality. Irish Protestants and Irish Catholics told mutually incompatible stories about Northern Ireland, fortified them with Protestant and Catholic ingredients, and fought each other through most of the twentieth century. One reason each of these nations compromised itself morally is that each failed to appreciate a God relevant to its particular story, a God intellectually and religiously plausible in an evolving society, and a God that was, in some respects, transcendent of, and therefore able to judge, its national history.

The first and best single response to the problems flowing from the American story is to begin to revise the theological grounds for the American spiritual culture. After all, the American spiritual culture will have no lasting authority unless it is understood to be based on something greater than itself. I will attempt to describe such grounds—specifically, concepts of God—in chapters 3 and 4. I will argue that these concepts of God pertain to America, are plausible in America, and describe a God transcendent enough to judge America.

3

_P_ragmatism

God is real since he produces real effects.
—William James, *The Varieties of Religious Experience*

CAST ON THE SHORES OR INTO THE INNER CITIES OF AMERICA, tested for their capacity to survive in what was or felt like a wilderness, American immigrants learned to prize practicality above all. Of course, they wanted their religious beliefs to resonate to established truths, but they knew their beliefs must be able to keep them alive or enhance their lives in adverse circumstances. Americans were not just practical; they were systematically practical, so it should have surprised no one when they became the world architects of the formal philosophy of pragmatism.

The Israelites as Proto-Pragmatists

In their practicality, Americans were like the ancient Israelites, who also wanted a religion that would help them survive in an apparent wilderness. Although the American Puritans have been called "proto-pragmatists,"[1] the title could equally well apply to the ancient Israelites. The most ambitious expression of the Israelites' pragmatism lay in their belief that God was real not because God was rational, sublime, or otherwise fit for divinity, but because God acted in Israel's history. This belief gave them a way to explain past outcomes and to predict future consequences.

It is true that sometimes God seemed indifferent to the Israelites' his-

62

tory. The authors of Ecclesiastes and of the poetry of Job, for example, were vexed by a history that seemed inveterately capricious and unjust. But their vexation made sense because they had assumed that God was involved in historical practice. Even the Psalms, which sometimes seem to praise God without reference to history, had supported this assumption when they celebrated the renewal of their thoroughly historical covenant with God.[2]

The Israelites' pragmatic theology made no sense unless it referred to a real history. Thus, ancient Hebrew pragmatism spoke of a history where God was known and identified through God's role in history. For the Israelites, God did not live beyond historical time and change, but as a changing reality within history. God was not represented symbolically through history, as though history were a window displaying God on the other side of history or a mirror reflecting God's eternal and universal Truth. There was nothing but the stage of history, and there were no wings to the stage. God was not a visible player, but God did play on that stage, and this could be demonstrated by how the stage action went. Even the creation of the world was a historical action: because God had created the natural context of history, God had the power to control the events of human history.[3]

God's usefulness in history was usually understood within a very specific framework. This was the framework provided by the covenant between God and Moses at Sinai, which became the principal expression of the covenant relation between God and Israel. God was valuable for the Israelites because God kept promises defined in the covenant, thereby making historical results predictable. The covenant stated Israel's obligations to God and set the terms for God's response when Israel fulfilled or failed to fulfill its covenant obligations. Israel's obedience to the covenant was rewarded with historical successes, and Israel's disobedience to the covenant was punished with historical failures.

The covenant's logic was spelled out in Israel's retributive philosophy of history—a philosophy that originated in Deuteronomy but that was generally adopted by Israel. God, it said, always applies retribution and Israel always absorbs retribution. The test of the covenant's truth was whether the covenant's predictions were actually fulfilled. For example, according to the biblical book of Joshua, when Israel violated the covenant by stealing "devoted things" of the enemies, God caused the Israelites to fall in battle and caused those who had participated in the theft to be stoned or burned to death. Further, Joshua implies, if Israel would repent and uphold the covenant, God would cause the Israelites to slaughter their opponents (Joshua 7–8). The book of Judges sets up the following four-part, causal sequence: (1) Israel's apostasy, through the worship of other gods, is followed by (2) God's judgment, causing Israel to be defeated in battle, which is followed by (3) Israel's repentance for its apostasy, which is followed by (4) God's deliverance of Israel, proved by Israel's conquest of its enemies. Thus, God's interactions with Israel occurred in history largely through God's acts of retribution. The covenant was the framework within which Israel's retributive philosophy of history worked; and the covenant's truth was tested by examining whether its predictions of retribution were actually fulfilled.

Given this historical pragmatism, it is not surprising that Jewish scholar Mordecai Kaplan would say, "The people of Israel was the first people to discover the God of history."[4] God not only acted in history, but God *was* God's action. God's overt historicity was described succinctly in the title of G. Ernest Wright's popular book *God Who Acts*. Wright's point was that the God of the Israelites is not the God who speaks, if speaking is a means of conveying a word that can be dissociated from acts and thereby "dissociated from history and dealt with as an abstraction" for theological contemplation.[5] God's famous answer to Moses' request for God's name is translated in the Revised Standard Version as "I am who I am" (Exodus 3:14). Jack Miles, a scholar of Hebrew Scriptures (the Christian Old Testament), argues that this should be translated "I am what I do," for God "is indeed defined by what he does." "Even to himself," Miles claims, "he is a mystery that is revealed progressively only through his actions and their aftermath."[6]

If God is what God does in history, what God does in history is, more than anything else, to impact the spiritual culture of Israel. Of course, God affected military and political history, but this history was important principally for how it affected the spiritual life and culture of Israel. Israel's theological reflections on military and political history were intended to correct and revise Israel's spiritual culture. And yet, when the Israelites felt the workings of their spiritual culture, they believed that as a people they were led neither by their spiritual culture nor by its covenant theology itself, but by the God who worked through them.

The Israelites assessed God's reality by reference to God's historical effects. For example, the important thing about a political or military victory or defeat for Israel was not the *theory* that God was directing physical events, but the *fact* that in victory or defeat Israel knew itself to be vindicated or punished by God. When the prophets judged Israel, they may have adroitly analyzed impending military and political events, but their intention was to show that, in fact, Israel had been or would be judged. When

Nathan found David guilty of killing Uriah, David was not miraculously struck down or removed from his kingly office, but he knew he had actually been judged.

The prophets' pragmatism was evident in their willingness to test their religious ideas by asking whether they were corroborated by history. This pragmatism was important because it gave the Israelites a way to guide their national life. If Israel wanted its history to improve, it should observe its covenant obligations. Faith affirmed God's reality, but it was not about that affirmation itself, but about how the nation could live better.

However, if acts of obedience or disobedience to God were to have no consequences or would have unanticipated consequences, then faith would be jeopardized. The book of Job toyed with this eventuality. While Job's counselors argued that his personal disasters implied that he was suffering divine retribution for grave sins, Job knew that he was basically innocent and did not deserve such treatment. Naturally, then, his faith in a covenant-abiding God was put to the test.[7] Throughout most of the Hebrew Bible, however, the pragmatic logic worked for the Israelites; obedience to God appeared to cause their life to flourish, and disobedience to God appeared to cause their life to deteriorate.

The Israelites' theological pragmatism lived on, in a sometimes diluted form, in the New Testament. Jesus argued pragmatically that, if people wanted to inherit the kingdom of God, they should treat his message as true. But Jesus was also interested in a pragmatic approach to more immediate questions. For example, false prophets could be identified, Jesus said, "by their fruits. Are grapes gathered from thorns, or figs from thistles? . . . Every tree that does not bear good fruit is cut down and thrown into the fire" (Matthew 7:17–20). In Matthew, Jesus generalized on this pragmatic criterion, saying, "The good man out of his good treasure brings forth good, and the evil man out of his evil treasure brings forth evil" (Matthew 12:35).

American Religious Pragmatism

Echoing this biblical pragmatism, American pragmatist William James joked: "By their fruits ye shall know them, not by their roots."[8] James was conscious that his fruits-roots alternative had American precedents. For example, Jonathan Edwards's *Treatise on Religious Affections*, said James, was "an elaborate working out of this [pragmatist] thesis." Edwards had argued: "*The degree* in which our experience is productive of practice shows *the degree in which our experience is spiritual and divine.*"[9] Edwards's contemporary, Benjamin Franklin, believed that in America bloodlines meant little (certainly Franklin's was not notable), so that a man's worth was determined, he said, by asking "What can he do?" With such a pragmatic orientation, it was easy for Franklin to accept the popular saying that "God Almighty is himself a mechanic," respected for the "utility of his handiworks."[10] Putting Franklin's statements on religion and morality together, one could argue that God was important to the extent that God instilled human virtue.

Pragmatic logic was adopted by many American Puritans, who tended to have a pragmatic streak—due, no doubt, partly to their deep consciousness of the parallels between their own story and that of the Israelites. Like the Israelites, they entered into a covenant that lay at the heart of their spiritual culture and required their loyalty. Linking their actions and consequences through the terms of their covenant with God, the Puritans knew that their material success in the wilderness was a reward for their covenant faithfulness and that their material failures—especially natural disasters such as rainstorms and earthquakes, or outbreaks such as smallpox—were punishments for their covenant violation. Historian Perry Miller notes the Puritans' "implicit recognition of a causal sequence: the sins exist, the disease breaks out; the sins are reformed, the disease is cured." Eventually, the punishments became less external and more internal; then punishment was found in spiritual rather than material deprivation, so that unfaithful Puritans were given over to hard-heartedness, sloth, sensuality, indifference, and hypocrisy. Later still, the punishment was manifested in the failure of their "public spirit."[11] This all was just as John Winthrop's early sermon aboard the *Arabella* said it would be: "the Lord will surely break out in wrath against us, be revenged of such a perjured people and make us know the price of the breach of such a Covenant."[12]

This pragmatic stance made particular sense to many later Americans, both because of their biblical past and because they found their Old World religious traditions inadequate as they faced circumstances radically different from those in which the Old World traditions had been developed. Consequently, the early immigrants could neither sustain European theologies nor test the truth of their own religious thought by its correspondence to those theologies. They needed to improvise on their received religious traditions, and in fact they did, developing ideas that often had little correspondence to ideas of the old countries.

For example, the Americans initiated successful evangelical "awakenings" and new forms of religious naturalism, and extended them intellectually, so that experiential and naturalistic theologies abound in America to this day. Theology based on religious experience prevails in the revival meetings that are regular events in some churches. And Jonathan Edwards's naturalistic theology was eventually followed by various species of what Catherine Albanese calls "nature religions" (wherein health is connected with a saving spirit in nature).[13] Theological naturalism is implicit in a variety of current movements, such as eco-theology, neo-paganism, process theology, and today's popular and well-funded science-and-religion dialogue.

Thus, both because they were influenced by Israel's retributive philosophy of history and because they needed to test ideas by their uses in a new environment rather than by their congruence with Old World customs, it is not surprising that Americans looked to historical success or failure for evidence of their salvation. On the whole, Americans came to adopt the Puritans' basically Calvinist style of thought, which emphasized the implications of behavior. Although Americans made much of salvation beyond history, their religious thinking was oriented less toward truths beyond history than the Platonic and Augustinian theologies were, and more toward truths found and tested in history, as the Hebraic and Calvinist theologies were.

In fact, Calvinist pragmatism became crucial in the unfolding not only of American theology but also of an American style of thought. American intellectual historian Bruce Kuklick, in *Churchmen and Philosophers*, demonstrates the heavy dependence of American thinking on the Calvinist orientation, which came to be "the most sustained intellectual tradition the United States has produced," providing "the one systematic body of thinking in America, as well as the only sustained intellectual debate."[14]

Calvinists had always found evidence for their salvation in their good works. For them, R. H. Tawney said, "good works are not a way of attaining salvation, but they are indispensable as a proof that salvation has been attained."[15] Like the Israelites, the Calvinist Puritans and their various American successors built their theology around what they believed was a covenant and around the recognition that fulfilling or not fulfilling covenant obligations had consequences. Therein lay the ideas and the logic for formal pragmatic reasoning: one could test whether one's internal salvation was real by looking at whether one's external life flourished.

John Dewey and
American Religious Pragmatism

With only slight exaggeration it could be said that Calvinism provided the world for which pragmatism became the method. It is no accident that the classical philosophical pragmatists' ways of testing their ideas of God by asking whether they were useful conformed to the ways of the Calvinist Puritans, who had long been interested in the effects of beliefs. Admittedly, the philosophical pragmatists discussed knowledge of God by reference to evidence rather than by reference to faith, and their God was set in the cosmology of modern science rather than in that of the Bible. Nevertheless, pragmatism owed its life largely to its Calvinist religious culture, even if also to the methods provided by its philosophical heritage.

John Dewey, whom Kuklick calls "the preeminent philosopher in the United States and the twentieth century's foremost American intellectual," is a prime instance of this Calvinist-pragmatist linkage. While the academics wanted to see Dewey as "the quintessential secular liberal," he was, in truth, according to Kuklick, a Calvinist in attitude, quietly importing "what were recognized at the time as religious values into a scientific conception of man and nature."[16]

Following the new mode of thought introduced by Darwin, Dewey understood society to be like a species threatened with extinction. Just as a species faces extinction either because it has undergone variations or because its natural environment has changed, a society faces extinction when it and/or its social and natural environment changes. When that happens, a society's only hope is to change itself and/or its environment. This adjustment cannot be accomplished piecemeal by tinkering with societies or environments until they better fit each other. What must be found is a view of "the universe," or the world, that will become a canopy under which society and its environment can be reconceived and altered, so that they can be related in new ways.[17] This view of the universe is critical to any society's efforts to avoid catastrophe and to attain a new life.

Although a society reaches this new vision by what it calls imagination, it has not simply invented that vision. Instead, the spiritual tradition that has helped form the society in the past now sets the initial rules for that society's vision of the universe. This tradition, which Dewey calls "the unity of all ideal ends arousing us to desire and actions,"[18] guides and sparks the social imagination, which will then go on to outrun the spiritual tradition, causing it to be slightly reenvisioned. Thus, the imagination, rather than working in isolation, responds creatively to a spiritual tradition that is living, active, and evolving. It can be argued that something like this occurred in the eighteenth century, as America developed an implicit vision under which it moved from being a parochial Puritan society to becoming a biblical/Enlightenment society with enough coherence and unity to revolt from England and to create a new democracy.

For Dewey, this spiritual tradition, as it leads the social imagination, does much that a transcendent God is believed to do for a society. The living tradition prompts a society to do what otherwise it could not do; it impacts the social imagination, informing it of the local past to which it must relate and spurring it to introduce needed novelty. Out of this comes a new vision, which contributes to the society's evolving spiritual culture. When traditions do this for societies, the society receives just the sort of influence commonly attributed to a God—and societies may, in fact, describe this influence as divine. Whether it is called a living spiritual tradition or a God, it amounts to the same thing when seen from a pragmatic point of view. It is not surprising, then, that Dewey sometimes called this living spiritual tradition "God."

For Dewey, God is the meaning or "the sense" of the whole that prompts a society to shape a new vision in terms of which it can grow. Dewey knew that religions tended typically to rivet themselves to an earlier vision, which is no longer useful under present conditions (i.e., to some dead God); however, Dewey argued that that need not be the case. Dewey contrasted such "religion" (loyalty to an earlier version of God and the spiritual culture) with "religiousness" (the faith that participates in the continuous revision of a society's spiritual culture). For Dewey, a religiousness is pragmatically meaningful and true because it can contribute to the growth of a spiritual culture.[19] But religiousness is possible only because, in addition to its own inventiveness, it is lured to evolve by the sense of the whole that can be called God. It is exactly God's influence on religiousness that makes God real; by all that is basic to pragmatism, this is the only conclusion that can be reached. If God prompts religiousness, and if religiousness prompts societies to readjust and save themselves, then God is real as the savior of societies. God prods societies to move beyond what is dead in their tradition and to generate new social ideals capable of saving the societies from extinction.[20]

To all this should be added the fact—seldom, if ever, noted by Dewey or by Calvinists—that this religious social process also has effects on God. When a society revises its spiritual culture and its environment, it alters, however slightly, the particular social universe whose meaning God is. If

God is the meaning of that whole social universe, then as that society changes, the Godlike meaning given to that society must change. This picture of God changing in response to a social process is hardly radical. Although it makes God to some extent malleable and although this violates ideas of the omnipotence, independence, and self-derivedness (aseity) of God, such divine responsiveness is necessary to a God who cares enough about to world to respond to it, as both Jews and Christians recognized.

Dewey was not original in using a pragmatic argument to establish the reality of God. He was preceded not only by the Calvinists but also by pragmatists William James and Charles Sanders Peirce, working out of the same biblical, Puritan, Calvinist tradition. Dewey was original, nonetheless, in showing through pragmatic argument how a historical God works in a social and historical context. Dewey's God was set thoroughly in history and was about public life and how whole societies should meet their challenges. Although James proposed a God who acted from within history, his God was a God of the private life of individuals, not of the public world of society.[21] Peirce's God could deal with public problems, but it existed outside the flow of historical change, in a world of eternal ideas.[22]

The work of these and other pragmatists was solidified and applied to biblical and religious history by a number of scholars of religion, but most early, most explicitly, and most expertly by that group of scholars at the Divinity School of the University of Chicago, a group called the "Chicago School." Chief among them were Shirley Jackson Case, Shailer Mathews, and Gerald Birney Smith.[23] They worked out of the Darwinian dynamic and believed that religion grew largely through responses to social changes. They called their method the "socio-historical" method. These and other religious thinkers gave theological clothing to what was already a basic American religious belief.

God as a Sacred Convention

Today, many decades after Dewey's death, how might a God who is active in history be described? Any concept of God must meet several conditions if it is to be consistent with biblical historicism, American Calvinism, and classical pragmatism. God must be a reality that is (1) located thoroughly within some history, even if not entirely within secular history. As located in history, God must (2) shape historical events and be shaped by historical events. However, to be called divine, God must (3) accomplish what historical creatures cannot accomplish for themselves. To do this, God must (4) in some limited way be free from strict determination by history and be able to innovate and to offer history something new. Within these limits, God might be conceived of variously. I have chosen to conceive of God in a basically Deweyan way, as an active, living historical tradition, one that has taken on a life of its own. However, it cannot be that simple, for if a tradition that has taken on a life of its own is to be real, as God is real, then it must be of a distinctive type.

God is real, I am proposing, in the way that a social convention is real. A social convention is not something eternal and universal, not an abstract and enduring essence or a universal law of nature. Rather, a convention is a social construct or habit that evolves in and from a society and then takes on a life of its own in that society, until it can accomplish for a society what a society cannot accomplish for itself.

To explain the nature of a historical convention, I turn to historian Thomas Haskell, who has proposed that "universal human rights" are social conventions. Universal human rights are historical, in that they have not always existed, they have evolved in history, and they are local (colored by local circumstances and, therefore, not actually universal even if they are meant to be). Such rights must be vigilantly protected precisely because they are historical—unlike, say, geometry, which seems to be nonhistorical in that it transcends or is true for any particular history, making it invulnerable to historical influences. Rather, as historical realities, human rights can perish, perhaps never to be re-introduced in a society. These rights began as pure fictions—things imagined by revolutionaries and the philosophers and theologians who listened to them. "But," says Haskell, "by saying that rights are fictions we need not mean anything more than that they are human creations, *conventions*, as opposed to natural or metaphysical objects."[24] Although conventions begin in imagination and are only temporal and local, they are known to be real because they actually change people's lives; they arise in history and have historical effects.

God is a unique type of social convention, unique because God is a convention that provides for a society its sense of the whole. As such a convention, God gives to a society its deepest, most comprehensive orientation in the universe, in terms of which it can work out its life, particularly its adjustment to its environment. This convention is the given, objective meaning-sense of the whole that gives to a society its personal, subjective faith-sense of the whole. Given this importance, this convention can inspire a society and sometimes instill awe.

I am calling this unique type of social convention a "sacred convention."

The sacred convention passes the basic test for anything that is real: it has historical consequences. It "takes on a life of its own" in that it is not simply the growing accumulation of influences it has received from society; rather, it becomes in some sense original, more than the totality of what it has received. That it has become original can be discovered when the effects of the sacred convention are known to be somewhat unpredictable, in the sense that they are not quite what one would expect, even if one knew all the influences it had received from the world. It takes on a life of its own somewhat like a child takes on a life of its own, when a child acts freely, or does things that no geneticist, social scientist, or parent could conceivably predict.

It may seem shocking to call God a convention, even a sacred convention, for "convention" conjures up mere social fashion, and calling God a convention would seem to make God no more real than a passing fad. There are, however, several balancing considerations.

First, any term applied to God is only an analogy; when this is forgotten, any God-defining term is sacrilegious. Second, to picture God as gradually evolving due to social interactions (as a convention does) is apt, because God, as God is commonly understood, is affected by human issues and actions. Third, the proposal that God is one kind of living convention is not novel. Eminent sociologists of religion such as Emile Durkheim and biblical scholars such as Shailer Mathews, without using the word, have suggested that God acts like a social convention.[25] However, Durkheim, Ludwig Feuerbach, and most social scientists of religion, as well as many romantics and existentialists, have assumed that God conventions are figments of the personal or social imagination and are not real. I would argue that they neglect the fact that, as a convention, God has a life of its own and affects societies in unexpected ways, so that by any pragmatic use of the term "reality," God is a living, historical reality.

As part of history, God can be understood in John Dewey's terms, as "the heritage of values we have received," the heritage that comes out of the past but that we, as historical creatures, can help reshape for our times.[26] When Dewey called God a "unity of all ideal ends arousing us to desire and actions," he knew that the ideals were, in part, received from an ancient past. He also knew that the ideals could not be good for an evolving history unless they were continually affected and altered by local, ongoing historical changes. On the other hand, the ideals, as they arouse us, are active in history. Beyond this and in ways that Dewey neglects, any vital heritage is living, so that it takes on a life of its own and acts in unpredictable ways, as did the God of the Israelites and of the Puritans. Both Israelites and Puritans detected the consequences of God's action in their histories. They believed that the social calamities from which they suffered were God's judgments on them. Although most people today would doubt that the course of physical history can literally be broken into by God's action, they could hardly doubt that the sacred convention altered the way the Israelites and Puritans understood their history and, thereby, adjusted their historical action.

The principal religious problem with calling God a living convention is that it seems to depersonalize God. How can a convention or a "heritage of values" be intimate with people? How can a social convention affect people personally, persuading them to think and behave in new ways? This is a question that cannot be dismissed if theological ideas are to have more than arid, academic meaning.

While this question seems intuitively correct, it is based on the false assumption that persons have intimate relations but that they are not, themselves, living social conventions. In fact, any living thing is social; it arises out of the social interactions of a natural and human society, functions as a member of that society, and responds to that society. It is constituted and formed by the past, continually altered by present conditions, and capable of moving beyond its social causes to change spontaneously and freely. Persons are created through sexual interactions, they are formed by historical and cultural influences, and, at least to some very small extent, they contribute to their own development and to the development of others.[27] Persons are, in short, social conventions—walking, talking social traditions, or collections of genetic and environmental inheritances from the past that acquire an organic integrity and that act somewhat freely in the present. They are formed and constituted by these inheritances much as a tradition is, and yet they change and innovate.

Like a person, God is formed by heritages and environments and moves beyond these heritages and environments to change in ways that could not be predicted. To say here that God changes is only to say that God is a growing convention rather than a static convention. To put it in contemporary language, God is not a social construction, created in a moment of time and remaining fixed forever, but a social convention, a social habit that evolves through time. Finally and in ways I cannot here elaborate, to see God as a sacred convention works just as well in natural history as in human history—for the divine vector of value in natural history is a convention, just as the regularities of nature described by physics, often called "laws," are historical conventions.[28]

Of course, although alive in the physical universe, God's body cannot be located or sensed. But this is hardly an unusual phenomenon. For example, Americans deal with nations, tracing their history and development and attempting to define them and predict their behavior. When Americans talk about the Russian nation, they are not referring primarily to a piece of land with certain geographical borders, nor to a simple entity that exists at a point in space or time. That nation is abstracted from a history of relations, and yet it both remains the same and changes in and through the transitions of leaders and wars. Through most of the twentieth century, Americans have felt the real presence of Russia in their personal lives, particularly as they lived under the threat of nuclear war. Yet this Russian nation had no locatable body; nevertheless, it has been real in all the myriad, invisible places it was experienced.[29] Similarly, to acknowledge that God is not sensed with the five senses and is not located in some particular point in space and time does not make God unreal.

In fact, a God who is a sacred convention is far more personal than the God of classical (Augustinian and Thomistic) theology, who is ahistorical, eternal, and universally the same—an absolute, self-sufficient, self-derived, entirely independent being. To be absolute in these ways is to be unmoved by anything that transpires outside itself, for if it were moved by anything, it would draw energy from beyond itself and be, thereby, dependent and relative. But as "unmoved" and therefore unaffected by any living things, the classical God had to be (though was not acknowledged to be) ignorant of all that lay outside itself, for all knowledge requires that one be affected by and dependent on the information that comes from outside oneself. As ignorant, this God was deprived of affections, because all affections depend on receiving information from outside oneself. Persons, as we know persons, are persons largely because they are vulnerable, dependent on, and affected by particular other people in their particular circumstances. To be a person—we say, "human"—means precisely not to exist in cold isolation, independent of and unaffected by the tragedies and joys of events in the world. Equally, as absolute, the God of classical theism is universally the same through time and space, acting uniformly throughout the world, having neither a particular history with, nor particular interests in particular groups of people (though this last point is also unacknowledged by classical theologians). This absolute God lacks all the historical thickness and entanglement with particular histories so important to the communities of the Jews, the Christians, and the Muslims.

Knowledge of God as a living sacred convention is the result of summarizing continuities from centuries of religious commentary on God's actions and allowing that entire tradition of speculation about God to form a composite picture of God. People are Jews, Christians, or Muslims precisely because they are informed by such commentaries on God, which they summarize and recognize. Although this known God is abstracted from a variety of particular historical interactions and might seem to be nothing but an abstraction, this does not keep God from being, in fact, a concrete reality to which people pray and on whom they personally rely. To know abstractly and yet to believe that what is known is concrete, is common. For example, people know other people only through abstractions. They see a friend through an abstract image developed over a long and varied history of friendship, and they rely on that abstract image as a representation of a very definite person. In short, they treat the friend as a living convention, conceived and born biologically in a physical history, formed in an ongoing physical and human social history, and occasionally acting spontaneously.

To know God abstractly is consistent with also believing that God is a motivating force in history. As a sacred convention, God can be personally known as the spiritual and historical impetus that incites a community to act morally and religiously. At one level, God may be the gist, *Geist*, or soul of a nation that inspires its spiritual culture.

The Sacred Convention and the Spirit of the Law

A sacred convention can, perhaps, be better understood through an extended analogy with what has been called "the spirit of the law."[30] In America, law is either common law or Constitutional law; the former is more fluid than the latter, but each is at times treated as though it possessed something like a spirit.

Most legal proceedings involve rules of common law, which ultimately are based on the social customs of a society rather than on any permanent document such as the Constitution. When these social customs are accepted as rules of common law, judges are free to shape and sometimes alter them. Common law comes into play when, for example, two people dispute over free speech—say, one person charges the other with slander or liable. Consulting previous law, a judge must reach a decision to resolve the contest. Typically, a judge will apply previous law; but if the judge finds that new circumstances are involved in the dispute, he or she can reach a decision that deviates from the legal precedent and, in effect, alters the rules of common law. Over time rules of common law can change so much that they lose altogether their original content and form. In his classic *The Common Law*, Oliver Wendell Holmes Jr. explains the growth of common law:

> The customs, beliefs, or needs of a primitive time establish a rule or a for-mula. In the course of centuries the custom, belief, or necessity disappears, but the rule remains. The reason which gave rise to the rule has been for-gotten, and ingenious minds set themselves to inquire how it is to be accounted for. Some ground of policy is thought of, which seems to explain it and to reconcile it with the present state of things; and then the rule adapts itself to the new reasons which have been found for it, and enters on a new career.[31]

Although both content and form of the law change, we still assume it is a particular law that evolves, as though it retained some "ground of policy" amid change. Holmes refused to call that ground an algorithm or an essence behind the law. But, obviously, something abides, even while the content and form of the law change.

I am calling the ground of policy that abides through change the living spirit of the law. Understood this way, the spirit of the law is one "organ" within the national "organism"; as such, it helps to explain how a nation endures even as it changes. Holmes claimed that, even though the com-mon law "cannot be dealt with as if it contained the axioms and corollaries of a book of mathematics," it does embody "the story of a nation's devel-opment through many centuries."[32]

If the spirit of the law were not alive, the evolution of common law would be mechanical, completely determined by past and present causes. Three forms of mechanical determination are imaginable: (1) the total determination of the law by the past, (2) the total determination of the law by the present choices and whims of judges as they rework the law,[33] or (3) the total determination of the law by a combination of past and pres-ent influences. But none of these forms of determination fully accounts for the actual evolution of the law. I am suggesting that "the spirit of the law" is an image that captures the aliveness of the law, making it partly pre-dictable but also partly unpredictable, just as living things are. People attempt to honor the spirit of the law the way they would never honor a fixed essence or a machine. If the law had no spirit, at the end of a trial on a question that seems novel, people would never await the verdict with hushed anticipation, as though the spirit of the law were reaching a deci-sion, much as a person makes a decision.

I am suggesting that the spirit of the law, as it resides in common law, is analogous to the sacred convention, if the sacred convention is seen as "the Spirit of History." The analogy between the spirit of the law and the Spirit of History suggests how the sacred convention, as the Spirit of History, can be real, can endure, and can also direct, in part, its own evolution. If the spirit of the law can, in principle, account for the inexplicable continuity and unpredictability in the life of the law, the Spirit of History also can, in principle, account for the inexplicable continuity and unpredictability in the life of a spiritual culture and, in effect, in the life of a historical group or nation—an unpredictability that always confounds the work of the historian. In each case, a spirit takes on a life of its own and moves in ways that are partly uncanny.

A more constricted and conservative spirit of the law is found in Constitutional law, which is based on the wording of the U.S. Constitution. If, for example, issues of free speech were to arise in matters of government or between people and governments, Constitutional law rather than common law would come into play—here, as a First Amendment issue concerning whether and how governments can regulate free speech. Constitutional law grows complicated partly because, although the literary form of the American Constitution is permanent, its meaning can change. However, even the meaning of the Constitution retains some minimal consistency through time, despite judges' ingenuity, which could, in principle, allow them to interpret Constitutional law just as they wanted, making this meaning mirror nothing but their own changing ideas and ideals. If this enduring meaning is called the spirit of Constitutional law, that spirit need not be described romantically, as some metaphysical "essence of the American spirit," some "grand and cloudy Constitution that stands in our minds for the ideal America, earth's last best hope, the city on a hill," the stuff of Fourth of July speeches.[34] The spirit of Constitutional law might be described by a few unstated Constitutional principles that live on and continue to be upheld, such as separation of powers, federalism, separation of church and state, checks and balances. These do not appear, in so many words, in the text of the Constitution, yet they live and hover over the interpretation of the Constitution and give to it a certain consistency.[35]

Similarly, the sacred convention retains a few indispensable elements that give it continuity through time—such things as God's covenant in the Hebrew Bible or God's enduring love in the New Testament. In contemporary America, the spiritual culture lifts up and focuses on such enduring elements in the sacred convention.

Yet these principles do not work like fixed essences. In the evolution of Constitutional law, there is an inexplicable freedom, giving unpredictability to its evolution, as though it had a life of its own. Even the "original intent" of the framers of the Constitution must sometimes be set aside to permit the law to work freely in new circumstances.

But whether the sacred convention as the Spirit of History is understood to be analogous to the more roving spirit of the common law or to the more sedentary spirit of Constitutional law, the sacred convention is that reality that influences a community's spiritual culture with both constancy and innovation. It is this spirit that people look to, not only with hushed anticipation but with fear and trembling, not quite knowing how it will speak in any new moment of history.

Faith, Revelation, and Prayer

When God is described as a sacred convention, the terms "faith," "revelation," and "prayer" take on meanings slightly at odds with the meanings they have had in more classical forms of theology.

In religious traditions of the West, *religious faith* can be understood as a community's or an individual's response to God. Among these communities is the national community with its spiritual culture, but also small communities such as churches and enormous communities such as what Samuel Huntington calls a "civilization."

Faith is knowledge, but it is more than knowledge. It is the communal sensitivity or sensibility that discerns the sacred convention as it is manifest in history. Somewhat as an appreciative teacher is able to read the attitudes that infuse a class or as a deft politician is able to intuit the changing sentiments of a political audience, faith senses the spirit that spurs and guides a community. Extravagant as it may seem, faith is the emotional, bodily, intuitive response to the sacred convention that is said to drive the entire historical process as it is seen from the standpoint of a community.

If a country is animated by a spiritual culture, then faith is the receptor of whatever it is that animates that spiritual culture. If a country's historical activity is more than an aggregation of separate events, so that it is unified by its spiritual culture, then faith is the perception of the reality that unifies the spiritual culture. If the sacred convention is the Spirit of History, then faith is the facility to discern or perceive the Spirit of History that is working on and through a spiritual culture.[36]

The faith based on a spiritual culture often stands at odds with the faith that arises from other communities. In organized religion, a church, synagogue, or mosque is the primary community out of which people discern, through faith, their God or sacred convention. This faith of organized religion does not necessarily eclipse and might not even compete with the faith that works out of a nation's spiritual culture, but it often does. For those many people who refuse to use the word "God," aesthetic, political, moral, or other secular organizations are the spiritual communities from which their faith works. Without referring to "God," these people have what John Dewey called a sense of the whole or what Paul Tillich called an "ultimate concern." Those who shun all spiritual communities may have a kind of individualistic faith, but it is unlikely that they can pass their spiritual individualism on to succeeding generations with as much facility as members of a spiritual community can. Each of these forms of faith can, and often should, rise up strenuously against the faith that is based in a nation's spiritual culture, as many did in Nazi Germany, as some Native Americans and other dissident religious groups have in America, and as most religious people do sooner or later.

Revelation can be understood as a manifestation or disclosure of the sacred convention that is given to a community and received by faith. If a revelation is acted on, and if this action has desirable historical consequences, then, in a more or less pragmatic way, that revelation is usually regarded to be true.

Prayer is the process whereby people attune themselves to the sacred convention. The exercise of prayer can intensify faith's receptivity to the Spirit of History. It can enhance a people's openness to, and thereby stimulate their active interaction with, the sacred convention.

Attributes of God as a Sacred Convention

To see God as a sacred convention is to place God thoroughly within history. This historicity of God, particularly as presented in biblical discussion of God and in the American pragmatic tradition, suggests distinct characteristics or attributes of God, in some respects different from those introduced by classical Christian theologians. These particular attributes have been recognized by a variety of religion scholars and theologians, particularly in America. Here, however, I must state these attributes without the development and nuance given them by these religious thinkers and with only a passing recognition of the worthy objections critics have leveled against these ways of describing God.

First, God's interaction with history entails the *moral ambiguity* of God. God's ambiguity would seem to be a consequence of God's interaction with a morally ambiguous human history. If God is among those forces that shape history, so that history is partly a consequent of a divine cause, then it is legitimate to reason backwards, from the historical consequent that can be seen, to the divine cause that cannot be seen. Because history's moral record is thoroughly ambiguous, this suggests that history's single most important moral influence is also morally ambiguous. Equally and more obviously, if God is seen as affected by history, then the moral ambiguity of history would seem to entail the moral ambiguity of God. Commentary on the moral ambiguity of God is longstanding and wide-ranging, emanating from skeptics such as Voltaire, some Holocaust survivors like Elie Wiesel, and a few theologians.

The moral ambiguity of God is not an idea strange to the Bible or to Christianity (see chapter 6). The Hebrew Bible repeatedly implicates God in evil and finds it appropriate that God repeatedly repents of what God has done. From a secular standpoint at least, the New Testament focuses on the execution of an innocent man and suggests God's implication in that execution. Many Calvinist and Lutheran thinkers have acknowledged God's involvement in history's evil. For them, a truly sovereign God must be responsible for all that occurs in history, including its evils.[37]

To comment on God's moral character is not only to anthropomorphize egregiously but also to speculate dangerously. Nevertheless, the moral ambiguity of God would seem to follow if God is understood to be a living, evolving sacred convention, affecting and being affected by morally ambiguous historical events.

Second, to call God a sacred convention suggests that *God's power is limited*, so that God cannot be understood to be omnipotent. Within recorded history it is apparent that people have always affected that convention, providing much of the imagery through which it has been shaped. As shaped by such powers of history, God's own power is limited. In addition, it appears that God's influence on history is one of many influences on history, again implying the limitation of God's power.[38] This leaves open the possibility that, at particular moments in history, God can have only limited influence on history, as well as the possibility that people can augment or deter God's effectiveness in history.[39]

In short, if God cannot do everything, then humans must do something, including those things that assist God (to quote William James, Why else *be* religious?).[40] For instance, in circumstances when some people are unreceptive to the Spirit of History (for example, they might be too hungry to be receptive), other people can alter those circumstances (feed them), making it more likely that they will be receptive to the Spirit of History. In such ways, action born of faith can literally make God more effective than God otherwise would be. Thus, James argued that religious "faith in a fact can help create the fact."[41] Just as a person, by having faith in the possibility of a friendship and by acting on that possibility, can increase the chances of that friendship developing, a person, by having faith in God's effectiveness and by acting on that faith, can increase the chances that God will be effective.[42]

To deny divine omnipotence may be antithetical to the mainstream of Western, including American, religious thought; but this denial is consistent with much other Western religious thought. The Hebrew Bible assumes that God's power is limited when it pictures Israel defying God's will and then pictures God as having to respond to that defiance. All biblical stories are historical in spirit, not playing out a predetermined script of an omnipotent God, but working in free space where human decisions are unpredictable and make a difference. To put it another way, if a God were to have all power, then the people involved in biblical history would have no power, making biblical history merely a puppet show, not the drama of free people interacting with a living God.

Admittedly, to deny God's omnipotence has come to seem sacrilegious, an arrogant human effort to diminish what is sacred. Consequently, magisterial efforts have been made to reconcile divine omnipotence and human responsibility, perhaps greatest of all by Jonathan Edwards in *On the Freedom of the Will*. However, it can be argued that to have God control all events, even tragedies, and to hold humans responsible for what they have been divinely predestined to do, and then to call God loving, is so contradictory that it is, in effect, far more sacrilegious than denying divine omnipotence.

Third, to understand God pragmatically and to place God in history is not necessarily to deny God's *transcendence,* and in fact can preserve it. If God is historical, God may not be metaphysically transcendent, if that means to stand above the realm of history; but God may be historically transcendent, if that means for God to supersede both what God once was and what people have understood God to be. Just as the spirit of the law cannot be tied to legal opinions or precedents of the past or to any essence of the law, so the divine Spirit of History cannot be tied to past divine actions or to past religious thoughts about God or to any fixed divine essence. Just as lawyers (with the possible exception of strict constructionists) believe the spirit of the law transcends any particular rendition of the law, so also many religious people believe their God transcends what God once was and what they had once thought God to be. Divine transcendence presupposes, in other words, that God, like other living things, can evolve, and that human understanding of God can evolve.

If this is true, then God is transcendent in a second sense. When God evolves, God becomes able to introduce into history what people had not given to God, what they had not even anticipated, and what they could not do for themselves. The history of God, in short, transcends natural and human history in the sense that God brings to bear on natural and human history what that history could not accomplish for itself. For example, the Hebrew prophets discerned in the sacred convention demands for justice that they attributed to God's will rather than to their own imaginations.

Fourth, to place God in history as a sacred convention usually requires *that God have an identity* that endures through the changes of history. The Hebrew prophets believed that God spoke in new ways in new historical circumstances, but never believed that the God who spoke in new ways was a different God. Equally, Jesus, like most of the Christians who eventually followed him, seemed to assume that his God was the God of his Jewish ancestors. For God's identity to endure amid change means that an earlier God does not die each time God changes—that is, moves beyond what God was in the past. To say "God is dead" when an earlier definition of God is no longer tenable is not, as it has been thought to be, radical. Rather, it is conservative, presuming that the only valid definitions of God are the old definitions, so that if God moves beyond these, then God has died. The sacred convention, like a person, evolves not through a sequence of isolated moments, but through a gradual progression of moments so deeply interrelated that it preserves a modicum of personal identity through change.

Fifth, a historical God *lives*, if to live means not only to change and transcend the past but to change in ways that are unpredictable. To be alive is to be in some sense not mechanically determined, or to be in some limited sense free. God is free in the sense that when God changes, those changes cannot be fully anticipated even through exhaustive examination of the history of God. For this reason, the sacred convention can be said to take on a life of its own. Like any living thing, including the spirit of the law, the divine Spirit of History is partially independent of, as well as partially dependent on, past and present historical situations. By comparison, non-living things seem[43] completely dependent on or malleable by historical influences. Thus, as noted earlier, when societies attempt to discern the sacred convention's current meaning, they sometimes wait to see how it will disclose itself in the spiritual culture, just as those who attend a trial sometimes wait to see how the spirit of the law will disclose itself in a courtroom verdict. In short, societies sometimes seem to wait for God to speak; and, when God speaks, God often speaks in unexpected ways. It was with such anticipation and confusion that many religious people, from conservatives to liberals, asked themselves what God was saying through the terrorist events of September 11, 2001. To others, this seemed naïve. However, by examining history for its theological meanings, the "naïve" were pursuing a style of religious interpretation that was consistent with biblical practice, particularly with the practice of the Hebrew prophets.

Sixth, a historical God should *not be an idol.* Idolatry arises when people identify their own interpretation of God with God itself, and then worship their interpretation. By doing that, they deny the possibility that God is unknown, in the sense that God has a life of its own and that God transcends the particular historical situation of the idolater. Idolatry, whether conservative or liberal, encourages a people simply to identify God with its own interpretation—with, for example, their interpretation of the early church or the Reformation, or with their interpretation of moral or scientific laws. To make God into an idol deprives God of the capacity to live and to transcend history.

Today the identification of God with nation may be the most destructive form of idolatry. Religious nationalism identifies God with something intrinsic to the nation, such as its spiritual culture, rather than with the sacred convention (the Spirit of History) that transcends the nation. Religious nationalism is the particular temptation of nations that are overtly religious, such as ancient and modern Israel, Puritan and modern America, and several contemporary Muslim theocracies. In the twentieth century, fascist Germany and Soviet Russia, although ostensibly nonreligious, each elevated a spiritual culture based on an ideology and treated it more or less uncritically, as though it were itself the ultimate reality. By denying God's transcendence of the nation, religious nationalism exempts the nation from the ultimate judgment it desperately needs.

From Fiction to Fact

I will recapitulate and extend what has preceded by describing a remarkable and critical commentary on all that I have claimed in this chapter. It comes from Sacvan Bercovitch, an eminent Canadian scholar who drifted down into the United States and became an American citizen. Speaking about his own migration into America and about the American people's dream that their nation was given meaning by God, Bercovitch said,

> I felt like Sancho Panza in a land of Don Quixotes. It was not just that the dream was a patent fiction. It was that the fiction involved an entire hermeneutical system. Mexico may have meant the land of gold, and Canada might be the Dominion of the North; but America was a venture in exegesis. You were supposed to discover it as a believer unveils scripture. America's meaning was implicit in its destiny, and its destiny was manifest to all who had the grace to discover its meaning.[44]

Bercovitch saw America as a nation whose very identity is a process of self-explanation, a religious exegesis of the markings formed by its own path through history, markings decipherable only by those who have received the grace to find God abroad in the land. Of course, Bercovitch warns, this venture in exegesis, which finds God alive in America, is all a "patent fiction"—and so, in effect, is "America's meaning." Thus does Bercovitch offer his criticism of American religious pretensions about American meaning. He does so as a skeptical Sancho Panza in a land of credulous Don Quixotes, as a man of facts, not fictions; as one who seeks true knowledge, not false grace; as a modern scholar, not an obsolete exegete. His criticism of acting on patent fictions rejects any theory that might describe God as a social convention—which, after all, begins as a fiction.

With a strange but well-practiced logic, religious people commonly are first overwhelmed by critiques like Bercovitch's, only to realize that, far from nullifying their religious interpretations, such critiques provide a welcome basis for their needed revision. Thus, the doubts about the meaning of his future led the wandering, childless Abraham to renew his religious hope; and the disillusionment of Jesus' disciples, caused by the crucifixion of their spiritual leader, became the basis for their revision of their Jewish faith. Both overcame these obstacles to faith with new religious interpretations, and those interpretations were understood to be responses to a reality that transcended their interpretations.

For Bercovitch—a professor of American imaginative literature as well as a scholar of American Studies—to dismiss an American interpretation because it is a fiction is surprising, to say the least. After all, the imaginative literature that is his stock in trade begins as pure fiction, but then becomes real—if what is historically effective can be counted as real. Fiction can change readers and, sometimes, entire nations. Imaginative literature does this in countless small ways and sometimes in great ways, as happened with Harriet Beecher Stowe's *Uncle Tom's Cabin*, Mark Twain's

Huckleberry Finn, Upton Sinclair's *The Jungle*, Ernest Hemingway's *Farewell to Arms*, Alan Ginsberg's "Howl," Joseph Heller's *Catch 22*, and Toni Morrison's *Beloved*.

Many things begin as fictions. Every new biological species begins as a fiction. After all, what is a "spontaneous variation" for Darwin if it is not a biological fiction, a made-up possibility that corresponds to nothing previously found in the biological world, asking a surrounding environment to select it anyway? Every cultural fact begins as a fiction. Cultures are built from innovative ideas, and innovative ideas begin as fictions—mere possibilities that correspond to nothing known in the cultural world, asking to be accepted by a society, to be institutionalized and converted into a cultural fact. How do nature's and culture's traditions evolve, if they do not evolve from novel and/or imaginative possibilities? Of course, most natural or social fictions are never accepted, never get to become facts, and are left behind as dead mutants because no historical environment will accept them. But a few are tested over and over again, until they become actual, history-making realities, actual in the way any social reality is actual. How did the American Constitution or the early Christian church arise if not as a people's dreams, only later becoming history-making institutions? To put it in the words of the hardheaded American pragmatic theologian Reinhold Niebuhr, "The truest visions of religion are illusions, which may be partially realized by being resolutely believed."[45] If they work, these visions, which begin as "patent fictions," become scripture, bolstered by exegesis and a hermeneutical system and, finally, become settled historical reality. All of this Bercovitch seems to deny.

I have added the theory that a sacred convention becomes not only real, but takes on a life of its own, acquiring the capacity to change and to test a society in new and unpredictable ways. If history is made of fictions, then the God of history is that historical fiction that becomes a sacred convention, instilling in a people a view of the universe and arousing them to desire, action, and self-criticism. In some ancient past, the biblical God may have begun just as nineteenth-century psychologist of religion Ludwig Feuerbach said Gods always begin—as a society's projection, accepted as a fact. But if this religious projection becomes a living tradition, a powerful convention effective in the life of a society, then by all that pragmatism can aver, it is a truth, a reality as solid as any historical reality can be.

The God experienced by Americans began as an imaginative construct and became a sacred convention with a history beginning in the ancient world. This religious reality had something to do with how the American people acted as one people. With how they exaggerated their own importance as "a city on a hill." With how they believed in democracy and human rights. With how they bloodied themselves in the Civil War and dehumanized themselves in the industrial revolution and in the rise of consumerism. With how they fostered and opposed racial prejudice, sexual prejudice, and oligarchic domination. With how they fought the great wars of the twentieth century and responded to the September 11 disaster.

4

$\mathcal{M}$ystery

Luther was the first moralist who broke with any effectiveness through the crust of all this naturalistic self-sufficiency, thinking (and possibly he was right) that Saint Paul had done it already. Religious experience of the lutheran [*sic*] type brings all our naturalistic standards to bankruptcy. You are strong only by being weak, it shows. You cannot live on pride or self-sufficingness. There is a light in which all the naturally founded and currently accepted distinctions, excellences, and safeguards of our characters appear as utter childishness. Sincerely to give up one's conceit or hope of being good in one's own right is the only door to the universe's deeper reaches.

—William James, *A Pluralistic Universe*

A FTER HAVING TAKEN A STUDIOUSLY PRAGMATIC APPROACH to life for as long as anyone in history, William James, one of the founders of pragmatism, underwent at the end of his life a reconsideration of pragmatism, which he here cloaked in a reference to Luther. His lengthy exploration of the religious experience of others had led to none of his own, and his efforts to arrive at a personally satisfactory philosophy of religion had come to bankruptcy. He was sixty-eight years old, and the decades-long heat of pragmatic analysis had baked his inquiries into an impenetrable crust of prideful accomplishment; I believe that James saw and accepted that. His attempt to build his way to belief in God must have felt like religious failure, as the attempts of the first Christian and the great Reformer had to them.

Then James concluded that this acceptance of failure could open the door to the universe's deeper reaches. This was the same William James

87

who earlier had confidently pronounced: "On pragmatistic principles, if the hypothesis of God works satisfactorily in the widest sense of the term, it is true."[1] In so many words, he had said that a possible God who auditions before James and passes James's own test has permission to be the actual God. But this same William James now accepted the poverty of his own judgments and the death of the God to which they had led. Unexpectedly, out of that poverty he found a door to theistic riches.

James's abandonment of pragmatism, with its practical tests of meaning and truth, was part self-mockery. He never officially disavowed pragmatism, and he remained a muted pragmatist to the end. But he does seem to have stopped making pragmatism a sufficient response to religious questions. He would marshal pragmatism to drum out the unfit recruits from the corps of religious possibilities but, beyond this, pragmatism was itself religiously unfit. Sufficient religious experiences were to be acquired only when self-sufficiency was thrown over.

The "Conclusions" to his last book, *A Pluralistic Universe*, suggests that in the nick of time (he had only months to live) James discovered the irony that, if one entered the darkness of atheism, one could return with theism. A person can "run to failure," experience a "deathlike termination of certain mental processes," only to discover "a life that supervenes upon despair," James said. The Greeks and the Romans "brooked no irony" and admired achievers; but, for Luther, achievements finally issued in nothing. James agreed, and referred to "new ranges of life succeeding on our most despairing moments." One could experience, he said, this new life "*in spite* of certain forms of death, indeed, *because* of certain forms of death—death of hope, death of strength, death of responsibility, of fear and worry, competency and desert, death of everything that paganism, naturalism, and legalism pin their faith on and tie their trust to."[2] This movement *through* the death of religious hope to the *birth* of religious faith is James's version of what I am calling "the irony of atheism."

If that irony holds, what is the value of America's pragmatic approach to religious truth? Like the earlier, more thoroughly pragmatic James, I have argued that God, which I called a sacred convention, is real because God helps to answer the questions of a pragmatic society. Pragmatic scrutiny precedes, tests, and authorizes faith. We will imagine God; we will wait to see the results of our imaginings in the formation of religious tradition; and then through pragmatic tests we will ascertain whether that God holds up under the attack of our pragmatic testing and whether, therefore, that God can be accepted "in faith." Interestingly, even pragmatists tend to argue that, if God is effectively to judge society, God must transcend society. But if a God is made God because this God works for society, can this be a God who truly transcends society?

When pragmatic scholars of religion sit at the table of religion, they tend to consume their host—and the partaking of the host is not exactly sacramental. As scholars should, they explain everything they possibly can with the instruments of their academic craft. They apply their tools to the fullest possible extent, and they do this to protect society from its own gullibility. But, in the process, they make God their servant.

If in the garden of religion the pragmatists' scholarly tools break, they often break over the earlier-noted, rocky idea that, in Augustine's terms, "I believe in order that I may understand,"[3] or that "faith precedes understanding." According to that idea, God will be found only when efforts to explain God intellectually are abandoned. Referring to secular ways of explaining God, Swiss theologian Karl Barth argued that nineteenth-century German liberals were "subjugating" the Christian message to "the prevailing worldview" of the secular critics of religion.[4] Similarly, historian of American religious thought Gary Dorrien can summarize his sympathetic study of nineteenth-century American liberal theology by saying, "The nineteenth-century liberals refused to accept religious teachings that offended their moral, intellectual, and spiritual sensibilities."[5] In effect, many German and American liberals sought an understanding that precedes faith.

When I suggest that, at some point, faith must precede understanding, and that pragmatists and other liberal theologians do not reach that point, I do not mean to abandon the liberal approach and its insistence that theology be somehow reconciled with secular standards of truth. Liberal religious thought, including pragmatic religious thought, is to be credited with much that is good: its advocacy of social, historical, and literary analysis of the Bible and doctrine ("higher criticism"); its affirmation of the importance of human experience as a source of knowledge about God; its willing acceptance of the Jesus of history alongside the Christ of faith; and its insistence on minimal continuity between religious truth and the truths of science, culture, and reason. Thus, in the 1930s, when liberal theology was retreating under heavy attack, theologian John Bennett was right to warn that "we must not lose [these liberal achievements] in the present stampede."[6] Those achievements are being sustained and extended in various forms of postmodern religious thought, and neither should they be lost.

However, critics of liberalism, including its pragmatism, have made points that stick. Reinhold Niebuhr, for example, argued that humanism left people "homeless"—an apt metaphor in light of our own study of Americans who seek a sustainable "home." Whatever the self knows religiously, this self in its freest, most self-conscious form has the remarkable capacity to be a subject and, at the same time, to turn itself into an object to be studied by itself as a subject. The human self irresistibly stands above itself, surveys and analyzes itself and then unhappily deems the objective description it has made of itself insufficient to its needs as a subject. This self-conscious self is too imaginative and critical to fit into the home that its own conscious thought has built—and so it remains homeless.[7] Sooner or later, it escapes and transcends all those religious homes that its liberal, humanistic, and even conservative mind has built, so that it is left in religious despair. Close examination of its religious accomplishment leaves this deepest self in despair. At the end of his life six centuries earlier, Thomas Aquinas reached just such a position. He said, "I cannot do any more. Everything I have written seems to me as straw in comparison with what I have seen."[8]

Like James, Niebuhr refused to break his pen and abandon critical, even liberal, religious thought, and went back to writing pragmatically about politics and social practice. He knew, however, that, taken alone, liberal and pragmatic theology could not suffice religiously. Its results were so devoid of a sufficient God that they were virtually atheistic. Of course, the liberals never viewed themselves as atheists, for they went on talking of God and discussing religious experiences. But, to speak anachronistically, the liberal frame of mind, including the pragmatic frame of mind, would have been for Paul and Luther effectively atheistic, for its God had little, if any, power that secular culture and thinking had given to it. The liberals' ostensibly transcendent God could appear to be radically immanent, reducible to what secular thinking would allow.

In the last analysis, much liberal religious thinking is the victim of secular understandings, if secular understanding is defined as it was in chapter 1—as the reduction of religious truth to what is permitted by or can be explained by secular learning, especially that of the social sciences. Sincerely, and sometimes with excellent effects, liberal theologians honestly grappled with the certain implications of contemporary learning. However, the unintended result was that they justified religious truth by explaining it in terms of, or reducing it to, nonreligious and secular learning. The problem was that, for all serious and practicing religious peoples, God must, in some respects, transcend secular culture and contemporary learning, giving to them what they could not give to themselves. A God who cannot transcend secular culture in this way can be affirmed but it makes little religious sense and, from a religious standpoint, the affirmation is virtually atheistic.

The religious pragmatists may escape this problem, but I do not see how. For pragmatists, as I know them, a concept is meaningful if its adoption has distinct and measurable consequences, and it is true only if its consequences meet needs that originate with and register in ordinary human society—that is, with and in the secular world. For religious traditions, the truest need and desire for the divine are instilled not by the secular world but by the presence of the divine and by faith in that presence; that is why it is commonly said that faith must precede rather than follow understanding. Therefore, for the religious traditions a concept of God can be meaningful and true if its consequences meet needs and desires that transcend needs and desires that originate with people—or, to say the same thing, that originate with God. At first, at least, that same concept may not be pragmatically true because the needs and goals faith sets may not make sense to people who take their goals from themselves or from the secular world, as pragmatists typically do. Of course, as the earlier William James said, if a concept of God meets needs and accomplishes goals set by the secular world, that God may, in some technical sense, be pragmatically meaningful and true. However—and this is my point—that same concept, because it serves rather than transcends secular needs and goals, may make little religious sense and may be, from a religious perspective, atheistic.

However, for James the religious failure of pragmatism's God was not the end of his end-of-life reassessment. By admitting to religious atheism, he was able to arrive at "the only door to the universe's deeper reaches." In this was the irony of atheism—the irony that atheism can be the prelude to or set the conditions for a new theism.

The Irony of Atheism

The workings of the irony of atheism can be found in the formal thought of several great American religious thinkers, but they are also evident in the informal experience of people who have no particular interest in academic religious thought. These people all begin by adopting a kind of unintentional atheism and end by affirming a new theism.

Before discussing these people, I must make a terminological adjustment. Many of those who adopt this "new theism" do not believe God is a being; they believe God is something more like a spiritual presence, a divinity, or a mystery. I am aware that some would not call them theists, for the term "theism" commonly refers to a belief in a God-being. My dilemma arises from the fact that we live in a society that believes that all those who are not theists are atheists; however, those who have traveled through the irony of atheism are not atheists, even if they are not always conventional theists. My only option is to extend the term "theism" to include the beliefs of those whose faith is in a mystery that may or may not be a being.[9]

Of those great American thinkers who went through the irony of atheism, I begin with the eighteenth-century theologian Jonathan Edwards. In his youth, Edwards began reading British philosopher John Locke's *An Essay Concerning Human Understanding.* Locke had replaced Descartes' effort to ground truth in reason (in certain ideas innate to the human mind) with the theory that truth should be grounded in observation—that is, in the observation of the five senses. Young Edwards adopted Locke's new empiricist epistemology, agreeing that the testimony of the senses provided the best source of knowledge. This could have driven young Edwards to deny God—for God could not be sensed by the five senses— and to confine himself to knowledge based exclusively on information gained by the five senses. However, Edwards embraced Locke's empiricist thesis with an adolescent fervor, until he found in his own perception something quite unanticipated by his mentor. Edwards found that he perceived in ways other than through the five senses. He had "a sense of the heart," whereby he perceived within the qualities of the external world a divine presence, which he called "being in general." Edwards went on to claim that, just as "there is a difference between having a rational judgment that honey is sweet, and having a sense of its sweetness," there is a difference "between having an opinion, that God is holy and gracious, and having a sense of the loveliness and beauty of that holiness and grace."[10] Ironically, Edwards dove so deep into Locke's potentially atheistic empiricism that he came up with a theistic empiricism.

A century and a half later, philosopher Charles Sanders Peirce began his career as a tough-minded critic intent on reaching a new kind of clarity, whatever the costs to belief might be. In 1878, his "How to Make Our Ideas Clear" proposed driving pragmatic method to the point where he could learn "how to give birth to those vital and procreative ideas which multiply, . . . advancing civilization and making the dignity of man. . . ." Too often, unclear thinking had led to the imposition of false beliefs by authoritative bodies like the church or the state; it had led to people's clinging to obsolete ways of thinking and to an unwarranted trust in innate (*a priori*) ideas. The church, for example, had encouraged people to believe that the wine in the sacrament was Christ's blood. The real need, Peirce said, was to understand things by their consequences. "We can consequently mean nothing," said Peirce, "by wine but what has certain effects, direct or indirect, upon our senses; to talk of something as having all the sensible characters of wine, yet being in reality blood, is senseless jargon." Peirce summarized by saying, "Our idea of anything *is* our idea of its sensible effects."[11] Here Peirce had a solid, scientific instrument that threatened to reduce religious experience to ordinary sensible effects; and he seemed headed for atheism.

But by 1906, driving the scientists' methods more relentlessly than did most scientists, Peirce was moving from an apparent scientific atheism to a theism modeled on science. What, he asked, actually, as opposed to theoretically, gets the scientists on the trail of ideas that can be tested pragmatically? How—not in principle, but in fact—do they pick up the scent? This was a strictly empirical and pragmatic question, but it led to the conclusion that scientists explore very unrigorously, using a kind of "instinct"—for example, discerning the cosmic order vaguely, even while being unable to define it conceptually. By instinct, Peirce meant not some biological drive, but a fuzzy intimation. Now, just as scientists have an intimation of the cosmic order, Peirce asserted, believers have an intimation of the reality of God. They get off the theological scent when they "precide" (make precise), distorting a religious idea by making it clearer than it should be. Then those who refute concepts of God typically attack "precided" concepts of God, which were religiously false to begin with. However, the "reality" of anything, including God, is "that which holds its characters on such tenure that it makes not the slightest difference what any man or men may have *thought* them to be, or ever will have *thought* them to be. . . ."[12] Thus, by driving his precise scientific method hard enough, Peirce arrived, ironically, at a point where precision did not work, and where people could discern the divine reality through instinct.

Of course, the testimony of the religious instinct must be tested pragmatically, comparing what happens when one holds a belief in God with what happens when one does not. But the technical argument of pragmatism "is as nothing, the merest nothing, in comparison to . . . an appeal to one's own instinct, which is to argument what substance is to shadow, what bed-rock is to the built foundations of a cathedral."[13] Therefore, just as Edwards had practiced empiricism until he could run the other direction on Locke's path toward atheism, Peirce pursued scientific observation until he could run the other direction on science's path toward atheism.

Peirce's friend, young William James, began his life as a medical student by coupling British empiricism with a belief in strict causality, so that in the 1870s he became a deterministic materialist and felt the cold breath of atheistic despair. He turned his attention to the nature of human experience and virtually invented experimental psychology. This left his atheistic forebodings quite intact, for it appeared that theology could not stand up to the scrutiny of a strictly experimental psychology. But James then drove his empiricism so hard he found reasons for religious truth.

The story is complicated. First, James's unflinching empiricism led him in *The Varieties of Religious Experience* to respect, even if not to believe, exotic religious testimonies that most scientists would have dismissed as too bizarre for serious consideration. For James these were experiences, after all, and should be honored as experiences, rather than cast aside simply because they were offensive to science's materialism, sense-data empiricism, and quantitative thinking. His pragmatic testing of theistic beliefs remained foremost, however, so that his own conclusions in 1902 at the end of *Varieties* were decidedly agnostic, if not atheistic. As I noted at the beginning of this chapter, however, six years later, in *A Pluralistic Universe*, he came to very different conclusions. There he sympathized with Martin Luther's conclusion that, ironically, it is just when you pursue self-salvation through to the bitter end that you recognize the folly of your ways and your need for a salvation that comes freely. Analogously, James had analyzed experience pragmatically, pushing his analysis to a point where it was virtually atheistic; but then he saw his methods and experience itself "give way to a theism now seen to follow directly from that experience more widely taken." Experience itself suggests, James concluded, that we are, in fact, acquainted with a reality continuous with our "tenderer parts," "a *more*," "an invisible spiritual environment from which help comes."[14] Thus, one way to portray the career-long odyssey of William James is to see him, like Edwards and Peirce, pursuing his method wherever it led, until it led from atheism to a new theism.[15]

Using a romantic rationalism rather than empiricism, Ralph Waldo Emerson made a similar move. Having grown hostile to Christian theology, Emerson called on his fellow citizens to rely on themselves rather than hope for rescue by a God beyond history. To do this, we must immerse ourselves, he said, in nature and history until they yield the purely naturalistic and historical answers we need. But, pursuing this humanistic, naturalistic, and historicist outlook to its end, Emerson arrived at a point where he affirmed that when human experience, nature, and history are truly plumbed, we find a Deep to which our own "deep" must respond. Like German philosopher G. W. F. Hegel, Emerson pushed secularity hard enough for it to reach spirituality. He discovered, in fact, that when any particular reality of the world is pushed hard enough, it leads beyond itself to the experience of an Absolute that informs whatever is merely relative.[16]

None of this was original to American religious thought. Again and again, such ironic reversals are found in Western religion. As theologian Paul Tillich has noted, just when there is nothing beyond the "here and now," just when people honor without reserve the phenomena before their eyes, at that moment they turn, inexplicably, "to the religious forms of faith."[17] For Tillich, this leads to the appearance of "the God above the God of theism," of "the God who appears when God has disappeared in the anxiety of doubt."[18] Ironically, the triumph of atheism prepares for the unexpected survival of ultimate reality.

Speaking more aggressively, sociologist Max Weber focused on the purely secular "intellectualization" in which "there are no mysterious incalculable forces that come into play, but rather through which one can, in principle, master all things by calculation." Quite consistently for those who take this stance, religion is false precisely because it defies intellectualization and honors what evades intellectual analysis, dignifying its evasion by calling it mysterious. But rather than back away from intellectualization in disgust, Weber said, one should follow the devil "to the end in order to realize his power and his limitations."[19] Surprisingly and ironically, Weber concludes that, through accepting this intellectual disenchantment of the world, one is enabled to find the world reenchanted. Twentieth-century sociologists, such as Peter Berger, pursued much the same point, arguing that "only after he has really grasped what it means to say that religion is a human product or projection can he begin to search, *within* this array of projections, for what may turn out to be signals of transcendence"[20]

Decades earlier, Søren Kierkegaard had described this phenomenon from his very different, existentialist perspective. Thinking like a good secular philosopher of his time, he first acknowledged that the existence of God was objectively uncertain, then "that objectively it [the existence of God] is absurd." But then he concluded that precisely "this absurdity, held fast in the passion of inwardness, is faith."[21] Only through first experiencing the absurdity of God in a kind of atheistic terror, Kierkegaard concluded, can one acquire religious faith.

All of this works more obviously at the level of aesthetic experience. On certain rare occasions, people give themselves to a piece of music without reserve, so that the music sweeps them away, eradicating everything else. That music at that moment becomes entirely sufficient; nothing else matters and everything else is transcended. Even if it is sacred music, the idea of God, the ceremonies of the church, the dogmas of organized religion escape notice—along with the artistry of the performers and the particular structure of the composition. The secular performance of this music at this moment is entirely sufficient and nothing else is needed. But just as it becomes everything, music's specific musical identity can fall away and become, in itself, nothing. At that point, ironically, the utterly secular hearing of pure music can become anything but that; it can open the listener to what feels sacred, dwarfing the music itself.

Fiction writer Flannery O'Connor suggests that something similar can occur in reading a story. It is precisely when the readers have been induced to give themselves over to the story's facts that the story can become more than a fact. When the story is made nothing but a story, the story can become more than a story. This outcome is not the result of getting away from the facts, but the exact opposite, from taking the facts with utter seriousness. The writer who subverts the facts to prove the existence of the supernatural has forgotten, O'Connor says, that "the natural world contains the supernatural." The Christian writer, O'Connor argues, has a greater, not a lesser, obligation to write a secular story, portraying the natural world just as it is, honoring its own laws and limits. It is when this is accomplished that the reader can be opened to a sense of mystery that operates within the natural world.

The irony, O'Connor says, is that "art transcends its limitations only by staying within them."[22] Only when there are no tricks, only when a secular history stands forth without reservation—so that, for example, no character can do anything out of character—only then will a secular history be transcended. O'Connor, believing her readers were so numb they had to be hit over the head, tells stories about killers, egoists, cheats, and liars. It is when her stories confine themselves to such petty, ugly, warped human lives and when the readers enter those lives that her stories can transcend those lives.

In this respect, the narrative theologians of the "Yale school" of theology were unwittingly to concur with O'Connor. For them, the New Testament story becomes more than a story only when efforts to prove that it is anything other than a story are set aside, only when the reader stops trying to make it a symbol or an argument, stops trying to have a religious experience by reading it, and simply enters it as a story.[23]

O'Connor hoped her readers would discover "mystery through manners, grace through nature." When religion is reduced to its nonreligious and ordinary-historical causes there appears "a depth where these things have been exhausted." O'Connor believed "there always has to be left over that sense of Mystery which cannot be accounted for by any human formula."[24] In short, the religious meaning of a story is most likely to appear in a secular representation that needs no religion, no God—a representation of the world that, in fact, could explain religion away by substituting its own sufficiency for anything that might be added by religion or God.

For O'Connor, what arises then is called "mystery" for at least two reasons. First, it is mysterious in a negative sense, as something that makes no sense to rational or natural explanations. It is mysterious in the sense that it enters just when it is least needed to understand the sequence and shape of natural events, when the secular is all-sufficient and an atheistic stance seems appropriate. Second, it is mysterious in a positive sense, as something that stands out as, perhaps, forgotten but as profoundly real. It is mysterious in the sense that it transcends ordinary explanations, offering what is strange to, or inexplicable by, secular modes of thought.[25] Here mystery is not simply the place where secular thought gives out, but is a rich and affirmative presence.

Mystery within History

In a letter to a friend, Flannery O'Connor tells of when she was taken to a party hosted by the famous novelist Mary McCarthy, who was, O'Connor writes, a "Big Intellectual." Far into the party, O'Connor—physically plain, unknown, hardly published, and definitely not a "Big Intellectual"—had said nothing. She felt, she said, like "a dog . . . who had been trained to say a few words but overcome with inadequacy had forgotten them." Toward morning the conversation turned to the Eucharist. As a Catholic, O'Connor felt that here was something she was "obviously supposed to defend." Before she had a chance to speak, McCarthy reflected on her Catholic childhood, allowing that she had once connected the ceremony with the Holy Ghost, the "most portable" person of the Trinity. But now, as a mature woman, she had come to think of the Eucharist as a symbol and conceded that it was "a pretty good one." Out of the shadows young O'Connor offered in a very shaky voice, "Well, if it's a symbol, to hell with it." Writing five years later, she had nothing to add, "except that it [the Eucharist] is the center of existence for me; all the rest of life is expendable."[26]

Of course, O'Connor had long understood the value of a symbol. As a novelist, she spent her life making symbols, particularly religious symbols. O'Connor meant not simply "if it's a symbol, to hell with it," but "if it's a symbol only for a secular meaning and that's the end of it, to hell with it."

For O'Connor, religious symbols use ordinary things to show God to be what ordinary things cannot be.[27]

Making the same move as O'Connor, but with regard to "history" rather than "symbol," many religious people would say that if the divine is nothing but the workings of some arcane aspect of ordinary history, then "forget it." Or they would say, if that's all religious history is, "I can do without it." American poet T. S. Eliot referred to the irony that, first, from a secular perspective, a secular history is sufficient and religious knowledge is unnecessary, but that, at some point in their lives, some secular people conclude that what was once unnecessary has become necessary. They are inclined to say, "And what you do not know is the only thing you know."[28]

O'Connor amplified the irony of atheism. For her, this irony and the mystery it introduces do not violate or contradict secular, ordinary history. In fact, often mystery is recognized when a secular history is genuinely important and richly appreciated—so important and so rich that at first it seems capable of explaining everything. If a mystery opens a "sacred history," then, although a sacred history may be a mystery to a secular history, it need not contradict secular history.

If a mystery's sacred history is not antirational, antinatural, or antisecular-historical, then the miracle stories of the Bible need not argue that the sacred has violated the structures of secular, ordinary history, even if it has violated that history's values. Mystery need not, in a Hellenistic fashion, introduce the eternal or nonhistorical in order to correct the purposes at work in ordinary history. Interpretations that make miracles violate ordinary historical processes stand at odds with the Bible's most important idea, which is that God is incarnate in ordinary historical eventfulness and gives meaning *to* rather than *obliterates* its structures.[29] To make a secular history meaningful by destroying it is, to quote the critics of the Vietnam War, like destroying a village to save it.

Nor does a mystery fill a gap in secular, ordinary history, so that that history more or less requires the introduction of a mystery to make it historically complete. This would be a God of the gaps, who provided a missing link in history's or nature's natural sequence of actions. Such a God is logically required and, if this God were not introduced, it would have to be replaced by a natural process with a nonreligious name. The God that conveniently fills that gap is a servant of normal practice, not (as God should be) something which, although implicit in that practice, is more than that practice, giving it a meaning it otherwise lacks.

In most writings on science and religion, a God who fills the rational or empirical lacunae of the naturalist's world usually turns out to be nothing but an arcane or overlooked aspect of science's own picture of natural history. Physicist Freeman Dyson, for example, argues that the order of the actual universe is, among all possible universes, so unlikely that it verges on the impossible. The actual order of the universe, he says, stands virtually alone as the only possible order among an unimaginably large number of other possible orders, all of which would have made human life impossible. To explain that the present order has arisen through randomness or accident is to introduce a possibility so at odds with reasonable probabilities that the explanation is implausible.[30] Dyson is left, then, with little choice but to explain that the existence of the universe's actual order is not accidental but was purposely designed. With such a hypothesis it becomes possible to understand how "the universe as a whole is hospitable to the growth of mind." The source of this design he names the "Anthropic Principle," which he allows could be called "God." Thus, natural history requires that there simply must be something like a God in natural history.[31] My point is that such a God—found in much "natural theology," including some "process theology"—is only a previously undiscovered part of the necessary natural order and belongs to the sciences. As atheist physicist Steven Weinberg has aptly noted, what has this to do with the God of most religions, who transcends the necessities of secular history?[32]

For O'Connor, far from filling a gap in ordinary understandings, the irony of atheism comes when ordinary motivations and circumstances are "adequate" to explain the story's action, making the introduction of mystery logically unnecessary.[33] Similarly, William James argued that "reason . . . would never have inferred these specifically religious experiences in advance of their actual coming. She could not suspect their existence, for they are discontinuous with the 'natural' experiences they succeed upon and invert their values."[34] Thus, for O'Connor and James, God transcends natural powers, but not through contradiction and not as something that is rationally required. I am suggesting that this transcendence comes through irony, an irony that moves beyond the atheism that arises from secular knowledge.

However, although religious prophecies and parables, for example, are puzzling from the standpoint of a secular history, they arise in relation to that secular history and speak to that secular history. They are not inert, irrelevant truths but are commentaries on history that have historical consequences. Hebrew Bible prophets demonstrated that military and political events in the life of Israel made better sense when understood through religious faith. Although the judgments and promises of God were not required logically to fill a gap in the causal chain of military or political events, they were needed to understand the ultimate meaning of those events, especially how they worked within the larger cosmos of the Israelites. For example, the many predictions of the fall of Israel could not be inferred from the secular history of politics and military affairs but were true in reference to those affairs. Equally, Jesus told parables that could never be derived from secular history but that, to the eyes of faith, made sense of secular history. As William James asserts in this chapter's epigraph, religious ideas become true only when the inhabitants of a secular history realize, through faith, that they are weak, lack "self-sufficingness" and are unable to fulfill their deepest needs. In effect, the meaning of faith arises when it is least needed logically and most needed existentially.

Knowledge of Mystery

In all this, the meaning of "faith" has shifted, becoming less the religious appreciation of something already understood and known, and more the initial attachment to something unknown, a mystery. How an attachment could be significant without being understood was a problem for most philosophers. But a collection of twentieth-century American philosophers and theologians developed a way of addressing that problem.

I will call these thinkers "radical empiricists," borrowing a term from William James. At the end of his career, James grew deeply sympathetic with his old acquaintance Benjamin Paul Blood, whom James called a "pluralistic mystic." Blood had averred that in some matters it is best to say "*we do not know*. But," Blood added, "when we say we do not know, we are not to say it weakly and meekly, but with confidence and content. . . . Knowledge is and must ever be *secondary*. . . ." In the astonishing last paragraph of James's last written (but not last published) essay, he elided his position with Blood's and wrote, "There is no complete generalization, no total point of view, no all-pervasive unity, but everywhere some residual resistance to verbalization, formulation, and discursification, some genius of reality that escapes from the pressure of the logical finger, that says 'hands off,' and claims its privacy, and means to be left to its own life." It is, he said, "the 'inexplicable,' the 'mystery.'"[35] The question was, how did James know such a mystery, at least well enough to speak about it? How could he, or Blood, or anyone appropriate a mystery "contained" (to use O'Connor's word) deep within the natural world but not apparent to natural knowledge? How can something that is not inferred from or provided by a secular history still be historical, working and belonging to history?

James needed a new way of knowing, a new epistemology that he was to call "radical empiricism." We have already hinted at this way of knowing in our earlier examination of the pragmatists, arguing that it arose ironically, after the acceptance of an atheism that would rule out such a way of knowing.

This is the form of perception that Jonathan Edwards called "a sense of the heart," that Peirce called "instinct," and that James used when he discerned "a more." The radical empiricists discovered a kind of sixth sense, a form of perception added to the perceptions of British empiricists John Locke and David Hume, who had strictly confined all perception to the perception of the five senses. The Americans' new empiricism was just as important as their pragmatism had been, but is today generally neglected by historians of American philosophy.

The radical empiricists developed an epistemology that could make sense of the testimony so common to scriptural Judaism, Christianity, and Islam, all of which used perceptions of history to justify their beliefs. For them, God had been encountered not behind closed eyelids and not behind closed doors in dark, silent chambers, but in the open spaces of the desert, in the clouds on mountaintops, in the outcomes of military battles, in green pastures and beside still waters, in outdoor sermons before hungry crowds, and at a bloody execution on the outskirts of Jerusalem. In those circumstances, God was perceived, but not through the five senses.

The radical empiricists proposed that people do perceive things that are not clear, distinct, and sensuous, but that are diffuse, vague, and non-sensuous. It was as though, for example, relations between people, though intangible, became more important than the quite tangible impressions of people, or as though the atmosphere of a room became more important than its dimensions. The non-sensuous perception of such data was registered primarily in the affections, and yet these affections referred beyond the self, even to the spatial-temporal world of history.

James came to believe that clear and conscious sensations of facts were less important than the relations among the facts—the "near, next, like, from, towards, against, because, for, through"—none of which could be sensed. These relations convey the desire underlying a sensed activity, the goal it seeks, and the dangerousness, beauty, and utility that it conveys. For James, these are "affective phenomena" or "appreciative attributes," missed entirely by Locke (and, later, by the twentieth-century positivists, who would confine perception to reports of the five senses). Perceiving these relations, we do not just invent, guess at, or think about the values of the external world, but actually feel or perceive them.

In *Varieties of Religious Experience* and *A Pluralistic Universe,* James argued that religious experience itself could be a form of non-sensuous perception. Religion is a person's "total reaction upon life," and religious perception is "that curious sense of the whole residual cosmos as an ever-lasting presence, intimate or alien, terrible or amusing."[36] Within that cosmos, the divine is perceived as "a wider self," "a more," but the divine is missed by our exact knowledge much as human language is missed by the cat dozing at our feet as we converse in a library. James found a way to reconcile two separate worlds, one of the religious and spiritual affections of the heart, the other of the irreligious and physical facts of the external world. Admittedly, James did not reach this point single-handedly, but with the guidance of many Europeans—perhaps, most obviously, the French philosopher Henri Bergson (1859–1941).

James's radical empiricism was extended by the English-American mathematician and philosopher of science Alfred North Whitehead and by fellow pragmatist John Dewey. When Whitehead, already a famed mathematician and philosopher of science, came to the United States at age sixty-three, he published in rapid succession at least seven books, each of which gave abstract knowledge a basis in vague physical experience. Claiming he was returning to the real empiricism of Francis Bacon, the founder of pragmatism,[37] Whitehead argued that any particular perception by the five senses began in an initial, primitive, largely unconscious reception of the emotional impact of surrounding circumstances. He pointed, for example, to the incomprehensible sense of attraction or repulsion experienced as one enters a room, making one feel like an iron filing entering a magnet's field of force. Because of this and often against their will, people find themselves making spontaneous, half-conscious judgments that are colored in ways they cannot understand. Conscious and clear sense impressions and rigorous thoughts are, for Whitehead, entirely derivative from this initial phase of a reaction; they are the unreliable abstractions from this rich soup of feeling.

Whitehead believed that the religious response began as a feeling, not as an idea but as a vague intuition of the sacred. It was a perception of the one reality, which Whitehead called "God," that stood beyond the chaos of the mundane world—the one reality that organizes and evaluates what otherwise is confused and meaninglessness experience and lures it to more intense satisfaction. Hence, God, is best known directly, through mostly unconscious perception rather than abstractly through sensation or thought. "The fact of the religious vision, and its history of persistent expansion," he said, "is our one ground for optimism. Apart from it, human life is a flash of occasional enjoyments lighting up a mass of pain and misery, a bagatelle of transient experience."[38]

John Dewey followed suit, talking about a form of "immediate empiricism." It was this that allowed one to have a "sense of totality," "of an extensive and underlying whole," of an "imaginative totality"—or, most simply, "a sense of the whole." Perceived aesthetically, this wholeness is an art work; perceived religiously, this wholeness to the universe can be called "God," for it accomplishes what God is said to have accomplished.[39]

In short, these American thinkers concluded that visual, auditory, olfactory, tactile, and taste experience, while highly significant, did not exhaust the forms of perception. They called attention to a mode of experience that preceded and was more basic than sense experience. Several mid-twentieth-century theologians—particularly Henry Nelson Wieman and Bernard Meland—carried this discussion into theology, claiming that religious people can perceive a force of creativity and evaluation that lends religious value to the world.[40] Together they represented a distinctively American and radically empirical way of accounting for religious experience.

Impishly, these American philosophers and theologians had stood Plato, Descartes, Locke, Hume, and Kant on their heads. The Europeans had separated body from mind, matter from spirit, fact from value, treating mind, spirit, and value as the more significant reality, even if (as they were for Locke and Hume) the less reliable reality. Always, for them, the clear, distinct, and sharp—whether it be sense knowledge or spiritual knowledge, whether one is a narrow empiricist or a rationalist—was that which was most reliable and authoritative. The radical empiricists collapsed this dualism into a mind–body singularity and argued that vague, barely conscious feeling was no longer the contaminated effluvia of reliable knowledge but the solid rock on which clear and distinct knowledge is built. In fact, together the radical empiricists revolted against both the empiricist and rationalist traditions of modern Western philosophy and laid down a new, distinctly American style of thought.

They gave Americans a way to discuss how mystery is encountered and known, and they did this without pretending to describe mystery itself. Knowledge of this mystery that was neither incompatible with sensuous perception, nor reducible to that perception. These American religious thinkers were impatient when sharp sense data were given exclusive rights; they insisted on an alternative form of perception—as did several American poets.[41] Whitehead, for example, chided those who elevated clarity and distinctness above all else, calling them people committed to "a healthy, manly, upstanding reason; but, of one-eyed reason, deficient in its vision of depth." He admitted that these strict empiricists helped eliminate intellectual sloppiness and contributed to sanity, acting on "the world like a bath of moral cleansing." "But," Whitehead added, "if men cannot live on bread alone, still less can they do so on disinfectants."[42] The other side of the radical empiricists' impatience with one-eyed reason was their patience with mystery, acknowledging that it is perceived only vaguely, without the benefit of sharp reason.[43]

As I will explain in chapter 5, John Dewey applied this radical empiricism not only to an individual's way of knowing but also to a society's way of knowing, arguing that communities, even entire societies, could, as an organic unit, experience mystery much as individuals did. For Dewey, a society's radical (root) experience was not limited to, say, the group compassion felt during the Great Depression, the national courage had during the Second World War, the collective guilt felt during and after the Vietnam War, and the peril known after the terrorist events of September 11, 2001. It is we as a society that also experience "the unity of all ideal ends arousing us to desire and actions," "the mysterious totality of being the imagination calls the universe."[44]

Mystery in the Bible

We read, "Once upon a time, this happened to these people and they did this." A realistic story is believable because each item in the story follows naturally, even if sometimes unexpectedly, from all that precedes it. All events are justified by their location within the limits of the story's world. In fact, for careful readers, anything inexplicable in the story's terms, anything that violates the story's limits, does not belong in the story. Typically, a story can be explained or at least understood in terms of secular history and, for this reason, has no need for a sacred history or a transcendent God. It is out of that self-sufficient, ordinary, secular story that the irony of atheism works.

The Jesus of Matthew, Mark, and Luke lived most manifestly within the limits of a secular history. He was not best known in his ostensibly supernatural or even extraordinary roles nor for his confidence in religion. It was not as a miracle worker, nor as a Messiah-in-waiting, nor as the man born of a virgin, nor as the descendant of King David entering Jerusalem before Passover that Jesus was most clearly manifest. In fact, these stories, taken alone, sometimes tempt people to see Jesus falsely, as simply triumphant over history. The devil, in his request that Jesus throw himself from the pinnacle of the temple and then save himself, suspected that even Jesus might share that triumphalist illusion. Rather, the Jesus of the Synoptic Gospels was primarily one who lived within history; who drank from, rather than let pass, history's bitter cup; who was helpless before his captors; who was willingly doomed by the ordinary consequences of his public activities. This Jesus of secular history was crucified in a secular history and died out of love for the people of a secular history. He seems to have accepted his confinement within a secular history when he cried out on the cross in virtually atheistic distress, "My God, why have you forsaken me?" Jesus' prayer implies a skeptical attitude toward God, as it asks God to give people bread, to forgive people as often as they forgive others, and to refrain from leading people into evil. The prayer suggests that we need to urge God to do even these obvious things, as though otherwise God might not. Nor did Jesus trust most of the religious authorities of his day. While all of this does not make Jesus an atheist, it does imply an immersion in the secular world and a pessimism about the usual theistic truths.

By normal standards, Jesus' *modus operandi* was virtually an atheistic *modus operandi*, so that he could live through the irony of atheism, first divesting himself of a standard theism, then undergoing an ironic reversal toward a new theism. Jesus may not have intended to found a new religious stance, but he had that effect. After the crucifixion the Gospel stories took an ironic turn; in the resurrection Jesus unexpectedly transcended the limitations of secular history. By sacrificing himself to secular history, the Jesus of a secular history became also the Christ of a sacred history. The man who died bereft of God was blessed by God. This ironic movement was followed by another ironic movement: because Jesus had manifestly entered a sacred history, he was able, ironically, to affect a secular history, giving it new meaning.

The irony of atheism, implicit in Jesus' life, gives self-sacrificial love a particular religious significance. If Jesus' followers would give food to the hungry, give drink to the thirsty, welcome the stranger, clothe the naked, and visit the sick and those in prison, they would give themselves single-mindedly to a secular history for the sake of a secular history. However, in those acts they would transcend a secular history without entirely leaving secular history, for they would recognize, said Jesus, that "when you did it to one of the least of these . . . you did it to me" (Matthew 25:40). They would discover in secular history the Christ of sacred history; and then they too would participate in sacred history. If people would give themselves to the secular world without thought of reward, they would acquire a meaning that transcends the secular world. A sacred history makes the love of a secular history not tragic, as it seems to be in the story of the crucifixion taken alone, but blessed, as it appears in light of the resurrection story. Further, and to double the irony, the total embrace of a sacred history leads people back to a secular history, renewing their life of self-sacrifice in secular history.

This interpretation must, like all interpretations, be adjusted to today's circumstances. Some feminists have argued that more self-sacrifice is hardly what women need, given their history of unwarranted sacrifice;[45] and the same response might come from members of other historically disadvantaged minorities. Such people, coming from a history of sacrificing themselves for privileged people, resist sacrificing themselves to such people even more. I argue that the irony of self-sacrifice works, nevertheless, when members of disadvantaged minorities sacrifice, as they tend to do, for the sake of other members of such minorities—counterparts to the hungry, the unclothed, the imprisoned.

Returning to the New Testament, the parable of the Good Samaritan elaborates the irony of self-sacrifice. On the road to Jericho, a Samaritan traveler stopped to help a man who was beaten and lying beside the road. The Samaritan gave of his time and money to help the stranger, sacrificing himself to an ordinary and unknown person who was without resources and who, as the Samaritan's historic enemy, was unappealing. But by giving himself, beyond the call of duty, to this bedraggled figure, the Samaritan became, in the eyes of Jesus, not a fool but a religious hero (Luke 10:29–37). Again, according to the Synoptic Gospels, to give oneself to secular history, as though there were nothing but secular history, is often a prelude to entering sacred history.

In Romans 3, Paul extends the point by arguing that, when people fully accept Jesus' death as the supreme expression of love for secular history, then they too die for secular history. Ironically, it is only at that point that they discover that this act enables them to acquire a meaning transcending what secular history can provide.

For Paul, one will acquire true faith only when one despairs of finding salvation through efforts to fulfill religious laws or moralities. One, in short, had better not look to the God present in the law even if there is a God present in the law—or, for that matter, in nature. Instead, one should live as though this God of the law, of nature, or of any form of a secular history were religiously useless. Although Paul might not have put it this way, it is as though one must first fully acknowledge that one had embraced a secular means of self-salvation. Then one must despair of finding in those secular means any feasible means of true salvation and, in that sense, no trace of the divine. Only after one has known such atheistic despair, has abandoned efforts at works righteousness, and has known oneself to be doomed, can one discover true faith made possible through God's grace. Then one is ready to accept that theistic grounds for fulfillment might be found outside secular history, but in the sacred history opened by Christ's crucifixion and resurrection.

Speaking in a Pauline vein, New Testament theologian Rudolf Bultmann argued that today it is after one has given oneself utterly to scientific naturalism and to utterly secular (existentialist) philosophy, and has found in them nothing religiously valid, that one is prepared to receive religious meaning. "God's grace," said Bultmann, ". . . can only be conceived of as grace by those who surrender their whole existence and let themselves fall into the unfathomable, dizzy depths without seeking for something to hold on to."[46] But then one does find grace, even though one expected not to. "God encounters us," Bultmann said, "nowhere else than precisely where from our human point of view there is nothing."[47]

Here, Bultmann follows Paul and Luther, as he claimed to,[48] but also Augustine. Whether it was Paul defending Judaism, Augustine pursuing philosophical learnedness, Luther attempting complete ritual self-abasement, each finally realized he had given himself to secular forms of self-salvation and to a world filled with human achievement but empty of God. This was the lesson Paul was conveying to the Romans, Augustine was conveying to Pelagius, and Luther was conveying to Erasmus. Ironically, it was after one became preoccupied with self-salvation and had admitted it, that one was prepared for salvation through grace. Only after having given up on God's saving presence in secular history—atheistically, it might be said—did people find the saving presence of God in sacred history. Then "as in Adam all die, so also in Christ shall all be made alive" (1 Corinthians 15:22).

In the Hebrew Bible a similar interpretation of love was offered. The Israelites would not understand their situation by looking at themselves as a light to the nations, as a people who supposedly heeded the prophetic judgment and were ready to inherit the ancient promises given to Abraham. Rather, the Israelites would understand their true situation if they saw themselves as a people who had refused their covenant relation with God. They would understand themselves only when they abandoned their religious pretensions, recognized their historical failure, and came to terms with the fact that, lacking God's protection, they had been conquered in 722 by Assyria and in 587 by Babylon. They knew who they were when they saw themselves, like Cain, as "wanderers on the earth," a dispersed people, exiled to a virtually Godless history. Ironically, it was when they saw their desperately secular and virtually atheistic condition that, ironically, they were able to recover their faith in God.

I assume that it was this paradox to which T. S. Eliot referred in "East Coker" when he said one must "wait without hope." "Wait without thought, for you are not ready for thought: / So the darkness shall be the light, and the stillness the dancing." Eliot adds, "In order to arrive at what you do not know / You must go by a way which is the way of ignorance." "In my end," he concludes, "is my beginning."[49]

Mystery and the
American Spiritual Culture

What does the irony of atheism imply for American spiritual culture? It could suggest that Americans should give themselves to the national community, to its political, social, economic, and cultural processes, as though life with that community were all that counted. Such undistracted devotion would be atheistic, prompted by nothing but the worth of the community—as though, to use Immanuel Kant's language, it were an end in itself. The irony of atheism suggests that this atheistic gesture will be followed by an appreciation of a mystery that transcends and evaluates America and its people.

I have suggested that such a mystery can be experienced through, but not derived from, non-sensuous perception. This way of describing faith is only one way to describe faith but, for Americans, it does have the advantage of following from the empiricism of a representative collection of American philosophers and religious thinkers who were, in turn, responding to the American situation. Nevertheless, through that thicker empiricism and what poet William Carlos Williams called "the roar of the present," people have been opened to what James called a "more," which is appreciated, finally, as a mystery that is irreducible to and transcendent of ordinary experience.

If in the irony of atheism and in the appreciation of mystery there is an American approach to religious truth, how is this related to American pragmatism and its sacred convention, described earlier?

The sacred convention suggests a God so immanent that, while serving many of the functions of God, it fails to open a people to what the religions call the sacred or the holy. In fact, we have seen that it could lead to an atheistic stance. It has the advantage of being understandable from the perspective of a secular history and the disadvantage of failing to meet certain important religious expectations. What Alfred North Whitehead says about proofs of God can apply to what I have said about the sacred convention:

> Any proof [of God] which commences with the consideration of the character of the actual world cannot rise above the actuality of this world. It can only discover all the factors disclosed in the world as experienced. In other words, it may discover an immanent God, but not a God wholly transcendent. The difficulty can be put in this way: by considering the world we can find all the factors required by the total metaphysical situation; but we cannot discover anything not included in this totality of actual fact, and yet explanatory of it.[50]

Of the immanent God that is a sacred convention it might be said, what rises will fall: what rises from ordinary history will also sink into ordinary history. This God can lead to atheism, for it is valuable only because of and to the extent that it can fulfill history's human or natural objectives.

But I have argued that this theological atheism can open a community to a sense of mystery that cannot be reduced to a secular history. The immanent God, reduced to a secular history, can lead to a mystery that, as an aspect of a sacred history, remains within history more broadly understood. To paraphrase Flannery O'Connor, the limitations of ultimately secular theological conventions can be transcended only when we accept them and live within them. This implies that a kind of atheism, explored fully and critically, can inspire a new theism. How this happens, O'Connor says, is incomprehensible: "faith is a 'walking in darkness' and not a theological solution to mystery."[51]

The Irony of Theism

Here, however, this inquiry does not stop. Americans remain pragmatic and are seldom willing to settle for the sheer contemplation of any truth, let alone a truth that is a mystery. The experience of mystery may be religiously sufficient, but it is not morally sufficient. People cannot simply revel in mystery, as if they were not obligated to return to practical action in the secular world. Flannery O'Connor did not want her readers to walk indefinitely in what for all the world seemed to be darkness, but for her readers to return to the world with new eyes. (She was no gnostic; in fact, she hated gnosticism and treasured "what is."[52]) She believed that "contact with reality" would deepen the mind's "sense of mystery," but she also believed that "contact with mystery" would deepen the mind's "sense of reality."[53] Influence flowed both ways, so that contact with mystery would eventually have pragmatic and moral consequences. It is often the moral heroes of the twentieth century, such as the Catholic social reformer Dorothy Day, who become morally effective after and, perhaps, because they were in touch with a reality that seemed, at first, mysterious and impractical.

I am suggesting that there is a second ironic swing: just as there is *an irony of atheism*, whereby the acceptance of the secularity of the world opens the door to a new theism, there is also *an irony of theism*, whereby the acceptance of a mystery opens the door to a new commitment to a secular world. Ironically, just after the mystery arising from a sacred history is accepted as religiously sufficient, a secular history can take on new importance. The fact is that Paul, Augustine, and Luther were not content to bask in the mystery of grace, but were compelled to apply faith to works—not to moral acts that earned salvation but to moral acts that followed naturally from faith. By this ironic move, secular history and pragmatism, even pragmatic theology, can acquire the sacred depth they seemed previously to lack.

Equally, through this unexpected movement, the same sacred convention that had seemed to lead to atheism can take on profound religious significance. In effect, if through the irony of theism a people is able to return to ordinary history, then not only will this be morally significant, but it will also give religious significance to a God who, from the standpoint of a secular history, was only a social convention. The spiritual culture that seemed to be alive only when in touch with a sense of mystery can become alive as the home of a convention that has arisen in the ordinary history of that culture. The God-convention that once seemed reducible to a secular history, can become sacred after all. Thus, this most important dialectic, as G. W. F. Hegel suspected, runs two ways, from the irony of atheism to the irony of theism, from a secular to a sacred history and from a sacred to a secular history.[54] Historian of religion and death-of-God theologian Thomas J. J. Altizer saw as early as the mid-1960s the significance of this dialectic in the American context.[55]

In the chapters that follow, I will suggest that such a dialectic occurs in popular American culture. Jazz, football, and the movies can be reduced to merely secular phenomena. But, ironically, they can open to a sacred depth just when they seem most secular. Finally, however, this sacred depth can have an ironic effect of its own, giving to jazz, football, and the movies the religious significance they seem to lack.

PART 2

America the Visible

Introduction to Part 2

Three Inventions

The effort to discern meaning in all the confusions and cross purposes of history distinguishes Western culture and imparts historical dynamic to its striving.
—Reinhold Niebuhr, *The Nature and Destiny of Man*

God's temple is human history. . . .
—Gustavo Gutiérrez, *A Theology of Liberation*

I F THEY ARE NOT TO BE INEFFECTUAL INTELLECTUALS, RELIGIOUS critics must risk what Niebuhr called "the hazardous assertion of a meaningful history."[1] With great appreciation for this hazard, I will probe the body of recent American history at three eminently visible points, attempting to discern its underlying and invisible organs, particularly its spiritual culture. I briefly sketch three American popular arts—jazz, football, and the movies—and attempt to show what those arts seem to assume or suggest about the American spiritual culture and about the God, or Ultimate Reality, active in that culture.

These three popular arts are ideal for this assignment because each is distinctively American. While jazz, football, and the movies each have foreign ancestors, each was actually born in America. While jazz and the movies are played and made in other countries, they are still played and made best in America, mostly because they have the advantage of being indigenous to America. While each of the three is secular, each reveals the American spiritual culture and its God with the vague significance of a gasp, a Freudian slip, or a blush.

Jazz, football, and the movies each presuppose an imaginary but unacknowledged world in which their activities make sense. The character of this world was largely determined by the American story, which I have named the story of America as a nation of displaced people. The players and makers of these arts almost never discuss the character of America, let alone its religious meaning. Nevertheless, in the following three chapters, I will study these arts, peeling back their surface in an effort to discover the worldviews and the moral and religious attitudes that set the preconditions for their flourishing. I will argue that these worldviews and attitudes go a long way towards explaining why these three popular arts were invented in America.

While jazz, football, and the movies can easily migrate to other societies, their rise in America was due in part to conditions indigenous to America—not to the American spiritual culture alone but also to a variety of beliefs normal to a displaced people. One result of these conditions has been the likelihood that, at some point, the enthusiast will derive from jazz, football, and the movies the cold shock of atheism and go on to experience a sense of mystery.

The American spiritual culture is sometimes more vividly expressed through secular activities such as jazz, football, and the movies than through the overtly sacred activities of organized religion. With some slight exaggeration, American religious historian Catherine Albanese notes: "As the religion which is perceived as religion occupies a smaller compartment in the heads and lives of its practitioners . . . , the 'real religion' of the American people lies to a greater degree outside the confines of traditional definitions. To state the matter baldly, the American penchant for teeth-brushing or flag-waving may have as much or more to do with religious orientation than church and synagogue attendance."[2] Also with slight exaggeration, Flannery O'Connor has claimed that "the artist penetrates the concrete world in order to find at its depths the image of its source, the image of ultimate reality."[3] Overworked Americans are able to allocate only a few hours each week to what they freely choose to do, and these choices often indicate who they really are and what they truly believe. When they give these hours to jazz, football, and the movies, they tip their religious hand, where religion is their "total reaction upon life," as William James suggested.[4]

In their devotion, jazz fans show their appreciation for, among other things, improvisation; football fans suggest their ambivalent negotiation with violence; and movie fans manifest their desire for self-creation through fantasy. In each case, the enthusiasts telegraph their view of what is most (religiously) significant in their world.

Of course, each of these activities is not first of all about ideas, especially not religious beliefs. Art critic Terry Teachout would want to protect these popular arts from all those who "believe that art is valuable only to the extent that it makes the world a cleaner, better-lighted place." But the arts should not be overprotected from analysis, as they would be by dance critic Arlene Croce when she says, "I never saw a good ballet that made me think."[5] While good art is not primarily about ideas, it can certainly assume and imply ideas or, at least, assumptions about the world. Americans, like other people, patronize the arts for a number of reasons, one of which is to examine the assumptions implicit in the arts. When an art is serving precisely the aesthetic goal audiences want it to serve, it is also a barometer of the American spiritual weather.

Thus, because jazz, football, and the movies are widely appreciated in America, they may tell about America's spiritual culture and the working ground for that culture. They may tell something true, even if not necessarily good; something common, even if not universally appreciated. They may make visible what too often has been, to coin a phrase, "one nation, invisible."

5

Jazz

Improvisation is inherent in America's errand into the wilderness, the conquest of a continent. And as [Wynton] Marsalis says, improvisation was the warp and woof of black experience. If you were a slave, the language, food—all of life—was strange, and if you could not improvise, you would be in a world of trouble. Trouble was the birth of the blues, music that is, in the words of music critic Gerald Early, "about sculpting meaning out of a situation that seems to defy your being able to find meaning in it."
—George Will, *Washington Post*

White people were hearing something in jazz that said something deeply about their experience. I'm not sure that it would have been this way if we were not a country of immigrants, and so many people felt kind of displaced. You had the music that kind of captured some of the feeling of that. I think that that was part of its amazing appeal, was how it spoke to feeling out of sorts and out of joint and maladjusted.
—Gerald Early, *Jazz*, PBS

Ellington's music represented the musical equivalent to the American spirit of affirmation in the face of adversity. It was constantly creative. It generated resilience, which made an experimental attitude possible, meant you developed an experimental disposition.
—Albert Murray, *Jazz*, PBS

SEVERAL MEN AND ONE WOMAN DRIFT INTO AN ELEVATED, dimly lit space in a smoky room and take seats in front of an audience. They come without directions. In a mostly scripted world, they have no old

117

and published score to carry them back to a musical treasure from a better past. They offer not what they bring, but what they do—now, with each other. Their music is this performance at this moment, their new interpretation of an old theme rather than their re-presentation of a fixed composition.

At first exclusively and still predominantly, these jazz artists were and are African American. They developed a musical style ideally suited for uprooted and displaced persons. As a people, they were largely dispossessed of their heritage, and that dispossession was more complete and devastating than that of any other group of Americans, except possibly Native Americans, because it came through force and was intended to ensure the loss of memory. If Americans are displaced persons, African Americans are proto-Americans.

True, like other Americans, blacks retained as much as they reasonably could from their former lives, particularly memories of their music and their religion, two things physical confiscation could not eradicate. Nevertheless, the black loss and displacement were far more thorough and the place prepared for the blacks far more daunting than for other immigrants. Involuntary immigrants from Africa, they needed ingenuity, particularly the musical ingenuity that led to twentieth-century jazz.

At the same time, however, jazz is natural to all Americans. Speaking about jazz, African American culture critic Stanley Crouch has said, "So all we get, really, from the Negro is just an intensification of the central ethos of the society."[1] After some resistance, most Americans were to make jazz their most distinctive form of serious music, their own classical music. With its emphasis on ingenuity, jazz was perfectly suited to answer the emotional needs of people who were uprooted and then deposited in a culture devoid of old, established traditions.

The key here is ingenuity. For jazz, ingenuity is improvisation, a specific response to a pervasive dispossession, an affirmation amid confusion. As I have told the American story, it has three episodes: (1) the experience of having left a place with an ancient and structured culture; (2) the recognition that the place that has been inherited is a place without an ancient and structured culture that the immigrants could appropriate; and (3) the realization that Americans had to choose between living without a culture and creating one, and they chose creation. All three episodes are preconditions for the importance of improvisation in America. As I have noted, African Americans were proto-Americans largely because these episodes were for them so deep-running.

Jazz, Improvisation, and Black Experience

Of the many components of jazz, none is found in all jazz, except possibly swing. Jazz may employ syncopation, complex rhythmic forms, polyphony, active and evolving collaboration among performers, dance and ritual, work-song styles (especially call and response), and voice-imitating instrumental timbre; and it usually presupposes suffering (particularly manifest in the blues). But it is swing—that "buoyant, lilting feeling that pulls the listener along"—that pervades all jazz and that is ultimately indefinable, making jazz itself ultimately indefinable.[2]

Added to and implicit in these components of jazz is improvisation, which is not present in some jazz but is the most important single element in the historical development of jazz. Improvisation was particularly prominent in the earlier history of jazz, when it was performed on a certain set of tunes out of the communal past and when it was collective, involving the interplay of all members of the jazz band. Although it remained crucial to the historic, spontaneous, and collaborative spirit of jazz, improvisation became less obvious when arrangements were written down (as with Jelly Roll Morton), and the collective development of improvisation was diminished when soloists stepped forward (as did Louis Armstrong). Nevertheless, improvisation remained extremely important, whether in performance or in big bands' sheet music, which was usually improvised somewhere—often by the band members collectively, during a rehearsal.[3] Improvisation operates especially in jazz that depends on the blues idiom or on a blues-type structure, tonality, and mood.[4]

Improvisation is emblematic of jazz's constructive response to American displacement. Of course, jazz is to be enjoyed and can never be reduced to a therapy. But even when the therapeutic aspect was covert and enjoyment was overt, jazz's improvisation had a function; it was—and still is—a way to thumb one's nose at the pain of displacement and to revel in musical expression. African Americans were ideal improvisers because of the extremity of their displacement. The slavers had stripped them in body, of material culture and of records of their past, leaving them with nothing of their physical African past that they could import and sustain in the Americas. Improvisation allowed musicians to compensate for the loss by focusing on what they could control, their performance itself.

It is true that Africans preserved their memories. Although they had no written tradition to work with, as did those who Americanized European music, Africans brought with them traditions of rhythm, often trivialized by ignorant observers but, in fact, too sophisticated for comprehension by most European ears. One historian argues, "Every piece of African music has at least two or three rhythms, sometimes four or five"; he refers not to successive rhythms but to simultaneous rhythms.[5] The Africans also brought with them the knowledge of how to play lute-like, fiddle-like, and harmonica-like instruments, as well as drums, banjos, guitars, flutes, thumb pianos, xylophones, bells, castanets, gong-gongs; in addition to distinctive styles of singing, including falsetto, shouts, groans, and guttural tones.[6] Thus, it was easier in America than might be expected for slaves to convert shells, hollowed-out sticks, combs, and other found objects into musical instruments, making their first American act of improvisation the improvisation of instruments.

The African Americans' improvisation was especially strong because it built on the improvisation already practiced in Africa. Around the beginning of the nineteenth century, explorer Mungo Park reported that African singing groups often improvised both tunes and texts; and science writer Thomas Edward Bowditch reported that the unfolding of a song was left largely "to the fancy of the performer."[7] However, although the African influence may have given improvisation a head start in America, it was not strong enough to make jazz only the Americanization of an essentially African form.

Jazz might be described as the Africanization of a synthesis of immigrant forms of American music created under the uniquely American pressure of extreme displacement. African Americans were exposed to a mind-boggling diversity of musical traditions, imported to America by others. This musical cacophony deprived them of a dominant tradition and structure that might replace the dominant tradition and structure they had left behind. Thus, whether to fill the void of a tradition left largely behind or to organize the surfeit of other people's traditions, whether to create wealth out of paucity or structure out of excess, if music was to be expressed, improvisation was required. It is not surprising, then, that "if there is any one aspect of performance that almost all the contemporary sources agree upon, it is the fact that the slaves improvised their songs."[8]

The profusion of traditions was most intense in New Orleans, the birthplace of jazz. Blacks encountered there such musical variety that they had no obvious musical mandate to build on, nothing like the clear line of succession and tradition evident in the development of much European music, even after it emigrated to America. Between the years 1764 and 1800, control of Louisiana passed from France to Spain and back to

France; settlers from Germany, Italy, England, Ireland, and Scotland also left their mark on New Orleans. The blacks themselves brought not only African but also Caribbean music—for many had migrated from Africa to Haiti, were pushed from Haiti by its revolution, migrated to Cuba, and then to New Orleans. All of this made Louisiana, says jazz historian Ted Gioia, "perhaps the most seething ethnic melting pot that the nineteenth-century world could produce."[9]

Added to the musical paucity and surfeit were the physical and psychological brutality of slavery, the failure of Reconstruction, and the humiliation of twentieth-century racism—all together making the black's need for simple cultural identity more than vivid. It was this combination of needs that jazz's improvisation most directly answered. Paradoxically, it was cultural deracination that laid the ground for an African American creation of cultural identity. Ralph Ellison, one of the leading interpreters of African American experience in the twentieth century, has said, "the American Negro" is defined by race and by racism, but also by culture. "He is the product of the synthesis of his blood mixture, his social experience, and what he has made of his predicament, i.e., his *culture*." Calling what the black has made of his predicament "a sense of life," Ellison claimed that that sense has seldom been expressed on a more "intellectually available level" than in the blues.[10]

If there was to be music, then something like raw improvisation was required. The score was that there was no score—or, at best, a confusing variety of scores. Black cultural critic Albert Murray titles a collection of his essays *The Blue Devils of Nada*, acknowledging that it is the devils of nothingness that present the most formidable opposition, the opposition that the blues most directly addresses. In the words of one blues song:

> Ain't it hard to stumble,
> When you got no place to fall?
> In this whole wide world,
> I ain't got no place at all.[11]

Improvisation is a pragmatic device for confronting the fact that life is felt to be "a lowdown dirty shame." In this context, Murray says, it is appropriate to offer "a functional definition of improvisation as heroic action, as a way of responding to traumatic situations creatively."[12] But also, as has been noted, jazz is more than socially and psychologically pragmatic or useful. It is instrumentally valuable largely because it is intrinsically valuable; it is therapeutic partly because it is enjoyable, enjoyable enough to overpower rather than yield to the effects of displacement. Not even the blues is simply a tale of woe about something gone wrong. "The Negro American's sense of life," Ellison has said, "has forced *him* to go beyond the boundaries of the tragic attitude in order to survive."[13]

Jazz, Improvisation, and American Experience

Jazz and its improvisation are finally not only a black response to displacement; they are an American response to displacement. Ellison argues that the black cultural sense of life is "one of the keys to the meaning of American experience. For if Americans are by no means a *tragic* people," Ellison says, "we might well be a people whose fundamental attitude toward life is best expressed in the blues."[14] Jazz reflects both the enduring cultural deprivation of the displaced American and the high creativity required to cope with that deprivation, instilling what Ellison calls a "tragic-comic attitude toward life." Without this combination, says Ellison, American experience would not be what it is. "Our jokes, tall tales, even our sports would be lacking in the sudden turns, shocks, and swift changes of pace (all jazz-shaped) that serve to remind us that the world is ever unexplored, and that while a complete mastery of life is mere illusion, the real secret of the game is to make life swing."[15]

More specifically, African Americans and their improvisation affected all Americans. The black experience was not so much an *influence on* American experience as it was an *influence within* American experience. The blacks *were* Americans—partly because their displacement and their need for improvisation were indigenous to the American circumstance. Although the lyrics of the blues reflect a unique, almost four-hundred-year history of suffering in many respects foreign to those who were neither black nor Indian, it is still true that all Americans were displaced. All were prompted to improvise a new culture, and all, in that respect, were primed to appreciate jazz and its improvisation.

Although the aspirations of blacks have been repeatedly thwarted, black culture has left its mark on the entire American culture. By word or deed in the Revolutionary period, in the Reconstruction era, and in the civil rights era of the 1950s and 1960s, blacks called for equal treatment. Even when their efforts were spurned, they left their mark on the national psyche. In the 1970s, black historian Vincent Harding referred to the white Americans' "black inner history" and to America's "black inner voice."[16] By the 1990s, Harding could entertain the possibility of an American story that people of color and whites might share. Beginning with face-to-face interethnic conversations, one day it may be possible, he speculated, "to grope toward what might become at least the proposed outline for a new master narrative, perhaps even a new 'holy history.'"[17] Here Harding stands with other black public intellectuals, such as Ralph Ellison and Cornel West. Ellison has argued that ". . . whatever else the true American is, he is also somehow black."[18] West introduced his widely read *Race Matters* by calling for American leaders "who can situate themselves within a larger historical narrative of this country and our world, who can grasp the complex dynamics of our peoplehood and imagine a future grounded in the best of our past."[19] If, finally, Americans of all colors and ethnicities can be placed in a single narrative, then it seems likely that the improvisation native to blacks will come into view as native to all Americans.

Is it naïve to believe that blacks are profoundly important in America— which is, after all, "the white man's country"? Perhaps, but perhaps not. As Albert Murray argues, when black people "speak of their own native land as being the White Man's country, they concede too much to the self-inflating estimates of others. They capitulate too easily to a con game which their ancestors never fell for, and they surrender their birthright to the propagandists of white supremacy, as if it were of no value whatsoever, as if one could exercise the right of redress without first claiming one's constitutional identity as citizen!" Murray goes on to say:

> *American culture, even in the most rigidly segregated precincts, is patently and irrevocably composite. It is, regardless of all the hysterical protestations of those who would have it otherwise, incontestably mulatto.* Indeed, for all their traditional antagonisms and obvious differences, the so-called black and the so-called white people of the United States resemble nobody else in the world so much as they resemble each other. And what is more, even their most extreme and violent polarities represent nothing so much as the natural history of pluralism in an open society.[20]

As immigrants through and through, all Americans had the choice between improvising a culture or living without one. It is the tendency to choose improvisation that has led to much of what is distinctive about America. Displacement, in short, became a powerful motivator, driving a variety of improvisational activities in America, prominent among which was jazz.

There are other ways of describing the motive for improvisation and the birth of jazz in America. I will name four and suggest how these other motives for improvisation, while thickening the story, might be seen as themselves products of displacement.

First, the American immigrants inherited (or seized from Native Americans) a physical geography that cried out for improvisation.[21] For many early European immigrants, America was a wilderness, a frontier, or a newly settled place, quite unlike the heavily domesticated cities and farms of Europe. Early Midwesterners and Westerners stared at barren plains and built houses that in much of Europe would be seen as only temporary shelters. Unlike the people they left behind, Americans had no long-domesticated and storied countryside, no ancient churches and monuments. To the new immigrants, the frontier felt like a physical wilderness partly because it was devoid of a culture that they could understand. For them, this barren physical context not only invited but virtually demanded definition; and improvisation in everything from architecture to philosophy became the means of definition. While this may appear to be an independent explanation for improvisation, it is not, for the physical geography felt empty partly because it was experienced in the midst of a cultural emptiness that, in turn, derived from the story of the American as displaced person.

Second, improvisation as a style was inspired by several, distinctively American folk types. As historian Constance Rourke has argued, these folk types are the black, the Yankee, and the backwoodsman/Indian. Each was a wanderer and each had broken bonds with other people—the black through slavery, segregation, and a clear sense of alienation from white culture; the Yankee through revolt from Old World civilizations; and the backwoodsman and Indian through an ongoing rejection of advancing eastern American civilization. All three indigenous American types have been afflicted with what Rourke calls a "mood of disseverance carrying the popular fancy further and further from any fixed or traditional heritage."[22] Each faced the choice between life without culture and a highly improvisational development of culture, and they tended to choose improvisation. These three prototypes for the American personality are products of the story of the American as displaced person. Different as their experiences of displacement were, the black, the Yankee, and the backwoodsman and Indian could not have been the distinctive characters they became, except for their distinctly American cultural displacement.

Third, a peculiar combination of social developments encouraged improvisation. Each of these involved breaking free from standard practice and indulging in improvisation, and each could be partially explained by the American experience of displacement. Among these developments were: (1) the demise of Victorian restraints, (2) the gradual liberation of women, particularly for self-expression, (3) the encouragement of innovation in the modern arts, (4) the continuing lust for wandering best captured in the literary idiom of the "road story," and (5) the evolution of American sports that depended on spontaneity.

Improvisation as a motif in the road story and in American sports warrants special comment. As Rowland Sherrill has demonstrated, the mood of cultural severance is represented in literally hundreds of road books in print today, with titles such as *Blue Highways, Travels with Charley, Zen and the Art of Motorcycle Maintenance,* and *On the Road.* Americans not only accept Cervantes's observation that "the road is better than the inn," they revel in life on the run, improvising themselves as they travel.[23]

In the sports world, basketball and hockey are native to and popular in the United States and Canada, two countries with similar histories of immigration and displacement. With the possible exceptions of soccer and rugby, there may be no sports in the Western world less scripted and more dependent on spontaneous improvisation than basketball and hockey. Like jazz players, basketball and hockey players quote old patterns (not old tunes, but old plays), and they improvise on those patterns through constant player interaction, rearranging and reinterpreting, moving so fast and with such complication that to the uninitiated the game seems chaotic.[24]

A fourth motivation for improvisation, also deriving indirectly from displacement, can be found in the ideology of American free enterprise, which decries government regulations and planned economies as well as glorifies the lone-wolf entrepreneur or the innovating company as they invent new ways to meet consumer needs. Free trade, antitrust laws, and anti–wage-and-price-control laws are designed to protect improvisation. At the extreme, the free enterprise system is *laissez faire,* calling for an economy literally composed by the free-play of entrepreneurs as improvisers. That system venerates not the person who carefully and intelligently imitates a long-established trade, but the maverick who spurns tradition, invents a market, and ventures into uncharted waters. Its hero—more often in image than in practice—is not the master craftsman in an old art, the violin maker or the blacksmith, but the Thomas Edison who creates new technologies, or the Bill Gates and the Sam Walton who create new retailing strategies. It can be argued that today's independent stock market players, the "day traders," offer a commercial counterpart to life on the road, only their road is the road of the World Wide Web. They may live off the staid institution of the public stock market, but they jockey their way around investment institutions, improvising their stock portfolio from day to day. While vital and wealth-producing, the economics of improvisation is often simply evil, particularly as it fosters, or at least fails to address, poverty, disparities of wealth, the loss of social capital, a self-interested and materialistic ethic, and the long-term needs of the society. Nevertheless, for good or ill, capitalism in its purer state is improvisational. And again, I would argue that capitalism itself is largely a function of the immigrant's displacement, which encouraged this free-wheeling, unplanned mode of economic activity.

Improvisation and the American Spiritual Culture

In short, improvisation is important in the American nation, and jazz is one way in which that importance is manifested and encouraged. My larger point is that, if the spiritual culture is to be congruent with the nation it underlies, the spiritual culture also should be improvisational.

But how can that be? Spiritual life and religion are typically understood to represent continuity with the past, not improvisation on the past. Religion and, in effect, a spiritual culture are said to be religious largely because they faithfully uphold biblical or ecclesiastical precedents and traditions or, more extremely, the eternal and immutable truths so commonly associated with an eternal and immutable God. If this is so, will it not be difficult, if not impossible, for a spiritual culture to give improvisation a serious role? And, if that is the case, how can America, for which improvisation is crucial, be informed by an appropriate spiritual culture?

There is a clear answer to this question in the history of Western religious thought. Though the fact is not emphasized, improvisation has not only not been foreign to but quite important in Western religious thought and practice from the very beginning. Improvisation can be traced to ancient Israel—in effect, to the earliest ancestors of Judaism, Christianity, and Islam. Consequently, the American spiritual culture became improvisational not despite its religious past but partly because of its religious past. Thus, America's spiritual culture can be both traditionally religious *and* improvisational. In fact, American improvisation cannot be understood except by a reference to an extensive, traditional, pre-American, and pre-dominantly biblical past.

As it happens, jazz itself demonstrates this. Jazz's own improvisation is attributable not only to America's history of displacement but to America's religious heritage. Although jazz's black church lineage is indisputable, many blacks, whether from loyalty to church music or from loyalty to jazz, have felt a disturbing tension between the two forms. Nevertheless, as has been frequently noted, jazz and its improvisation grew out of the black church. (Jon Hendricks, one of many black jazz singers who began by singing in the church, has maintained, even if too simply, that the only difference between a gospel singer and a blues singer is that the first says "Jesus" and the second says "baby."[25]) The black spirituals began as a commentary not only on the experience of slavery but on the hope born of the biblical message, as that had been conveyed by Christian churches. The blues amplified the frustration expressed in the spirituals, but they also sustained hope—a hope based, it would seem, on the possibility that history would not always keep blacks down but could be improvised upon to permit new freedom. Jazz, dependent on both spirituals and the blues, commented further on both the oppressive social history of the African Americans and on their basically religious hope. Black gospel music—standing beside spirituals, blues, and jazz—treated biblical motifs with great respect, particularly the exodus-born belief that people could break free from the shackles of their past and develop a new history.[26] In short, all these black musical forms, both in church music and jazz, depended on a basically religious hope.

The African American use of musical improvisation makes it obvious that improvisation involves a view of the world that begins as a view of history. Black theologian James Cone argues that the blues are both religious and concrete—"rooted in the black perception of existence...."[27] This perception, born both of history and of religion, leads to a style of thinking and living. It is the style of jazz, as it picks up a song from the past, extends it, works beyond it, sometimes even violates its original and standard version. For the jazz player, the past is an occasion for spontaneous interpretation rather than a norm to be replicated in present performance.

This same perception can be found in the American spiritual culture, which arises out of a similar history and religion. For that culture too, the past is more a medium on which to improvise than a prototype to copy, more what you light out from on your way to the future than what you delve into in search of eternal riches. For jazz and the American spiritual culture, that perception is attributable both to the American history of displacement and to the pre-American history of religion.

To demonstrate the unexpected religious origins of improvisation, I will examine the *concept of history* as it developed in Western religious thought, for the history of that concept is part of the chronicle of Western religion. Within the vast complexity of Western religious thought, the concept of history grew in response to the questions, How does or should historical practice transpire? What is the purpose of people's social activity in space and time? What should be aimed at and attempted by people as they work out their fate in the temporal course of history and in their historical negotiations with God? In Western religion, there were two major concepts of history that arose in answer to those questions, and in one of these concepts of history improvisation played a major role.

To summarize, central to American jazz and to the American spiritual culture is improvisation; and improvisation makes assumptions about the world. These assumptions go back to the American history of displacement, but also to the Western origins of American religious thought, particularly to one of two concepts of history within that thought.

Two Ancient Meanings of History

What might be called external history and internal history are the histories that take place in the public world of social and physical happenings and that take place in the private world of the historian's mind.[28] In the West, these histories have had two meanings. For one set of historians—call them "Hebraists"—the past is to be consulted but then intentionally exceeded, so that the present interpretation is valued not for the faithfulness of its imitation of the past but for the creativity of its improvisation on the past. For these historians, as for jazz performers, the value of the study of the past rests in the ingenuity, the inspiration, or the cunning of its re-creation of the past. For another set of historians—call them "Hellenists"—the past is to be intentionally preserved in the present interpretation, so that the interpretation is valuable for its capacity to replicate what is forever valuable in the past. For these historians, as for most classical musicians, the notes, time, and dynamics of the past are to be replicated, sometimes as if they stood for some permanent truth. In short, speaking in broad generalizations, there are two kinds of historians, which I am calling Hebraists and Hellenists; one honors improvisation and the other honors replication.[29]

HEBRAISTS

The pre-Israelites (the people whose descendants formed Israel) were displaced persons in a new land. In order to survive in the new land, they needed to improvise a culture. The Hebrew Scriptures begin by acknowledging that their great ancestor is a displaced person: "a wandering Aramean was my father" (Deuteronomy 26:5). Israel's real history begins with the displaced person par excellence, rather than with a confederacy of twelve tribes standing poised to cross the Jordan, armed with a fully developed religion built on the stories leading up to and following from the Egyptian captivity. The pre-Israelites were wanderers into and within a strange country, rather than a conquering army poised to establish their rule and their religion in a new territory.

The conquest story, which dominates the narratives from Genesis to Exodus, is built on the exodus-Sinai tradition. The tradition had a historical basis, but it pertained to only that small number of the future Israelites who left Egypt, received through Moses a revelation at Mount Sinai, and subsequently underwent adventures in the desert. The idea of a pre-settlement confederacy of all the tribes of Israel, commonly shaped by these experiences, is more fiction than fact. The drama of the sudden conquest of Palestine by a single people (described in Joshua, especially chaps. 1–12, and Judges) was most likely the creation of a few biblical editors, designed to explain how Israelites had gained control of the land of Palestine.[30] The belief that Joshua was the leader of the conquest was also a creation of authors writing long after the settlement of the pre-Israelites in Palestine; they wrote primarily to provide a clear and unambiguous link between the pre-conquest peoples and the settled Israelites.[31]

Most recent scholars of the Hebrew Bible argue that the Israelites had no common pre-conquest experience or tradition. Lacking this, the future Israelites straggled into Palestine with different histories, or they were culturally dissatisfied and alienated inhabitants of Palestine; but in either case they were displaced persons.[32] The emerging scholarly consensus is that the settlement of Palestine by the people who would one day form Israel began with the gradual encroachment of a few separate nomadic clans. They first spent the rainy seasons (winter and spring) in the border territory between the desert and the occupied plains. When summer heat would parch the vegetation in the border territory, the clans would venture onto the plains, where farming occurred, and, with the permission of the established people, would pasture their cattle in woods and neglected fields. Gradually, the new occupants began to inhabit some wooded areas, particularly those that were neither populated by Canaanite city-states nor controlled by the Egyptians. Eventually, they turned the woods into arable land and practiced agriculture. Only at a later phase, as the clans of nomads began to move into even more desirable areas, did military skirmishes begin, eventuating in a few peaceful alliances between the clans and the native peoples. In all this, the future Israelites were a very loose collection of clans groping for existence and meaning in a strange land.[33]

Gradually, these people developed a religion that gave meaning to their displacement and that promised corporate unity and identity. Some had brought into Palestine the traditions of the patriarchs Abraham, Isaac, and Jacob. Others brought other stories, among which were stories of an exodus from Egypt, an experience at Mount Sinai, and long years of wandering in the wilderness. The immigrants eventually amalgamated and reconfigured these stories in order to develop a coherent tradition that would give them hope and meaning to help them cope with the experience of displacement.[34]

In the ensuing decades and centuries, the Israelites added stories from the past, but they always revised those stories. They used stories that counted for them as old traditions, but when their circumstances changed, they reinterpreted their stories to make sense of the new circumstances. Equally, the God of the old stories was interpreted in new ways as history changed. Clearly, traditions were not fixed, freestanding truths in their own right, but were changing interpretations of God's will relative to changing historical situations. For a tradition about the past to speak to the present, it had to be newly interpreted—that is, improvised on—to answer present needs.

Such improvisation can be illustrated by looking at the changing meanings of the law of the Israelites in the Pentateuch (the first five books of the Hebrew Scriptures). The law did not express the fixed and uniform will of an unchanging God, but was a compilation of particular, time-specific renderings of the will of God (many having begun as oral traditions). The laws always "presupposed a particular state of affairs, as laws normally do in human history,"[35] beginning with problems that arose during the settlement and then with other social and historical situations. A group of current scholars is persuaded that, "as such, the law is not understood in a static sense, as if the law were given once and for all. In view of Israel's ever changing experiences on its journeys, laws will be given and revised and ever taken away."[36] Because of changing historical situations, each generation of Israelites was presented "with the ever-identical and yet ever-new task of understanding itself as Israel," largely in continuity, but also partly in discontinuity, with its past.[37]

Hebrew Bible scholar Douglas Knight has called this continual improvisation Israel's "tradition process," arguing that it applied not only to how Israel's law developed but to how all of Israel's religious meanings kept being revised to fit new social situations. Knight gets at this participatory, tradition-creating process by drawing connections among: (1) changes in the social environment, (2) what is said of God, and (3) religious traditions. First, because the social environment was continually changing, something about tradition's view of God became inadequate. Second, a slightly altered view of God, more responsive to the new environment, was formed by a new "revelation." Third, this new view of God altered the religious tradition that was presented to the next generation. Knight concludes by saying that, while not necessarily moving towards something better, this process nevertheless "creates new meaning."[38]

Thus, the Israelites took their religious identity not from beyond history but from within history. It was past history that provided the old traditions. It was present history that provided the new, incongruous situations that required new interpretations. Obviously, when these new interpretations created new traditions, the new traditions were not rationally necessary or eternal, but were contingent on a new environment and were adapted through real decisions of real people at particular moments of historical time. Because always-new traditions would include new knowledge of God, the identity of God in the actual future was largely unknown.

The New Testament is largely a Jewish writing, so it is not surprising to see Hebraic understandings of history at work also in the activities of Jesus and of the early church. The Jews, finding themselves under the domination of the Roman empire, hoped for the restoration of a political kingdom or the arrival of an earthly kingdom of God. They yearned for a revelation that would be viable in and appropriate to these new expectations. So, once again, the historical context provided new questions that for some were answered by interpreting Jesus as the one who would redeem the Jews from their present catastrophe as well as from the woes they shared with their ancestors.

Thus, history for the Israelites and then for the early followers of Jesus was improvisational. The believer, the tradition, the present circumstances, and God conspired together to revise old traditions to answer new problems. None of this is to deny that Israelite and Christian histories have structure, aim, or unity, but to affirm that their structures, aims, and unity arose in and were altered as a result of historical activity. Even God was seen as a historical participant, one who makes promises, fulfills promises, reacts in anger, makes judgments, and forgives—but always with reference to old traditions, changing historical circumstances, and new possibilities for the future.

The Israelites had little choice but to be improvisational. They were

either new immigrants in another people's land or a resident and beleaguered minority within that land; they came with, or lived within, a variety of disparate religious traditions, and yet they needed a unified religious
tradition to make them one, sustainable people. They did not feel they
were established or native peoples standing on ancient heritages. To put it
in the language of one scholar, it is emphatically clear that "at all periods
Israel was vitally conscious of not being autochthonous [indigenous] in
Canaan."[39] Even those future Israelites who had not migrated to Canaan
but who had lived there all along were conscious of not being culturally
indigenous. Further, the Israelites had no transcendent, stable, and unify-
ing ideals outside history to guide them within history. They had nothing
eternal to provide an unambiguous mandate for their changing historical
existence. They did only what they could do: they improvised meanings,
especially religious meanings. But they did not do this in isolation or in a
vacuum; their improvisations were revisions of the stories of the fathers
and of the exodus-Sinai experience, not creations out of nothing. Like jazz
performers, they improvised on old melodies.

The Israelites did not act alone, but in dialogue with their God. The
Israelites' God was affected by what happened in secular history but was
never entirely reducible to or determined by secular history. God was
always more than what the sum of historical influences might have caused
God to be, so that God was historical but God's history included the possibility for God to act freely. At times, Israel's God seemed to resist historical pressures, to stand over against what the Israelites expected and
wanted God to be, and then to judge the Israelites. Because of this, their
God acquired authority, so much authority that it was called almighty lord
and king. At other times, the Israelites opposed their God, called God to
task, and saw God repent of God's errors (see chapter 6). In effect, the
Israelites improvised on God, just as God improvised on them.

HELLENISTS

In the ancient world, this picture of history stood beside another picture,
this one advanced by the Greeks, for whom history was understood to be
imitation. It is this difference between improvisation and imitation that
separates history for the Hebraists from history for the Hellenists. Of
course, there were important exceptions. First, from the fourth to the sixteenth century most Jews lost interest in history, placing the Law (Torah)
simply beyond history, as though it were eternal, absolute, and unqualified
by historical context.[40] Second, there were a few Hellenists, both Greek and
Roman, who were more interested in improvisation than in imitation.

For the imitating historian, the work of the historian should be as unaffected by his or her present historical situation as possible. The imitating historian looks at the past and tries "to get it right," to replicate or imitate it, for only through faithful replication of the past can history and the God of history be understood. The imitating historian regards outright improvisation on the past as simply bad historical writing. In theology, the imitating historian tends to treat improvisation as heresy.

For Greek historians Herodotus (484–424 B.C.E.) and Thucydides (460–399 B.C.E.), history was, more than anything else, a body of evidence about the past, and the task of historians was to make themselves faithful recorders of that evidence. Herodotus said he wrote so "that men's actions may not in time be forgotten nor things great and wonderful, accomplished whether by Greeks or barbarians, go without report."[41] Thucydides disparaged "the vulgar," who are careless "in the investigation of truth, accepting readily the first story that comes to hand." The good historian should rest only after "having proceeded upon the clearest data, and having arrived at conclusions as exact as can be expected in matters of such antiquity."[42] Both Herodotus and Thucydides, however, mixed their witness with strong interpretation. In their histories, both consistently favored the Greeks over their enemies; Herodotus included legends he knew were apocryphal and Thucydides invented speeches for his long-dead heroes. Despite this, their high seriousness about memory and objectivity made them want to see the past as something to imitate, not to improvise on.

Even though they were unlike the Hellenists, the Israelite historians did not believe their history was sloppy. They, too, wanted to get history right, but "right" meant something different to them. The right history was faithful interpretation of God's changing will, not an objective replication of the past. The Israelites were more interested in how their historians related to God than in how they related to historical evidence. It is not surprising, then, that the Israelites sometimes allowed several conflicting accounts of history to stand, because they knew that each, in a different way, could be a faithful interpretation.

But the difference between Israelite and Greek, Hebraist and Hellenist, goes deeper than this. It is true that the Israelite historians felt personally involved in the historical past and allowed themselves freely to interpret the past, while the Greek historians often, but not always, attempted to remain personally detached from the historical past and tried rigorously to copy it. However, this difference of approach was caused by a difference in the meaning of history, and this difference in the meaning of history was caused by a difference in the nature of history itself, a difference that was essentially religious. For most Israelites, God lived within history, so that history contained God, whereas, for most Greeks, God was located outside history, so that history only referred to God. When Israelites related to history, they were relating to God, whereas when most Greeks related to history, they were relating not to God itself but only to references to God.

The Greeks, said historian Arnaldo Momigliano, "liked history, but never made it the foundation of their lives." Greek historians' inquiry could be dispassionate about history partly because history itself did not determine the value of their lives. Their religious truths were refined in rhetorical schools, mystery cults, or philosophies, none of which depended directly on historical evidence, let alone on creative historical interaction, interpretation, or improvisation. Plato, for example, believed that the search for truth had to begin in the flux of history, but he also believed that history itself contained nothing essentially important. History was little more than a window to truths on the other side of history—to universal and eternal truths unaffected by time, place, and circumstance.

For the Israelites, "history and religion were one," said Momigliano.[43] They constantly improvised their historical relations with God, and their spiritual as well as their physical existence depended on these improvisations. History provided not only evidence of God, but the arena in which God acted. In particular times and places, the living God decided how to treat the Israelites, and the Israelites decided how to respond to that treatment. God's decisions and the people's decisions affected each other, and they all transpired within history.

Nevertheless, both Greeks and Israelites believed that the evidence for truth was first found in history, and this led them to place high value on narratives. The Israelites used narratives to portray chronological developments in history, while the Greeks often used narratives as metaphors to portray timeless realities beyond history. For the Israelite, the narrative was not a metaphor for truths beyond history, but a representation of historical (including divine) realities themselves. In other words, for them history was as deep as it gets; it was history all the way down.

Imitation and the Theological
Meaning of History

As it turns out, the imitation theory of history has prevailed in the West, making most Western historians and theologians Hellenists. The imitation theory of history was adopted by the Romans, sustained by the Christian ecclesiastical historians and theologians, and then brought into the modern era, where it has remained the dominant or standard way to understand history. Although, as heirs to Hebraists as well as Hellenists, the third- and fourth-century founders of Christian historiography desperately wanted evidence of historical events, this evidence and those events were important primarily because they were metaphors for realities beyond history. As a Hellenistic Christian historian, one imitated or copied that evidence, and as a Hellenistic Christian believer, one adopted and lived by its metaphorical meaning.

Eusebius of Caesarea (265–339/340 C.E.), Christianity's first great historian, and Augustine of Hippo (354–430 C.E.), Christianity's first great theologian, came closer to following Herodotus's imitation theory of history than to following the Israelites' improvisation theory of history. Certainly, as heirs of the Israelite emphasis on history, Eusebius and Augustine insisted on historical study and were sharply critical of those who neglected the Scriptures. But as occupants of a Hellenistic culture and as heirs to Greek ideas of imitation, they (1) separated spiritual realities from history's material realities and (2) located spiritual realities outside and above history.[44] Accordingly, while history was to be understood in terms of this world, the religious truth of history was to be found in things unseen, in realities beyond history.

As a historian, Eusebius recorded the evidence, seeking not to improvise on history, but to replicate in his writings the facts of the church from its earliest Old Testament origins until the time of his writing. He sought to "escape error and danger," humbly to follow those who left "faint traces, in which in their several ways they have bequeathed to us particular accounts of the times through which they passed." He merely "plucked, as it were, from meadows of literature suitable passages from these authors of long ago."[45]

As a believer, Eusebius was witness to the Word, particularly as represented by Jesus. He examined historical evidence of the church and then, as a Hellenist with Platonic sympathies, treated that evidence as a metaphor for the workings of God's Word, seeing church leaders as "the ambassadors of the divine word," just as the great prophets and apostles were the "vessels" of the Word.[46] For Eusebius, Old Testament laws, for example, were not new responses to new situations, but only particular representations of the universal and eternal Word. And the criterion for the success or failure of the church's life was not the creativity of its response to new situations, but the consistency of its replication of the one eternal Word.

For Eusebius, the Word was manifest in historical Scriptures and celebrated in the historical church—much as for the classical Greeks religious truths were manifest in the rhetorical schools, mystery cults, and philosophies of actual people. But the Word itself was eternal, and therefore nonhistorical. It is true that the Word became manifest in Jesus and the early church, and these historical manifestations became the working criteria the later church and its historians were to live by. But, in effect, the church and the church historian were imitating the historical manifestations of the history-transcending Word and will of God.

Less than two centuries after Eusebius's *Ecclesiastical History* (written in 324 or 325), ecclesiastical history went into eclipse and was gradually replaced by theological history. The transition was smooth, however, because the theologians of history also supported the imitation theory of history, only with greater philosophical self-consciousness. Thereafter, the Hellenistic ideal of imitation was dominant in Christian thought until the twentieth century—as can be illustrated by brief comments on how history was treated by Augustine, Martin Luther, Thomas Aquinas, and twentieth-century theologian Paul Tillich.

Both Augustine (354–430) and Luther (1483–1546) took history seriously, but were more theological than Eusebius. In Augustine's words, they understood that "whatever evidence we have of past times in that which is called history helps us a great deal in the understanding of sacred books."[47] Historical observation was important not only because it made scriptural understanding possible, but because it showed in stark clarity the human plight in what Augustine called the City of Man and Luther called the earthly kingdom. Also, for both men, history was the temporal medium in which God's eternal will was manifest and was enacted. However, historical existence could do no more than reflect the divine will that lay beyond history. Taking this point to its logical conclusion, Augustine and Luther believed that persons could not freely initiate in history anything that might contribute to their salvation; even their disobedience to God was controlled by God. Those who assumed that people, through their free decisions and good works, could even slightly contribute to their salvation were heretical; they believed that historical beings could improvise—whereas, in fact, they could do nothing but imitate the will of God. Hence, for Augustine, Pelagius was a heretic, and for Luther, Erasmus was a heretic; for Pelagius and Erasmus believed that persons could, to some extent, improvise on and improve their old selves and, to that extent, save themselves.[48] They failed to recognize that people were helpless creatures of God's eternal will. For Augustine and Luther, the work of the theologian as well as the believer was to accept that an essentially unchanging tradition reflected God's unchanging will. The only appropriate response to God's will was to witness it in faith but also in helpless passivity. For Augustine and Luther, unlike the Israelites, history could not be improvised on, at least in matters of salvation.

Thomas Aquinas (1224–1274) adopted a somewhat different approach, one that had the potential to be slightly more congenial to improvisation, even though it remained fundamentally imitative. God's will, Aquinas said, is truly embedded in history, rather than beyond history, and can be discovered through the combined uses of sense experience, memory, and reason. In addition, God creatively affects history, giving the world its final, formal, efficient, and material causes.[49] Unlike Augustine and Luther, Thomas seemed to assume that humans are able to carry history in directions God had not intended. All of this would seem to give humans both knowledge of a historical God and the power to interact with God and to affect the course of history and salvation—or, in short, to improvise on history.

However, in the last analysis, for Thomas, God's influence on history is always controlling and incontrovertible. Thus, though Thomas acknowledged that humans are free to affect history, the question of how freedom is possible is moot. God is self-caused, eternal, unchangeable, and omnipotent, and therefore, in principle, impervious to human, historical influence. And because God's influence is universal and irresistible, it is hard to see how, unless it be mysterious, human freedom could be effective. In short, Thomas seemed to believe that, at least in matters of salvation, humans could not significantly improvise on history.

Paul Tillich (1886–1965), a German theologian who emigrated to America, is often seen as a modern successor to Augustine and Luther and for good reason, especially with regard to his interpretation of history.[59] For Tillich, historical events are finite and the study of history is conducted through a rigorous examination of finite events. But because God is infinite, history becomes theologically significant only when faith "transfers historical truth into the dimension of the truth of faith."[51] But this turns historical events into symbols of faith, which are valid to the extent that they become transparent to the infinite, which is nonhistorical. Consequently, "historical revelation is not revelation in history but through history," said Tillich.[52] Jesus, for example, is the finite, symbolic, historical medium through which the eternal Christ appears in history. Although God participates in history, God cannot be thoroughly within history, for that would confine the Infinite to what is finite. Human culture and its acts of improvisation are no more than the finite forms in which God is man-

ifest, leaving the substance of the divine unaffected by human interpretation. That is, although human communities do improvise on traditions,
these improvisations cannot alter the Infinite itself or affect the deepest
content of faith.

Although Tillich is a leading theologian in the modern era, his theory of
history falls in line with almost two millennia of theological preference for
historical imitation over historical improvisation. Admittedly, he and
many other recent theologians differ from classical and Reformation theologians when they acknowledge that history is indeterminate (rather than
necessary), deeply ambiguous, and capable of generating new forms of
religious meaning, new finite husks for the eternal grain.[53] Nevertheless,
they have retained a belief in the timeless validity and universal applicabil-
ity of God's own truth, revealed in the Bible, and a belief that historical
behavior cannot alter the God who transcends history. When they turn to
history, they are usually critical and balanced historians, but for them history remains only a medium for an ahistorical meaning.

Improvisation and
the Theological Meaning of History

Despite the dominance of the Hellenistic concept of history in the history
of Christian thought and religion, Hebraic history as improvisation was
able to surface in twentieth-century religious thought. This emergence was
more pronounced in America than in Europe, partly because, as I have
contended, American thinkers had looked more favorably on improvisation from the beginning. The Puritans believed they could bring into existence a new covenant with their God. They believed such religious novelty
could occur in their own history, partly because of what they did. Even
though many of them mixed this belief with a Calvinistic or Catholic theory of predestination, early immigrants to America often believed they
were doing something analogous to, but different from, what the Israelites
had done. They and then the millions of immigrants who followed them
were displaced persons, and they knew that in the vacuum of displacement
something new had to be created, and that whether or not it was created
depended partly on their own actions. In the twentieth century, this pro-
clivity for improvisation came full term and issued in new ways of studying history, especially the religious meaning of history.

Both before and after the American Puritans, theological improvisation had been kept alive in popular Christianity. Whether negotiating with God through prayer, ritual, or moral behavior, the academically uncredentialed laity tended to believe that they had real influence on the ultimate shape of historical events. Prayer got results. Miracles answered prayers. God, Jesus, Mary, the angels, and the saints could be called upon and counted on. In the American twentieth century, such trust in the effects of human initiative was most evident in Christian evangelicals and fundamentalists and among the more conservative laity in mainline denominations. They kept alive the improvisational theory of history, even while it was being neglected by historians and theologians and even as it directly contradicted modern science's imitative theory of natural history, according to which all physical events mirrored eternal, inexorable natural laws and mathematical principles. When most modern theologians and church leaders rejected popular Christianity for its lack of cultural sophistication and, sometimes, moral concern, they unintentionally ceded to the laity the Bible's improvisational concept of history.

Nevertheless, with the passage of time, American scholars began unwittingly to borrow these habits of popular Christianity once European philosophers and theologians had given them new life. Georg Wilhelm Friedrich Hegel (1770–1831) had argued that history does not point beyond history to a nonhistorical, nonspatial, nontemporal realm of pure ideas, but is itself the arena of all that is real and important. There is an implicit logic, purpose, or Spirit in the world, and it is made real and worked out only in and through the particularities of historical activity as they unfold. He called on people to participate in that historical process. Hegel's commitment to improvisation, as well as that of the semi-Hegelian Karl Marx, was curtailed, however, by their insistence that the historical logic was itself eternal and unchanging. While Hegel explicitly called on people to improvise history, he implicitly called on people to sit back and watch the logic of history work its necessary will, as though people had no choice but to fulfill something foreordained by God, or the Absolute Spirit. Marx as well as Hegel muted history by rejecting just that indeterminacy and freedom that had made history improvisatory for the Israelites.[54]

German religious thinker Ernst Troeltsch (1865–1923) took indeterminacy more seriously than had Hegel and Marx,[55] announcing in 1902 that the "new world" is developing "an unreservedly historical view of human affairs." He asserted that Christianity has "no historical uniformity, but displays a different character in every age," so that it displays "an immeasurable, incomparable profusion of always-new, unique, and hence individual tendencies."[56] At the same time, he worried that, without an Absolute in terms of which to judge history, all religions become "simply illusions or the products of human vanity." He thought he heard the first stirrings of capriciously arbitrary forms of historical interpretation. (His fears were fulfilled later in the twentieth century by, among others, historian Carl Becker's 1931 presidential address to the American Historical Association, "Every Man His Own Historian."[57]) Troeltsch was driven to conclude that all religions "must be products of the impulse towards absolute objective truth," and that all people share "a common ground in the Divine Spirit."[58] Thus, he introduced an absolute force that curtailed the indeterminacy that would always be unnervingly present in a history that is truly improvisational.

American scholars who developed less curtailed versions of historical improvisation had been prepared in two ways: (1) in the late nineteenth and early twentieth century, many had studied in Germany, imbibing influences of Hegel, Marx, Troeltsch, and others; (2) many were influenced by the rise of the distinctively American philosophies of pragmatism and radical empiricism. Most notably, William James concluded that personal, even bodily, history affected not only knowledge but reality itself; John Dewey made a similar argument for the effects of social history. Both became contemptuous of metaphysical claims that the world is ordered by absolute powers and universal principles. James, Dewey, Charles Sanders Pierce, George Herbert Mead, and many of their readers and students contended that ideas and events were products of personal and social histories.

At the Divinity School of the University of Chicago an improvisational theory of religious history began to be developed around the turn of the century and was sustained until the mid-1940s. Dewey and Mead, who both taught at the University of Chicago—Dewey from 1894 to 1904 and Mead from 1892 to 1931—influenced the Chicago theologians. The theologians set forth a "socio-historical" method of interpretation and founded what came to be the Chicago School of theology. According to these theologians, the church had always creatively reinterpreted or improvised on its past in order to formulate theologies more capable of addressing an emerging society's new needs; and the Chicago theologians called upon current religious thinkers to do the same in their own time. Their concept of history was more improvisational than any theological concepts of history had ever been in the modern era—and than they would be again, until the rise of postmodern studies of religion in the 1980s. In the interim, from the 1930s and 1940s until the 1980s, the Chicago School's influence receded along with that of other liberal theologians in America—largely overwhelmed, as they were, by German and American neo-Reformation theologians with their imitation theory of history.

The leaders of the Chicago School were Gerald Birney Smith (1868–1929), Shailer Mathews (1863–1941), and Shirley Jackson Case (1872–1947), all members of the faculty of the Divinity School of the University of Chicago. Like Troeltsch, Mathews believed there were many Christianities, each relative to its social context, none representative of what might be called an essential meaning of Christianity. "My studies," Mathews said, "have convinced me that Christianity was the religion of people who called themselves Christian; that is to say, who believed themselves loyal to Jesus Christ, but that there was no static body of truth which was a continuum to be accepted or rejected or modified."[59] Sounding much like Dewey, Mathews claimed that religious institutions and creeds arose in response to the mismatch between a community's old theological heritage and the new religious needs implicit in a new social environment. New creeds and institutions were improvisations, offering new versions of old traditions to address new environments. The improvisations were new theological truths—hence, the Chicago School named its work "constructive theology." For Case and Mathews, the New Testament and the early church were themselves constructive responses to new social and political crises. Through the history of Christendom, each new theory of salvation and each new concept of God was a response to an era's distinct problems. Smith reached similar conclusions, but focused on cultural rather than social and political life.

The Chicago thinkers believed that most modern European theologians—especially Søren Kierkegaard and Karl Barth—had adopted what I am calling an imitation theory of history. To greatly oversimplify, what came to be called the "crisis theologians" in Europe, as well as many "neo-orthodox theologians" in America, tended to import Reformation truths into the present, even though the present was immersed in problems quite unlike those of the sixteenth century. Case, in particular, fought not only crisis and neo-orthodox theologians, but contemporary liberal theologians who followed nineteenth-century German idealism. Despite their efforts to put doctrines in "forms acceptable to modern modes of thinking," these liberals, such as Paul Tillich, wanted to retain eternally valid truth, restricting improvisation to a doctrine's form but leaving untouched its content. Case went so far as to claim that such liberals implicitly encouraged the rise of twentieth-century mysticism and the growth of neo-Reformation theologies.[60]

By the mid-twentieth century, theologians of improvisation were out of favor, partly because they seemed optimistic about religious creativity in a century whose barbarism seemed to condemn all forms of human creativity.[61] In effect, their conservative opponents challenged them to say how they could trust the improvisations engendered by a race that had generated two World Wars, mass genocide, and ruthless forms of totalitarianism and capitalism. Following the Augustinian theory of history, Karl Barth and Reinhold Niebuhr concluded that scholars who claimed they could reinterpret God's will were either proud, hopelessly shallow, or bluffing, claiming to have wisdom they did not have.

In the last three decades of the twentieth century, many postmodern thinkers undertook what amounted to a revival of improvisational, or Hebraist, theories of history—although they seldom understood, let alone acknowledged, their dependence on biblical historians. Best represented by Jacques Derrida in France and Richard Rorty in America,[62] these thinkers saw history as a series of deconstructions of earlier ways of structuring the world and the replacement of those structures with the constructions of a new generation working out of its own dominant *Zeitgeist.* They openly rejected the possibility of either objective representations of historical facts or metaphysical visions of eternal and universal (or foundational) truths. They denied that there was any transcendent criterion for historical truth (except, apparently, the one hiding in their own metaphysical insistence that all truths are relative to historical situations). All criteria for new ways of organizing the world were rooted in personal or social preferences. Not surprisingly, Derrida and Rorty came from decidedly religious heritages, Derrida being a secularized sephardic Jew with Moroccan roots and Rorty being the atheist grandson of the famed American theologian Walter Rauschenbusch.

Such postmodern philosophy encouraged a revival of improvisation theories of history in American philosophy of religion and theology. Denying old deterministic forms of historicism, the proponents of these theories, principal among whom is Gordon Kaufman, could be called new historicists—where a "new historicist" is one for whom the origins, the creative improvisation, and the testing of religious truth are all historical. For a period, three of the four theologians at the Iliff School of Theology were historicists, making Iliff a temporary stronghold of theological historicism—a latter-day Chicago School west. However, this latest version of the Hebraist theory of history was quite un-Hebraic in its concentration on methodology, in its neglect of theological construction, and in its tendency to be preoccupied with nonreligious theories of history (neglecting the classical history of improvisation theories of history, particularly its biblical beginnings).[63]

Late-twentieth-century American feminist theologians and black theologians and philosophers of religion, without making an issue of it, have also worked out of an improvisation theory of history. They have seen how white, male European and Euro-American historians have improvised on the religious past to give it a meaning that accords largely with their interests. Feminist and black religious thinkers have deliberately reconstructed theology from the locations of African-American and women's history, recognizing, in effect, that this openly improvises on history.[64]

Improvisation and Mystery

Look beneath American jazz and you will find improvisation; look beneath improvisation and you will find displacement; look beneath displacement and you will find the American story. In America, improvisation has been a strategy for coping with displacement. Americans were hard-pressed to find any given and true score that was fit for imitation, so that, if there were to be a meaning relevant to their lives, it had to be in large part improvised. Further, as the black inventors of jazz knew better than anyone, if history's plan was always to be the one that past history had given them, the blues would be unremitting; if the blues were to swing, they needed the hope that only improvisation on history could provide.

Improvisation, like jazz, can seem disrespectful of the past and blatantly secular. As it sets aside traditional meanings and relies on the mood and spontaneity of the present, it can seem to radically secularize America, removing it from any received religious style. It is important to recognize, however, that improvisation is deeply biblical and inherent in one strand of Western religious thought, so that America's improvisation is not unnecessarily separated from its religious past. Because it too is shaped by that religious past, America's spiritual culture provides a link between America's secular improvisation and its religious past, but a neglected link. Improvisation was the style needed and developed by wandering pre-Israelites and the early Christians; and it is a religious style altogether appropriate for displaced Americans.

Improvisation, in short, is a religious motif and, as such, gives God the role of co-improviser with humans. For a Hebraist, the religious community does not think religiously in a vacuum, but depends on something to respond to. Religious people, whether they rely on improvisation or imitation, do not create ultimate meaning out of their imagination, but look to a reality greater than themselves. When they choose improvisation, religious people interact with a changing God, rather than imitate the unchanging will of an unchanging God. God and God's people are each participants in a living process, each improvising and each being improvised upon. Herein is the West's oldest image of God, and it provides the theistic framework out of which jazz arises.

This conclusion, however, raises the question, Does a theology of improvisation reduce God to history? An improvising God can appear to become God primarily because it so effectively answers the needs of a people who must improvise on the past. Such a God can appear to be itself justified by wandering people who need help in coping with a confused past or by pragmatic people who need help in coping with a world that threatens their survival. In both cases, God appears to be God primarily because God works for a secular history, passing the tests laid down by its improvisers.

But the God of religion is expected to offer to the world the meaning it needs, rather than to receive a meaning from a world that needs God. To worship God because God improvises so well can seem to make God the creature of what a secular history wants rather than making that history a creature of what God offers. The history of religious improvisation seems to judge God with a judgment arising from society, whereas God was to judge society with a judgment arising from God. It would appear that God has been reduced to or emptied into a human concept, and then deemed worthy of worship. Such a justification of God does flatter people, but it also seems to make human aims the end of history. This justification appears to be, in a word, atheistic, much as religious pragmatism can appear atheistic, as we noted in chapter 4.

However, this atheism, like that noted earlier, can fall victim to a dialectic I have called the irony of atheism. This can be seen even in the testimony of commentators on and performers of jazz. Just as pursuing God to meet historical needs seems awkward, many musicians have found it awkward to play jazz for purely musical needs. For some serious jazz performers, improvisation is not just inventiveness with intrinsic value; instead, it is an effort to express something beyond music—a *je ne sais quoi*, or "soul," or the blue reality to which the blues respond. The blues, as commentators like Murray, Ellison, and Crouch have said, cannot finally be reduced to musical process, no matter how exciting the process, but are insistently about the fleeting, sometimes tragic reality to which the blues attest. James

Cone has argued, "The blues are not art for art's sake, music for music's sake. They . . . came into being to give expression to black identity and the will for survival." "Black music," he has said, "is also theological. That is, it tells us about the divine Spirit that moves the people toward unity and self-determination."[65]

Speaking from the musician's standpoint, eminent saxophonist John Coltrane declared that jazz speaks more of the world than of itself. "The main thing a musician would like to do," he said, "is to give a picture to the listener of the many wonderful things he knows of and senses in the universe." Rather than believe that most musicians play only to improvise music, he believed that "the majority of musicians are interested in truth." And for Coltrane, that truth and that universe were religious in character. "My goal," he said, "is to live the truly religious life, and express it in my music. . . . My music is the spiritual expression of what I am—my faith, my knowledge, my being."[66]

As the life histories of jazz performers like Coltrane attest, a dedication nearing obsession and a recklessness, often leading to drugs and alcoholism, seem requisite to the execution of improvisation. The sophistication and alertness it requires are so great that most concert instrumentalists would shy away from its challenge. It is as though improvisation must seem to be all—as though for a time it must become music for music's sake—before that purely secular dedication can turn, ironically, to the kind of depth of which Cone and Coltrane speak. Then it can become a comment on something beyond, and more than an exercise in free interpretation.

Jazz and most religion in America are, in fact, built on improvisation, but that is not finally their meaning. Although on the surface jazz improvisation is nothing but improvisation on old musical themes that may themselves be improvisations, just as religious improvisation is nothing but improvisation on old religious themes that may themselves have been improvised, it is only the sterile scholar, whether in music or religious studies, who would make music or religion nothing but a self-reflexive exercise in style. Ironically, what began atheistically can lead to religious mystery.

In the morning of Western philosophy, Aristotle suggested that Greek syntax presupposed that the subject of a sentence is a mystery. The subject is an *ousia*, or substance, known only through its qualities.[67] But even if it itself remains a mystery, the subject can be lived with because so much can be *predicated* about it. Thus, for example, a friend may be gendered, bipedal, and cultured, but this does not remove the mystery of the person herself or himself, who retains a whatness, a suchness never fully revealed by these qualities. Similarly, religion and jazz speak of truths that can be constantly qualified by improvised interpretation but that themselves remain ineffable. Of course, by means of technical analysis the mystery of religion and the soul of jazz can seem to be reduced to process or technique. But that secular analysis, no matter how valuable, is not the last word.

A number of American philosophers and theologians have testified to the mystery that remained after all interpretation had been accomplished. For them, precise, pragmatic, empirical, and rational analysis could say much, but still leave untouched the core reality of things. Whatever might be adumbrated, vaguely and physically, the mind could only grope at awkwardly. For Alfred North Whitehead, after all analysis of a particular thing was accomplished, one had to settle with what remained "an individual 'It' with its own significance." In a similar vein and with similar discomfort, William James found beneath all his empirical labors a "plain, unqualified actuality, or existence, a simple *that.*" John Dewey reluctantly concurred, suggesting that through immediate experience people are confronted with something inexpressible, so that their erudition diminishes to stumbling comments like "that *was* an experience," or they speak of "*that* meal."[68] To put it another way, this is where their radical empiricism led them. This is the mystery they confronted when they reverted to the raw, bodily experience underlying the data of the five senses or the abstractions of speculation.

Dewey was biblical enough to look beyond the private experience of individual persons and to suggest that societies also can experience what is mysterious. He believed that a person is "born and reared in a community," so that, "upon the whole, collective modes of practice either come first or are of greater importance." Also, a community may continually improvise on religious rites, religious rituals, stories, legends, and myths, adjusting them to new circumstances, so that what it acquires might appear to be only its own communal illusion. However, the irony of atheism worked even for the sometimes-secular Dewey. Dewey claimed that "the community of causes and consequences in which we, together with those not born, are enmeshed is the widest and deepest symbol of the mysterious totality of being the imagination calls the universe." The religious imagination may arise from the community, which is "the matrix within which our ideal aspirations are born and bred." But this social matrix is not simply an intrinsically valuable process, improvisatory or not; it is a symbol for a mysterious totality.[69] The imagination and improvisation that aroused society were not operating with strict autonomy, but seem themselves to have been aroused, as symbols are, by a reality beyond itself.

These American thinkers were not, finally, original. They simply echoed the experience that has tended to follow the atheistic reduction of everything to history or to the experience of history. When all is reduced to history, ironically, all talk of the historicity of God, including the argument that God is a partner in improvisation is, at best, a thin surface over an ocean. Then, like oil, it is destined sooner or later to break up or be burned off by good, atheistic skeptics. Ironically, it appears that, after skeptics have struck their matches and lit their fires and the fires have burned out, then the oceanic depths can be experienced. That is, the mystery may be best apprehended after, rather than before, social analysis has reduced God to historical improvisation. To transpose Flannery O'Connor's claim for fiction, historical analysis will "transcend its limitations only by staying within them."

If the analysis of improvisation reduces God to a mere social and historical creation, then God can become what is testified to, ironically, after the reduction. If jazz and if religious history come down to secular improvisation, then they are truly religious to the extent that this secular practice reveals, ironically, the mystery that lies beyond improvisation.

But then an irony of atheism can lead to an irony of theism. The mystery that lies beyond improvisation can, in turn, give to improvisation, including the improvisation of jazz, a new religious meaning. John Coltrane's playing not only expresses a religious truth beyond itself, but becomes itself religiously important.

6

Football

The object of the game is the conquest of territory. The football team invades foreign land, traverses it completely, and completes the conquest by settling in the end zone. The goal is to carry the ritual object, the football, into the most hallowed area belonging to the opponent, his inmost sanctuary.... Not only does it dramatize the myth of creation, it also plays out the myth of American origins with its violent invasion of regions and their settlement. To a certain extent, football is a contemporary enactment of the American frontier spirit.

—Joseph L. Price, *From Season to Season*

IN THE GAME OF FOOTBALL, THE WEIGHTIEST MOMENT IS NOT the moment when the center snaps the ball, but the preceding moment, when players and spectators themselves center on what will follow the snap. This is the moment when the players freeze, the spectators hold their breath, and announcers, if they know the game, pause, however briefly. In the ideal game, the quarterback's voice can be heard. During this brief interlude in the game's action, people anticipate the violence that will follow the snap of the ball. Take away the imminent violence, and the prominence of the moment recedes, the quarterback's signals become just so much information, and the game is gone.

Violence is the *sine qua non* of the game. Throughout the history of football, the violent spirit of the game has endured, even as other elements of the game have changed. Touch football was never meant to be and will never become football. Commenting on football, sociologists David Riesman and Reuel Denny noted that Americans "fear and enjoy their aggression at the same time, and thus have difficulty in pinning down the inner meanings of external violence."[1] Football provides a ritual moment during which Americans can stop and at least weigh the meaning of their violence.

Apart from its setting in the American story, that violence is anomalous. Over and over, football reenacts the conquest of territory, overwhelms those who would fiercely defend it, and permits the temporary satisfactions of the end zone, as Joseph Price suggests. The game's violence arises from the historic disposition of the conquerors. They were not only immigrants but displaced people, uprooted from the ancient culture of a motherland, thrown into a society lacking an ancient culture of its own, and forced to improvise in order to lay out the lineaments of their own culture. They were acquiring their own landmarks, lineages, and ancient legacies, but they were built, cross-bred, or borrowed. Americans were never to trust that their own experience had been gradually civilized in the way others' had been; they had to make up their own rules and traditions on the run.

America's cultural improvisation had proceeded on ground that seemed to the immigrants to be wild—beginning with the Puritans' "howling wilderness." Here the true "founding fathers," said American studies scholar Richard Slotkin, were "not those eighteenth century gentlemen who composed a nation at Philadelphia. Rather, they were those who . . . tore violently a nation from the implacable and opulent wilderness."[2] They were the protagonists of James Fenimore Cooper's *Leather Stocking Tales*, who defined themselves through violence toward the Indian, the buffalo, and the bear. They were Captain Ahab from Herman Melville's *Moby Dick*, who was obsessed with killing a white whale.

Impromptu, culturally thin, and set in the wilderness, American improvisation was bound to be quick, dirty, and unrestrained. It is no accident that football's conquest is violent.

Football is not the freakish experience of a few mavericks but America's most popular sport. Even amid a slight general decline in sports television viewing, one hundred million people watch National Football League games every weekend, NFL commissioner Paul Tagliabue said in the 2000–2001 season. The NFL championship game is not only the premiere event of sports television, it is the premiere event of all television. Among the top twenty-five single events in television history, eighteen are Super Bowls; this overwhelms the largest audiences ever drawn by an Academy Awards ceremony (thirty-eighth place) or a baseball game (fifty-sixth place).[3] Nor is football a freakishly male experience. Thirty million of the one hundred million NFL viewers on an average weekend are women; 22.1 percent of women pick pro football as their favorite sport, as compared to 13.6 percent who pick pro baseball, 12.6 percent pro basketball, 6.5 percent figure skating.[4]

Points in the History of Football

This or any other assessment of why football is important in America is not scientific, but it can be reinforced by a brief review of a few events in the history of football.

The birth of American football can be understood in terms of two principles. First, American football evolved from English rugby, but without rugby's sense of tradition. Rugby's procedures were guided implicitly by ingrained cultural traditions, whereas in America such traditions were largely absent. Consequently, football needed explicit rules, and these had to be created and applied *de novo*. Second, the rules of football normally protected the violence of the game, for reasons seldom discussed by those who wrote the rules.

We begin with the origin of the game of rugby, from which American football descended. At the famous Rugby School in England (from which the game's name was taken), soccer matches traditionally ended promptly at five o'clock. One afternoon in 1823, just as the bell began to sound that hour, a schoolboy named William Webb Ellis caught the ball and, instead of taking the expected free kick, put the ball under his arm, ran toward the goal line, and reached it before the bell stopped ringing. "With a fine disregard for the rules," a commemorative stone later announced,[5] Webb violated the spirit of the ancient game and prompted the indignant outcry of his English schoolmates. But over time his goal certainly counted, for it led to the inauguration of rugby.

Thus, rugby was a child of European soccer, which was played in the twelfth century C.E., for example, as a contest of kicking a skull or an inflated cow's bladder between medieval towns. Earlier, soccer had been played in ancient Greece, was then adopted by the ancient Romans, and had been taught by Julius Caesar's legions to the natives of England.[6] Then, as we have seen, when the procedures of soccer were deliberately violated, rugby was born.

The English did not at first give the new game precise rules, but this was not a problem because the English possessed traditions of gentlemanly behavior, so that players' judgments could be trusted. This allowed them to translate the ambiguities of the game into civil agreements, even in the absence of hard and fast rules. For example, the English were able to trust players' informal judgments about whether a ball was truly "dead," or at rest, in the end zone and whether, therefore, it would count as a goal. In addition, the English permitted a ball to be carried only if it was not intentionally "heeled out" of the tangle of players called the "scrum," but popped out accidentally and thereby was delivered to a player who could then run with it fairly. Thus, William Webb Ellis's run with the ball, despite its illegitimacy, was soon legitimized; an unspoken cultural tradition of proper behavior and trust quickly sanctioned running with the ball.

As displaced people, Americans were not heavily imbued with the cultural traditions that allowed players' judgments to be trusted. Furthermore, said Riesman and Denny, "the emotional tone for resolving such questions without recurrent dispute could not be improvised." To compensate, the Americans were forced "to fill in by formal procedures the vacuum of etiquette and, in general, to adapt the game to its new cultural home." For this reason the Americans set forth a body of rules, and it was these rules that created American football.[7]

Turning to the second principle for understanding football, the rules of the game gave prominence to violence. One team was given full possession of the ball; quarterbacks were allowed to call signals; linesmen could crouch down; and body blocks replaced shoulder blocks. A line of scrimmage was established, demarcating one team's territory from the other's far more clearly than could a moving ball. Teams lined up on either side of the line of scrimmage, cleanly separating not only territory from territory but team from team as rugby's scramble and scrum never could. This same line replaced the guesswork of ruling a player "offside" when he got ahead of the ball, making his encroachment into the other team's territory indisputably clear.

The game began to resemble war. But because the rules were written in America for Americans, they echoed not only conventional war but war on the frontier. In American history, the original "line of scrimmage" had been the line between so-called civilization and so-called wilderness. Set in such a history, it is no wonder that football assumed violent proportions.

In 1827, the two lower classes at Harvard played a football-like game on the first Monday of the college year—a game so rough it came to be called "Bloody Monday." When the Harvard faculty stopped the annual event in 1860, their prohibition became the first in a long series of unsuccessful efforts to govern the game's violence. Eventually, tackling below the waist was introduced, causing linemen to draw close together to protect the ball carrier. In 1893 Harvard added new twists to what was called the "V trick," devising a tactic whereby the ball carrier was tucked into a moving wedge of players. Soon, chess expert and military tactician Lorin F. Deland invented and Harvard instituted the "flying wedge." This play was initiated even before the ball was snapped, as players formed two, unconnected, inward-slanting columns fifteen to twenty-five yards behind the line of scrimmage and began to run, their columns converging as they approached the line of scrimmage. Then, just when the ball was snapped, the columns met in front of the ball carrier to form a flying wedge that hit the opposing line at full speed and was capable of seriously injuring any defender foolish enough to oppose it. Other momentum plays were added, particularly the "guards back" and the "tackles back," whereby two guards or two tackles would stand well behind the line, begin their charge before the ball was snapped, and then envelope the ball carrier, sustaining a charge that had "the force of a pile driver."[8]

The flying wedge and the guards back and tackles back formations were abolished, despite the angry objections of Harvard and Penn. Rules were introduced requiring every player to come to a full stop before the ball was put into play. Naturally, the meaning of "full stop" was disputed instead of civilly agreed on, and new styles of mass formation were deployed, until an article in the *Chicago Tribune* called attention to the fact that, in the 1905 season alone, eighteen players had been killed and 159 seriously injured. The national populace was in such an uproar that even hypermasculine president Theodore Roosevelt was constrained to take action, calling representatives of Yale, Harvard, and Princeton to the White House and persuading them to denounce football's "brutality and foul play."[9]

Over the succeeding years, additional rules have somewhat diminished the lethality of football's violence, even while sustaining its brutality. Players have grown ever bulkier, and television broadcasts have brought the viewer ever closer to the sound of the action—to the point where the crash of shoulder pads and helmets could be heard as clearly as on the sidelines of a high school football game.

The extension of this violence into a national lifestyle is illustrated by professional football players themselves. Over one-fifth of all National Football League players in the 1996–97 season had accumulated a lifetime average of 2.42 arrests and had been arrested or indicted for one or more of the following crimes: homicide, rape, kidnapping, robbery, assault, battery, domestic violence, reckless endangerment, fraud, larceny, burglary, theft, property destruction, drug-related offenses, illegal use or possession of a weapon, driving under the influence of alcohol, disorderly conduct, resisting arrest, and trespassing. Players were particularly inclined to beat up their wives.[10] Frank Deford, senior contributing writer at *Sports Illustrated*, has concluded that professional football players "simply seem disposed to violence."[11]

Physical assault is football's standard means for stopping a ball carrier's forward motion—assault that on the street would be criminal. Bone-shaking, if not bone-breaking tackles, particularly if they are stealthy enough to go undetected, are implicitly praised and rewarded by professional player salaries that could be expressed in multiples of the salaries of U.S. presidents. All professional football players are handsomely compensated: in the 2000 season New England Patriots' Drew Bledsoe's annual salary, based on a distributed bonus, was $8,542,700, and Minnesota Vikings' John Randle's $7,750,000, and the official minimum salaries ranged in the hundreds of thousands of dollars.[12]

Violence came to play this central role in the history of football because America's own story made the game a ritual of conquest, undertaken by people who lacked an ancient culture and who saw themselves as improvising a civilization in a dangerous wilderness. The Americans, embarked on a venture in cultural improvisation, had to protect themselves by explicit rules, but these rules retained the violence of the conquest. The harshness of the culture was symbolized in football in one additional way: football rules stipulated that the contest would not end until one team was beaten. That is, with symbolic eloquence, the "tie" between the two teams would be thoroughly broken.

As Slotkin has carefully demonstrated through three lengthy studies, the Americans generally believed they were involved in a "savage war." This became "a basic ideological convention," which assumed mythic proportions and helped to make America "a peculiarly violent nation."[13] The archetypal American story, then, is about "regeneration through violence." It is, by definition, religious because it provides a "sense of total identification and collective participation."[14] The unofficial scripture for this religion appeared, we might say, to be what Alfred North Whitehead called the "Gospel of Force" when he asserted: "The Gospel of Force is incompatible with a social life."[15]

Seen in light of the benign peace and sacrificial love that Americans discovered in their official sacred scripture and ecclesiastical institutions, this violence began to appear not only reprehensible but simply evil. And yet, as Riesman and Denny note, Americans were ambivalent about their violence. Ironically—Slotkin's objections to the notion of regeneration through violence notwithstanding—Americans occasionally found just such regeneration.

Lincoln, Nixon, and Evil

Football's and America's ambivalent attitudes toward violence can be illustrated variously in American history. They are clearly evident, for example, in the speeches and writings of the two U.S. presidents most controversial in their respective centuries, Abraham Lincoln and Richard Nixon.

At first a politician who denounced moral and military violence, Lincoln became the commander-in-chief of moral and military violence. In 1854 Lincoln had said of the Kansas-Nebraska Act (which allowed the Kansas and Nebraska territories to choose slavery) that "it was conceived in violence, passed in violence, is maintained in violence, and is being executed in violence."[16] But Lincoln would come to indulge his own, selective preference for violence. He repeatedly and unsuccessfully prodded first General McClellan, then General Hooker, and then General Meade, all leaders of the Potomac Army, to stop pausing and fencing and to pursue Lee's Army of Northern Virginia unrelentingly, until it was destroyed. Finally, he found in Ulysses S. Grant a general with blood in his eye and put him in charge of the Army of the Potomac—a choice that shocked Mary Lincoln, who declared Grant "a butcher."

Gradually, Lincoln evolved into a prophet of God's own exercise of violence, an evolution apparent in his migration from the Gettysburg Address, the centerpiece of his first term as president, to the Second Inaugural, the centerpiece of his brief second term. Each speech described the aims of battle. In the first speech, Lincoln's focus was on preserving a single republic based on the Declaration of Independence's concepts of freedom and equality. In the second speech, Lincoln was concerned with the evil of slavery, saying that, from the beginning, all Americans "knew that this interest was, somehow, the cause of the war." The Gettysburg Address assumed that the Republic should endure ("testing whether that nation . . . can long endure"; resolving that the government "shall not perish from the earth"). The Second Inaugural was uncertain whether the nation should endure. For all Lincoln knew, this war "may speedily pass away," but, then, it could stretch into an impossibly long "two hundred and fifty years of unrequited toil"—implying, surely, the death of the Republic as a viable entity. In the Gettysburg Address's theater of battle, violence was the government's means to national unity, while in the Second Inaugural's theater of battle, violence was God's means of national punishment.

In the battle prescribed at Gettysburg, the nation needed unstinting devotion. In the battle prescribed in the Second Inaugural, the nation needed religious preparation, for its evil would soon be answered with divine retribution. The Inaugural suggested that, if men died for the sake of a republic, perhaps they died in vain, for the endurance of the republic was not the issue. If the nation should die, that was secondary compared to the importance of God's will.

The Second Inaugural became most emphatic when it claimed that the outcome of the war hinged not on people's prayers but on God's purposes. By 1865, Lincoln believed he could discover God's purposes in history's events and that these purposes were not his own purposes. In a letter to Thurlow Weed commenting on the Second Inaugural, Lincoln said that to deny the introduction of divine judgment into history would have been "to deny that there is a God governing the world."[17] Lincoln said he expected the Second Inaugural to stand up in the future, but that it would not be "immediately popular. Men are not flattered by being shown that there has been a difference of purpose between the Almighty and them."[18] In the Inaugural, he had reminded his critics that what he ascribed to God was not "any departure from those divine attributes which the believers in a Living God always ascribe to Him," and that they should remember that "the judgments of the Lord, are righteous altogether." By 1865, Lincoln was preoccupied with the possibility of national redemption rather than the assurance of national survival. The war's violence would be imposed, that is, by a Good that was *not* the people's own good.

Lincoln's rhetoric of violence had become apocalyptic. He anticipated the time when "every drop of blood drawn with the lash, shall be paid by another drawn with the sword." He quoted from Matthew 18:7 and charged that the current suffering of American states was "the woe due to those by whom the offence came." The war became "a mighty scourge," God's punishment for the offense of slavery. Lincoln's God was not a Platonic God who, like a fisherman, languidly dangles a lure of potential order before curious creatures, but a biblical God who, like a mighty warrior, violently directs his wrath against a violent people.

In short, Lincoln shifted from a preoccupation with saving the Union from political violence through military violence to a preoccupation with preparing a country for divine violence elicited by its own evil. In the process, he extended the American conversation on violence, directing it toward human evil and God's response.

Richard Nixon also shifted from a preoccupation with survival and the political order to a preoccupation with evil and the spiritual order. Although his was a faint echo of Lincoln's shift, it too moved, or should have moved, the American spiritual culture. Each president was deeply preoccupied with moral issues, even if, for some observers, one would represent the moral zenith and the other the moral nadir of presidential behavior. While both were intellectual, emotional, and at least implicitly theological in their interpretation of violence, Lincoln's interpretation seemed to be informed more by public experience and Nixon's more by private experience. Each understood that violence plays a prominent role in history and that it must be discussed, but Lincoln noted its pathos and saw it as a cause for humility, while Nixon noted its power and saw it as a cause for vigilance. Each man brooded about violence in private, but Lincoln's brooding gave him a reputation for wisdom while Nixon's brooding gave him a reputation for paranoia. Both men developed a virtual metaphysics of violence: Lincoln's eventually based on divine providence and retribution, and Nixon's eventually based on general characteristics of people and nations.

Because Nixon's views on violence, even international violence, sprang from personal experience, and because he was an exceedingly private man, most of his views have been represented by people who thought they could read his private life. Historian Garry Wills described the Nixon he interviewed on a DC-3, flying in the spring of 1968 to Chicago after a long day of primary campaigning in Wisconsin. During the flight, Wills was ushered forward to the cold front cabin of the plane, where Nixon was seated at a small table. Sitting across from Nixon, Wills asked him why he was running for president. Nixon—with his head in the darkness outside the pool of light illuminating the table, his fidgeting hands finally at rest, his voice shifting to a slow cadence—muttered in a voice barely audible over the roar of the DC-3, "There is an awful mood abroad—a desire to just blow everything up. There must be a new vision of America's role if we are to shake ourselves out of this nihilism."[19] Nixon did not deny the importance of other, more personal reasons for wanting to be president, but this was the reason Wills heard that night.

Journalist Tom Wicker maintained that Nixon's dark views, whether or not about violence, were typical of Americans. Wicker titled his book on Nixon *One of Us* and drew a parallel between the American people and their leader, both of whom are regularly misunderstood. A principal task of Wicker's book is to explain how this man who was neither handsome, nor charming, nor self-assured, nor particularly articulate, nor athletic, nor graceful, nor funny, nor at ease with people could come in 1960 within one percentage point of beating John Kennedy, who was all of the above. Nixon campaigned in a still heavily Democratic nation; he was thrown into the hospital for two weeks at the height of the campaign; and he was undermined, sometimes deliberately, by the popular Dwight Eisenhower, whom he had loyally served for the eight preceding years. Finally, the vote count in Cook County, conducted by the crooked (Mayor Richard) Daley machine, probably swung the electoral count in Illinois to Kennedy, which, in turn, swung the national election to Kennedy. In short, despite the handicaps, Nixon almost beat (or, in fact, did beat) Kennedy. Nixon drew votes, Wicker argues, because the people knew Nixon's life story. They knew he was a man with middle-class origins who had been forced to give the humiliating Checkers speech and who for fifteen years had articulated (and capitalized on) their fear of a violent confrontation with the Communist nations. Kennedy may have been ideal, living a life most people secretly wished they lived, but Nixon was real, as they were.[20]

In short, Nixon shared with others not optimism born of privilege and a natural place in the sun, but pessimism born of struggling against the odds. He saw darkness in the American populace, and they saw it in him. In his pessimism, Nixon stood with America's founders who, international relations theorist Robert Kaplan said, "thought tragically." The *Federalist Papers*, Kaplan argued, "are an unending story of a few people arguing about what could go wrong in human relations. . . . Throughout the *Federalist Papers* and the Constitution you see laws in a system built on a worst case scenario of human behavior."[21] It can be argued, in fact, that the founders had enough of Nixon's pessimism to design a federal system that could anticipate and unseat presidents like Nixon.

I have suggested that Nixon's predisposition derived more from private than from public experience. It is commonly believed that Nixon's father was grim and reticent, that Nixon felt humiliated by those who were affluent and socially adept (at his Whittier College, for example), and that Nixon may have received some unrevealed emotional wound as a boy. Henry Kissinger argues that Nixon had an "abiding fear of being rejected."[22] Nixon felt he had to make up for being not particularly talented or attractive by working harder than others—on what he called his "iron butt." He came back from abuse and defeat with the unruffled stoicism of a person who has always expected such treatment and has had to regularize his responses to it.

Near the end of his life, Nixon's grim political realism assumed larger proportions. Referring to the American electorate, he once said, "You've got to be a little evil to understand those people out there. . . . You have to have known the dark side of life to understand those people."[23] Nevertheless, he believed, they had never come to grips with the implications of their own sense of evil. In an article prompted by a long discussion with general secretary of the Soviet Union Mikhail Gorbachev in 1988, Nixon instructed his readers to remember to "serve our interests," "to force the Kremlin to address our concerns." Shaming his American readers and, this time, perhaps misreading them, he said that they "tend to believe that conflict is unnatural, that people from all nations are basically alike, that differences are products of misunderstanding, and that permanent and perfect peace is a reachable goal." Then he added, "But what moves the world for good or ill is power, and no sovereign nation will give up any of its power—not now and not ever. This is an immutable aspect of national character." Real accomplishment comes, he wrote, "not from avoiding the fray but from being in the middle of it, fighting for our principles, our interests and our friends." According to Nixon, the world is and always will be based on the self-interested use of power; we are fools if we forget that we must use this power in defense of "our principles, our interests, and our friends."[24] Nixon spoke not just of strategy but, he said, of "what moves the world," now and, apparently, forever. His allusions to "the fray," to "fighting," and to the international use of "power" are not only metaphorical; he was instructing his fellow Americans on the necessity for violent action and of a violence that moves the world.

Six years later, Henry Kissinger captured Nixon's realism, as well as his own, in *Diplomacy*, his massive study of U.S. foreign policy. Nixon understood, Kissinger said, that America's foreign policy should uphold self-interest by the use of power. In America's relations with other countries, America must pit its power against their self-interested power, and it must help beleaguered countries do the same. Americans can come no closer to harmony than that; to pretend to act out of higher, altruistic ideals is not only morally pretentious, but diplomatically confusing and militarily dangerous. Nixon, Kissinger said, understood that "peace and harmony were not the natural order of things but temporary oases in a perilous world where stability could only be preserved by vigilant effort." "Nixon did not accept the [Woodrow] Wilsonian verities about the essential goodness of man or the underlying harmony among nations."[25] At best, Kissinger said, diplomats could attempt to implement a balance of power among nations and to back that effort with the threat of violence.

In Nixon's world, the gravest international problems arose from threats of violent military action and were best quelled through counterthreats of military violence, leaving a balance of terror as the awful best means of enforcing peace among nations. This concurs with the worldview of the leading American Christian ethicist of Nixon's time, Reinhold Niebuhr, who argued that, because all people are proud and must protect themselves from others who are proud, "no form of individual or social power exists without a modicum of physical force."[26] Although Kissinger disparagingly calls Wilsonian idealism "theological," his and Nixon's pessimism about human nature was as sweeping in its application and implications as Wilson's idealism. In some respects, their pessimism belongs to the tradition of the ancient Hebrew historians and prophets, who found at the bottom of Israel's political and military troubles Israel's own vanity and unwarranted self-assurance. For Nixon and Kissinger, the Vietnam protesters, who called on America to abandon its morally tainted ally and to rise above self-interested power politics, were not only naïve but morally arrogant, more likely to cause general diplomatic instability and international distrust than to bring peace in Vietnam. In some respects, Nixon's pessimism echoes classical and Reformation Christian concepts of sin, of the sort found in Augustine's *Anti-Pelagian Writings* and Luther's *Bondage of the Will.*

Nixon's pessimism began to assume, in short, the proportions of a worldview, even a religious worldview. It was probably not theological, at least in the sense that Nixon meant his "what moves the world" to refer specifically to God; most immediately, "what moves the world" referred to "an immutable aspect of *national* character." Nor, surely, did Kissinger mean his "natural order of things" to refer to a divine order. Nevertheless, their generalizations are deadly serious generalizations about innate human behavior, working much like theological generalizations. Just as for the Israelite prophets human defiance of the will of God stood behind national catastrophe, Nixon's "what moves the world" and Kissinger's "natural order of things" stood behind their balance-of-power thinking and its grim justice. And just as for Israel other nations would occasionally be the agents of divine judgment, so for Nixon and Kissinger other nations would occasionally be the agents of *réal politique.*

The route from Nixon's childhood to his preoccupation with violence was suggested in his reflections on football. Despite being too light for football, he said he had "tried and tried and tried" to make the Whittier College football team, and he did make it but seldom played. He pursued football, he said, "To get the discipline for myself and to show the others that here was a guy who could dish it out and take it. Mostly," he said, "I took it."[27] In each of his first two books, *Six Crises* and the 1,122-page memoir *RN,* he tells of the instructions of the Whittier football coach, Chief Newman: "You must never be satisfied with losing. You must get angry, terribly angry, about losing. But the mark of the good loser is that he takes his anger out on himself and not on his victorious opponents or on his teammates." "There is no way," Nixon says, "I can adequately describe Chief Newman's influence on me."[28]

Football is a violent game. Nixon knew that, and most Americans know that. International relations are violent; and their violence is best controlled, paradoxically, when nations declare that they are always ready to use violence against other nations. For Nixon, violence, whether merely human or cosmic, came to express "what moves the world."

Nixon in his century, like Lincoln in his, presided over unprecedented uses of violence. In Southeast Asia, Nixon orchestrated a use of firepower that in its intensity was unprecedented and is still unequaled in human history. Lincoln presided over internecine violence, where the enemy's and one's own casualties and fatalities were all American casualties and fatalities. Although America then had a population of only thirty-one million, the number of fatalities in the Civil War is unequaled by the number of American fatalities in any other American war, coming to twice the number of American deaths in World War II.[29] Nixon's phase of the Vietnam war stimulated domestic protest, disruption, and cynicism that many say implicitly threatened the existence of the country, just as Lincoln's war explicitly threatened the existence of the country. Each war threatened America as it had never been threatened at any other time, except in the other war.

Nixon's and Lincoln's reflections on violence, therefore, uniquely warrant study. Each president was driven to make large generalizations that were explicitly theological or that functioned theologically. Each made violence a product of something not merely circumstantial; violence, in short, cannot be reduced simply to human sins, but results from something productive of evil. In an astounding gesture, Lincoln hung the Second Inaugural on its second-shortest sentence: "The Almighty has His own purposes." This, it turns out, is the sentence that unexpectedly explains the Inaugural's shortest sentence: "And the war came." Lincoln goes on to suggest that it may have been God who introduced slavery, saying, "If we shall suppose that American Slavery is one of those offences which, in the providence of God, must needs come." For Lincoln, God may not be evil, but can certainly produce evil. In his posthumously published *Beyond Peace*, Nixon reflects on his own First Inaugural Address, somewhat as Lincoln in his Second Inaugural had reflected on his. "In my first Inaugural Address twenty-five years ago, I said, 'To a crisis of the spirit we need an answer of this spirit.'" Then, speaking of present history, he uses "spirit" to refer to a human capacity, but perhaps also to more than a human capacity: "The violence, discord, viciousness, and slovenliness that so mar the quality of life in America are products of the spirit, and they require answers of the spirit."[30] Again, "the spirit" may not be evil, but can certainly introduce evil.

If one can generalize from the reflections of only two presidents—but two who are uniquely qualified to indulge in these reflections—human violence can be highly illustrative of a general condition. Lincoln and Nixon imply that violence is no accident of history, but is a pervasive element, perhaps more pervasive than any contingent human practice could ever be, perhaps suggestive of a general condition that might be called evil.

That suggestion can be thickened by a story that writer Joyce Carol Oates tells of herself. She has long been an avid aficionada of boxing—which, though invented in ancient Greece, is now a thoroughly American sport.[31] Oates interrupts her typical praise of boxing to describe her response to one bout one night. She tells of having a sudden but "sickened sense that boxing is, simply, wrong, a mistake, an outlaw activity for some reason under the protectorate of the law." This came to her as she "sat in the midst of a suddenly very quiet closed-circuit television audience in a suburban Trenton hall watching bantamweight Richie Sandoval as he lay flat and unmoving on his back . . . very likely dead of a savage beating the referee had not, for some reason, stopped in time. My conviction," she writes, "was that anything was preferable to boxing, anything was preferable to seeing another minute of it, for instance standing outside in the parking lot for the remainder of the evening and staring at the stained asphalt. . . ." At such times, she says, "one thinks: What is happening? why are we here? what does this mean? can't this be stopped?"[32]

One can imagine telling a similar story about football—setting it, perhaps, on a Friday night during one of this country's many injurious high school football games. The violence of football can seem not only wrong but somehow expressive of a general American preoccupation with evil. Momentarily at least, Oates felt that preoccupation, and frequently so did Lincoln and Nixon. Oates remained an ardent fan of boxing, and both Lincoln and Nixon remained passionately interested in America. Nevertheless, to put it in the words of Flannery O'Connor, they acquired "a knowledge that evil is not simply a problem to be solved, but a mystery to be endured."[33]

The Ambiguity of the Bible's God

Lincoln and Nixon saw violence in the ordinary, secular history of their country. Eventually, to explain why violence had arisen in this history, they had to look beyond this history, to a history large enough to contain the theological or near-theological language of evil. For them, free or accidental human decisions could not fully explain the deadly regularity and magnitude of violence; this made sense only if violence were prodded by something steady and in the nature of things. Lincoln's and Nixon's belief may have had something to do with the fact that the Bible they and their fellow citizens read portrayed a God who was morally ambiguous.

When the authors of the Hebrew Bible attempted to discuss violence in their history, they too invoked more than human causes of violence. Whether explicitly or implicitly, literally or symbolically, they spoke of evils somehow associated with their God. The point of the story of Genesis 22 is that Abraham traced his decision to sacrifice his son Isaac to a command of God. Although God eventually withdrew the command, God had already caused Abraham unwarranted suffering. When Jeremiah was abandoned to his enemies, he blamed God for not protecting him (Jeremiah 11:18–12:6; 15:10–21; 17:14–18; 18:18–23; 20:7–12; 20:14–18). When virtuous Job suffered the death of his family, his servants, and his cattle, the authors of Job traced those calamities to God, who had initiated this violence by a frivolous wager with Satan (Job 1–2). Although a coda to the story has Job's fortunes restored, his suffering was ineradicable and his slain family, servants, and animals were irreplaceable. When Saul showed mercy toward the Amalekites by failing to "utterly destroy all that they have," to "kill both man and woman, infant and suckling, ox and sheep, camel and ass," this was said to be disobedience to God's explicit commands (1 Samuel 15:3). When Aaron's sons unintentionally offered the wrong kind of sacrifice, the Lord devoured them by fire (Leviticus 10:1–3). When Uzzah innocently reached out to steady the ark of God to keep it from capsizing when oxen stumbled as they hauled it to Jerusalem, he was destroyed by God for having touched the ark (2 Samuel 6:6–7).[34] In none of these cases does God's use of violence seem warranted or justified; it seems evil.

Numerous Hebrew Bible stories, whether read as symbols or literal accounts, have a single meaning: God is one who must repent of and implicitly accept responsibility for violence. In Jeremiah 42:10 God says, "I repent the evil I did to you" (Jeremiah 42:10), and in Joel 2:13, Jonah 4:2, Amos 7:3–6, 2 Samuel 24:16, and 1 Chronicles 21:15 God repents of other particular actions. God repents of having created humans (Genesis 6:6–7) and of having made Saul king (1 Samuel 15:11, 35); even if it was they who fell from righteousness, God repents, as though God had initiated their action. Although *nicham*, which the Revised Standard Version translates as "repentance," does not have precisely the modern meaning of regretting a sin that was intentional, it does mean regret in the sense that an action has been taken that later on one wishes one had not taken. At the least then, divine repentance points to God's unforeseen or accidental mistakes, allowing that they are mistakes and God's own mistakes. At most, God repents of an "evil I intended to do" (for example, Jeremiah 18:8; 26:3; Exodus 32:12); of "the evil which he has pronounced" or "said he would do" (Jeremiah 26:3, 13, and 19; Joel 3:10); or God is said to "repent and turn away from his fierce anger" (Jonah 3:9).[35]

Jewish theologian Judith Plaskow explains much of the human violence in the Hebrew Bible by showing how God served as a model for that violence. As king, God favors one people over all others; as warrior, God sanctions the destruction of entire peoples. "As holy lawgiver, he enacts the subordination of women in the Jewish community. This God," Plaskow says, "authorizes the subjection of women, but also, and more specifically, the rape of females taken as spoils of war (Num. 31:17–18)."[36]

In short, biblical authors are not content to attribute violence to humans alone, but connect some acts to a historical reality transcending secular history. Although this reality lies behind events in secular history, it is itself historical and operates in a larger historical theater—one that includes the theater of secular history. This reality can be evil, because it engenders violence that is unnecessary and morally unjustified. Further, the authors associate this evil with God.

Despite the fact that the Hebrew Bible is far more loquacious about God's love and justice than about God's evil, it offers a God who is morally ambiguous, a source of secular history's evil as well as its good. The moral ambiguity of God can be understood as a necessary consequence of Israelite monotheism. If polytheism (many Gods) and theological dualism (God and Satan) are abandoned in favor of monotheism, then the one God is the sole ultimate agent, the carrier of both ultimate historical good and ultimate historical evil. This monotheism and this divine ambiguity are explicitly acknowledged in Isaiah 45:5–7:

> I am the Lord, and there is no other,
>> besides me there is no God;
>> I gird you, though you do not know me,
> that men may know, from the rising of the sun
>> and from the west, that there is none besides me;
>> I am the Lord, and there is no other.
> I form light and create darkness,
>> I make weal and create woe,
>> I am the Lord, who do all these things.

In the King James version, "I make weal and create woe" is translated as "I make peace, and create evil."

While the God of the Hebrew Bible is good, that Bible offers little evidence to support the idea that God is unambiguously good. For example, in Genesis God is never called loving, and in the exodus stories God seems more interested in demonstrating God's own capacity to prevail over the Egyptians than in winning justice for the people they have enslaved. Looking at the Bible panoramically, biblical scholar Jack Miles concludes, "If we were forced to say in one word who God is and in another what the Bible is about, the answer would have to be that God is a warrior, and the Bible is about victory."[37]

The God of the New Testament is more regularly good and less manifestly ambiguous than the God of the Hebrew Bible, but vestiges of the divine ambiguity can be found in the Gospels as well. The first words about the coming of the Christ—"Do not be afraid" to Zechariah and "Be not afraid" to the shepherds—suggest the expectation of violence (Luke 1:13; 2:10). As if to confirm this, Jesus announces himself by saying, "Do not think that I have come to bring peace to the earth; I have come not to bring peace, but a sword" (Matthew 10:34). While the crucifixion itself eventually serves an overriding good, the passion drama centers on an innocent man who suffers a sadistically slow and vicious death and who believes he has been forsaken and thrown into the hands of his enemies (Matthew 27:46). Schooled as a Jew and believing that an innocent man should not be punished, Jesus is naturally dismayed. The apostle Paul focuses on the violence of the cross, passing over the babe in the manger, the dove of peace, the watchful shepherd's crook, and the life-giving nourishment of the fish. While these illustrations do not show that the God of the New Testament is not a God of love, they do seem to demonstrate God's implication in violence, sometimes a violence that seems unjust.

When Christian ethicist Reinhold Niebuhr turns to the Hebrew Bible, which he reads symbolically, his monotheism causes him implicitly to represent God as morally ambiguous. In the Garden of Eden, the snake comes out of nowhere and tempts Eve and, indirectly, Adam to defy God, with the obvious implication that, had the snake not appeared, human sin might never have entered the Garden of Eden. But in that story, what, if not God, is the ultimate source of the snake? Obviously, the snake could not have appeared except at the initiative or with the compliance of the Creator. Nor can Niebuhr cleanly separate God from the fact that "sin is crouching at the door," tempting Cain to kill Abel (Genesis 4:7). The problem is not resolved when Niebuhr contends that "sin posits itself."[38]

In recent years, the case for the ambiguity of God has been enlarged by scholars speaking in defense of gays, lesbians, and people of color. While such scholars use God's justice to argue that these people should be treated justly, they also implicate the Bible's God in the injustice these people have suffered.

Some scholars have noted the homophobia of certain biblical passages and, by implication, of the God those passages invoke. In *Gay Theology without Apology,* Gary Comstock reviews several biblical passages and rejects the various attempts to exculpate their authors.[39] Among these passages are the famous lines from Leviticus (18:22 and 21:13): "You shall not lie with a male as with a woman; it is an abomination"; and, "If a man lies with a male as with a woman, both of them have committed an abomination; they shall be put to death, their blood is upon them." It is presumed homosexuals who are used to demonstrate the extraordinary evil of Sodom (Genesis 19:4–14). In Romans 1:26–27, Paul has God punish the infidelity of heterosexuals by turning them into homosexuals, making homosexuality a penalty.

Similarly, scholars of color have objected to the racial bias of several biblical passages and, implicitly, of the God depicted in those passages. There is the story of Hagar (Genesis 16 and 21), in which an African servant is used sexually by Abraham, is exploited openly by Sarah, and is ejected and made homeless—all without God's objection. Womanist theologian Delores Williams identifies a "second tradition" of African American biblical interpretation in which God clearly supports the survival of Hagar, but together these two traditions could serve to demonstrate the moral ambiguity of a God involved both in the abuse and in the salvation of Hagar.[40] Later, God rewards the wandering Israelites by causing them to fight and to seize land from an indigenous people, the Canaanites. Even if the conquest stories are historically inaccurate, they still argue that the God depicted in the Bible commanded the destruction of innocent, indigenous people and the appropriation of their land. Native American theologian Robert Warrior asks how Native Americans can trust "Yahweh the conqueror." While he does not claim it is contradictory to be both Native American and Christian, he does argue unequivocally that indigenous people would be foolish not to be wary of the God of the conquest stories.[41]

The Ambiguity of God in America

Invoking their quintessential sport, I have argued that Americans are fascinated with violence. I have illustrated that fascination through references to Lincoln and Nixon and have partially explained Lincoln's and Nixon's fascination through references to their country's premier religious document and its morally ambiguous God.

Underlying these attitudes about violence is the American story of displacement, its cultural wilderness, and the need it created to tear "violently a nation from the implacable and opulent wilderness." The Bible aside, this story encouraged belief in a God associated with evil—despite the fact that most Americans have yearned for and claimed to know a God who is unambiguously good. A few American theologians agreed that God might be associated with evil, thereby departing from the great majority of American theologians who preferred to speak of a God who is unambiguously good.

For German-American theologian Paul Tillich, God is "Being-itself," because God is present in all being. Therefore, Tillich was critical of the ancient Hebrew prophets who called God simply just; he objected not to their claim that God is just but to their inference that God is never unjust. By denying God's involvement in injustice, the prophets confined God to participation in only that part of being involved in justice and excluded God from that part of being involved in injustice. Tillich detected in the prophets a tendency to domesticate God, to reduce the divine to their own moral ideals and theories. To correct this, Tillich invoked what he believed was the way authentically religious people actually experience the divine. They experience what is Ultimate in all human concerns, the Being-Itself in which all beings participate, the Infinite implicit in all that is finite—or, in a word, the Unlimited as it is manifest in the limited. When faith simply identifies God with any moral category, including the category of the good, it improperly limits God to a category that is finite. Accordingly, Tillich argued, "the holy originally lies beyond the alternative of the good and the evil."[42] Tillich's intent was to recognize the magnitude of the holy, not to undermine what is good. After all, his own moral commitment to justice was established in the 1930s when he denounced the Nazis, acted in defense of German Jews, was among the first to be suspended from a university professorship by the Nazis, and was forced to flee Germany.[43] When he turned to more naturalistic theologians, Tillich found them equating God with all that is creative and disconnecting God from all that is destructive. Here too he detected a tendency for theologians both to limit the divine and to worship their own ideal of creativity.[44] Again, Tillich was not treating creativity lightly; after all, his own theology was, in large part, a theology of creativity. For these several reasons, then, he had no choice but to associate God with evil and destructiveness on the grounds that that which is truly ultimate is involved in everything and cannot be reduced to any human ideal or to any limited aspect of the world.

American empirical theologian Bernard Loomer agreed with Tillich on this point, for he too understood God to be involved in every aspect of everything. To experience God is to experience the life process. We all know, Loomer argued, that those who have been particularly creative have also been particularly destructive. In this world, the positive simply does not exist apart from its own negative counterpart. Because what is actual is always ambiguous, pure goodness must be an abstraction from what is actual. Consequently, Loomer refused to reduce God to the moral abstractions in terms of which God is typically discussed. Rather, he said, God is "the organic restlessness of the *whole* body of creation"; "the being of God is not other than the being of the *world*." As such, God is thoroughly ambiguous, working as "an expansive urge toward greater good" as well as "a passion for greater evil."[45]

Violence and the Irony of Atheism

If the American preoccupation with violence implies a morally ambiguous God, this is, finally, more theologically problematic than it already appears to be. Those who involve God in evil have taken away the one attribute that clearly distinguishes God from the world, the attribute of unambiguous goodness. Because God's reality includes everything, even evil, it becomes difficult to distinguish God from the world. The Israelites' God who is Creator of everything, or Tillich's God who is "Being-itself," or Loomer's God who is "the whole body of creation" can appear to be so unlimited that they are meaningless. What does "God" add to the totality of all being or creation? Why not just speak of "being" and "creation," and be done with it? If God is "the organic restlessness" of the world or "an expansive urge" toward greater good *and* greater evil, why not just stop at the restlessness of the world and the expansiveness of urges? Is God anything more than a metaphor for the ambiguity of history? Is God-language not merely a way to add an "aura of religious sanctity" (Slotkin) to the ambiguity of the Civil War, the ambiguity of international relations or, for that matter, the ambiguity of football?

In short, if God becomes just a way to expatiate on violence, why not stop with violence? It appears that at just that point where God becomes, as Tillich would say, ultimate enough to be ultimately concerned with, God evaporates into the secular air. The theological stakes that should hold down the tent of the American spiritual culture simply dissolve in history's rich soil. The spiritual culture can exist on its own, without God, or, to say the same thing differently, it can dissolve into the common culture. Nothing would be lost if God-language were replaced with a more complete secular language. In effect, thought about violence that leads to thought about the ambiguity of God becomes thought that leads to atheism.

That realization, however, can be short-lived. If violence, once deeply imbibed and dwelt on, can lead to atheism, this atheism, once deeply imbibed and dwelt on, can lead to an irony: it can open the way to religious mystery. This theological sequence inaugurated by violence may have its counterpart in a military sequence once stated by defense expert Edward Luttwak in a five-word sentence: "Make war to make peace."[46]

This irony can be approached logically by reference to the famous theological principle of the *via negativa*. The proponents of the *via negativa* have argued that whatever human thought affirms about God cannot apply to God because the reality of God surpasses what humans can think. Because the human mind is simply not capable of grasping the divine in its fullness, whatever that mind "knows" about the fullness of God is necessarily what is not true about God. Or, conversely, with the *via negativa* something can be known about God, which is that God is *not* what humans describe God to be. But, in effect, to know nothing about God is hardly distinguishable from a kind of atheism.

When this simple principle is applied to atheism, the result is ironic. If the *via negativa* nullifies positive claims about God, it just as effectively nullifies negative claims about God. In theological discourse, the *via negativa* has meant that we must put aside what we say is true about God because God, by definition, cannot be what finite humans find to be true about God. It follows that the same applies to a-theology: we must put aside what atheists say is true about God (particularly, that God does not exist) because the truth about God, by definition, cannot be what finite atheists say it is. In short, when atheism is taken as seriously as theism was by those who put forth the principle of the *via negativa*, then atheism should undergo the same reversal undergone by theism. If the *via negativa* applied to theism leads to a kind of atheism, and if there are only two options, then the *via negativa* applied to atheism leads to a kind of theism, but possibly a different kind of theism than was begun with.

However, the ironic movement beyond atheism is not confined to such logical discussion and can be found in the more metaphorical approaches taken by Bernard Loomer and Paul Tillich. While Loomer reduced God to a great generality about the world (God is nothing "other than the being of the world"), he also argued that that generality, once accepted, can awaken people to "a restiveness that impels us toward a fullness or an emergent 'more' that lies beyond our comprehension." In the last analysis, then, the truth about God is not the product of theological abstraction; rather, the truth about God is a product of the God who is "a transcendent and inexhaustible meaning that forever eludes our grasp."[47] Loomer's atheism stimulated, ironically, his theism of mystery.

This was a route already well trod by Paul Tillich and a legion of classical theologians. After having reduced God simply to the Being-itself in, with, and under all beings, the Infinitude in all finitude, and so on, Tillich turned against such abstract definition of God, calling it "theological theism." Taken literally, theological theism makes God an object of knowledge, reduces God idolatrously to the boundaries of finite knowledge and secular experience. But when this is appreciated, thought about God becomes virtually atheistic, for what it calls "holiness loses its meaning as the 'separated,' the 'transcending,' the 'fascinating and terrifying,' the 'entirely other.'"[48] However, it is just this atheism that leads one to the mystery that Tillich called "the God above the God of theism."[49]

Here Tillich stands in a line of religious thinkers, only two of whom I will name. The German philosopher of religion Rudolph Otto understood the holy to be "incalculable," "arbitrary," without any "concern whatever with moral categories," "*sui generis*" in the sense that it cannot be accessed by any intellectual categories. And yet, Otto said, it was just those who reach this a-theological conclusion whose experience of God becomes most direct.[51] Second, the biblical Job, who could not understand God's morality, withdrew theologically, saying, "I lay my hand on my mouth. I have spoken once, and will not answer; twice, but I will proceed no further" (Job 40:4–5). And yet, ironically, it was then that God was made newly manifest to Job.

Today, the ironic movement from violence to atheism, to a new theism of mystery can be found through the contemporary arts. For example, one consequence of hearing Henryk Górecki's *Third Symphony* is to move from atheism to theism. This symphony's lyrics and its musical development lament the violence perpetrated in the Nazi death camp at Auschwitz, carry listeners into the depths of that tragedy, and convince them that the Holocaust is history's final statement. History's evil is given free expression in the symphony and allowed to triumph over hope. A mother's unrelieved grief over the death of her son at Auschwitz is expressed in crushing musical detail. However, after following the symphony to its bitter atheistic end, listeners may feel strangely liberated; they may move beyond the atheism encouraged by the symphony and experience, as one commentator accurately observed, an uncanny "hope born of sorrow."[51]

Just as Flannery O'Connor observed that "fiction can transcend its limitations only by staying within them,"[52] so also, religious life can fall prey to the moral ambiguities of secular history, can die, and then be reborn. Americans are displaced, find themselves in a land that is not religiously significant, experience the evil implicit in that land, but sometimes find themselves more rather than less able to interpret their experience religiously. Lincoln fully accepted the horrors of the Civil War and acknowledged America's guilt. He saw the absurdity of America's theological reasoning, where both North and South "read the same Bible, and pray to the same God; and each invokes His aid against the other." He noted that it did, indeed, "seem strange that any men should dare to ask a just God's assistance in wringing their bread from the sweat of other men's faces." And he added astoundingly, as though completely lost, "but let us judge not that we be not judged." Yet the Second Inaugural may be America's greatest single political testimony of religious faith. Similarly, the Nixon who sank to ruthless balance-of-power politics and political vilification was the Nixon who, at the end, found hope in what he called "spirit."

Flannery O'Connor was quite aware that her preoccupation with violence was an affront to others, and she struggled to justify herself. Some of her comments refer to her literary technique. In a lecture in 1957, she presupposed that violence was unnatural, saying, "The novelist with Christian concerns will find in modern life distortions which are repugnant to him, and his problem will be to make these appear as distortions to an audience which is used to seeing them as natural; and he may well be forced to take ever more violent means to get his vision across to this hostile audience." On May 4, 1963, from her home in Milledgeville, Georgia, she wrote to Sister Mariella Gable about her novel *The Violent Bear It Away*: "If I set myself to write about a socially desirable Christianity, all the life would go out of what I do."[53]

But some of O'Connor's comments were more theological. She died at age thirty-nine, on August 8, 1964, just as her writing was becoming widely recognized. For thirteen years, she had known she had lupus, a disease that was yearly disabling and deforming her and that she knew would probably kill her at a relatively young age, as it had killed her father. As a highly intentional Catholic, she had to cope with the fact that she would be silenced inexorably, arbitrarily, prematurely, involuntarily, and, in effect, violently. And yet, as one interviewer noted, she had "a marvelous wit and an absolute absence of self-pity."[54] On October 14, 1963, ten months before her death, in a lecture at Hollins College, she said that violence was a part of reality to which the reader "must be returned at considerable cost." Then, near the end of the lecture, she justified her use of violence on grounds that were religious as well as rhetorical. "In my own stories," she said, "I have found that violence is strangely capable of returning my characters to reality and preparing them to accept their moment of grace."[55] And that moment of grace was a moment for all people. A frequent visitor, who saw much of her just prior to her death, said of this very American author, "If her characters often emerged as displaced persons, it was because she felt that all human beings are displaced persons standing in need of divine grace."[56]

As to football, every seasonal fall that violent game can jog its spectators into a recognition of their own religious fall. And yet at the end of a Friday night high school football game, as they walk through the chill autumn evening, they are often filled with fellow-feeling and high spirits.

7

$\mathcal{T}$he Movies

Whitman had expected this new art to come from literature, particularly poetry, and while his own work certainly qualified, it would not be poetry but the movies that would be America's own native form. Here was a medium free of any traditions whatsoever, much less the taint of European culture. Here was a medium that would sound the barbaric Yawp as no American form before it ever had or could.

—Neal Gabler, *An Empire of Their Own*

For faith is the assurance of things hoped for, the conviction of things not seen. For by it the men of old received divine approval.

—Hebrews 11:1-2

PEOPLE LINE UP AND DRIFT INTO A DARK AUDITORIUM, abandoning the true colors of day or night. The only light comes from a two-dimensional appearance on a vacant screen. Sound comes from electronic impulses magnified by hollow cones—called, with a fine sense of irony, "speakers." The light reaches the screen after having passed through separate celluloid etchings that jump in time with a flashing beam of light, twenty-four times a second. Between each flash comes a dark interval about half as long as the period of illumination, so that the audience spends an embarrassing proportion of its time in the dark. But never mind, for the human retina is so impressed with any image that comes along that it holds it, after it has left, for one-fifth of a second—just enough time for another image to replace the old image and to sustain belief that what is seen is continuous and, what's more, in motion. Capitalizing on

172

this human gullibility, flicks (separate, still pictures) become movies, a medium based on illusions created by machines. But the genius of the movies extends beyond the technological and the biological.[1]

Movies are important because they allow people to "look not to the things that are seen but to the things that are unseen" (2 Corinthians 4:18). When the apostle Paul asked people to "look" at what is "unseen," he called on the followers of Jesus to perceive what they could not perceive with their five senses. Admittedly, rather than shun the sensed world, the movies rejoice in it; nevertheless, like Paul, the movies finally rely on what cannot be sensed. That is, the faith of the movies lies not in their visual images, nor in their audible words and music, but in the combined, intangible effects of both of these. Movies trust that the real motion of the world is not to be sensed but, nevertheless, experienced. The movie's light and sound, like the Eucharist's bread and wine, are not themselves the important things, but they are the necessary conduits for the important things. The movies make possible "the assurance of things hoped for, the conviction of things not seen."

The audience, which for two hours appeared impassive, files out of the auditorium converted, by another movie possessed. As with the great stories told at houses of worship, the movie's story transforms receptive congregants into witnesses of a power greater than the medium's own sensate power.

Sometimes, the suppliants of the movie house are idolatrous, imputing meaning not to what is intangible in the movies but to what is tangible. Throughout the history of the movies moviegoers have worshiped the stars. But during the first decades of the movies, they were also enchanted by the mechanics of the movies, the novel device in the back of a penny arcade, outside a vaudeville show, or in a nickelodeon ("nickel madness," it was called). The audiences also were encouraged to venerate the studios, which in the 1930s to the 1940s were given grand names like "Universal," "Paramount," and "Columbia" or the names of their creators—Fox, Gold-wyn, Mayer, and the Warner brothers. The audiences were also lured by the movies' directors—like Josef von Sternberg, Howard Hawks, and Frank Capra of the 1930s, or Alfred Hitchcock, William Wyler, Preston Sturges, Orson Welles, Michael Curtiz, John Houston, and John Ford of the 1940s and 1950s. In the closing decades of the century, the audiences made idols of themselves. First, in a kind of postmodern Protestant revolution, some people believed the movies were about themselves, for whatever their interpretations, it was they who issued them and they who gave value to the movies. Subscribing to the priesthood of the moviegoers, they made the movies vehicles for interpretations, and all interpretations came back to them, the interpreters.[2] They made idols of themselves in a second and altogether different way. More and more Americans made themselves the stars of the movies. The real movie was not the one in the movie house but the one that was their own lives. The movie house became a schoolhouse, where they would be instructed in how to make their own lives as entertaining as a movie is.[3]

But despite such idolatry, American moviegoers have also sought meaning in the movies, some kind of note in the bottle from Hollywood. Sometimes they would turn to the movies to understand who they were as a people or as a nation. To explain how they did this, I will concentrate on two significant moments in film history: the reign of the studio system from the 1920s to the 1940s, and the recent rise of a new kind of movie of fantasy. In exploring this history, I am indebted to several specialists in film interpretation, especially to Neal Gabler's perceptive examination of "how the Jews invented Hollywood," the subtitle of his *An Empire of Their Own*, and of "how entertainment conquered reality," the subtitle of his *Life the Movie*.

The Studio Heads

From the 1910s to the 1950s, the movies tried to provide answers to what I have called Americans as displaced persons. I have used the label "displaced persons," because for four hundred years Americans have been like the famed DPs from Europe at the mid-twentieth-century. Almost all Americans have been uprooted from some cultural tradition of some Old World, have found only a weak cultural tradition in the New World, and have been forced to improvise their own tradition. The movies contributed to the process of improvisation, but did it radically by creating fantasies. For a society most fundamentally characterized by the paucity of its own traditions, the movies not only manipulated dim memories but created new images of Americans, such as the cowboy, the gangster, the sophisticate, the war hero, the boy and the girl next door, and the urban vigilante, all of whom coped with displacement. These were not images to be literally emulated but images to symbolize American solutions, sometimes even American religious solutions. Eventually, these images were treated as symbolically true, and then, unexpectedly, they acquired the power to alter American facts. The moviegoers did not become cowboys or gangsters, but took on the simple-mindedness, the idealism, the social protest, and the resentments of cowboys and gangsters.

This particular power of the movies is best portrayed not by the movies themselves but by the studio heads who made the movies. During the formative, "studio system" years of the American movies (the 1920s into the 1940s), the studio heads reigned supreme; they chose the directors, the actors, the producers and, most significantly, the meanings of the movies. They made the movies important in America and, by the time they had died or retired, their task was completed, and the studio system had been replaced by a combination of the star system and of directors as shapers of the medium. By the 1940s, the movies had become America's most socially influential art, and the studio heads had become the most influential twentieth-century interpreters of American meaning.

In this period, studio heads were remarkably similar. They were mostly Jews in a mostly Gentile country, and they surrounded themselves mostly with other Jews, so that in 1936 one study found that fifty-three of the eighty-five leaders in movie production were Jews.[4] They were first- or second-generation immigrants, mostly from Eastern Europe, who were born to families in difficult financial straits, often because of the ineptness or absence of the father. Carl Laemmle, the founder of Universal Pictures, was born in Laupheim, Germany, and came over as a boy, after his parents died. Adolph Zucker, the founder of Paramount Pictures, was born in Tokay, Hungary; his parents died when he was a child and, like Laemmle, he came to America alone. William Fox, the founder of the Fox Film Corporation, was born in Hungary, emigrated with his parents, and spit on his father's coffin. Louis B. Mayer, the head of Metro-Goldwyn-Mayer, was born in Russia; his family emigrated to Canada, and he then came to Boston alone. The Warner brothers, who founded Warner Brothers studios, were born in Poland; their family came to America by way of Canada, and their father was a peddler. Harry Cohn, founder of Columbia Pictures, was the son of parents born in Germany and Russia.

Their immigrant and outsider status made these studio heads hyper-American Americans in the sense that they were virtually perfect instances of displaced persons. In *An Empire of Their Own*, film historian Neal Gabler may first argue that, as Eastern European immigrant Jews, they were "anything *but* the quintessence of America"; he goes on, however, to acknowledge that these same men were successful largely because they, unlike some others in the movie business, knew how to give the audience what it wanted because "they *were* the audience."[5] So like the African

Americans who created jazz, these outsiders were, paradoxically, quintessential Americans.

The story of these studio heads was a story of displacement and how they responded to it. First, they were conscious rather than unconscious immigrants, who deliberately refused to import their Old World cultures. Most of them did not respect their fathers, who, in patriarchal societies, would have been the prime purveyors of cultural tradition. They lost themselves in an obsessive preoccupation with work, which helped them forget religion and ethnicity—a forgetfulness that could make sense for Jews in a dominantly, sometimes virulently Gentile nation. Second, not only were they unwilling to import a cultural tradition, but they found no vibrant New World heritage awaiting them, at least not one that was long-enduring and well tested. They shunned America's universities, communities, and cultural institutions, which were making some effort to improvise American versions of Old World traditions. Third, doing what displaced persons have to do, they dealt with the absence of a strong and distinct culture by constructing a culture, in their case a fictional culture through the movies, the one thing they thoroughly knew. They made, says Gabler, "a powerful cluster of images and ideas—so powerful that, in a sense, they colonized the American imagination. . . . [B]y creating their idealized America on the screen, the Jews reinvented the country in the image of their fiction."[6] The studio heads may not have created their America *ex nihilo*, but they had fundamentally altered the weak images and ideas that they, like the Israelite patriarchs before them, had received from what they believed was a cultural desert.

As poor, Eastern European Jews in a nation dominated by affluent, western European, often anti-Semitic Gentiles, the studio heads entered a country that not only had no place for them but that, on the whole, intended to deny them a place. They produced stories in which they could have a role, much as the Puritans had produced the story of themselves in America as God's new Israel. They extended the history of American improvisation, but unlike the standard improvisers on America, they revised American themes so thoroughly that their improvisations were fantastic. The studio heads worked on the American house, which had been built partly over a cultural void, but they worked not simply by remodeling but by adding rooms. To make the country more congenial to people who, like themselves, felt their displacement acutely, they created almost pure fictions that pretended to be solid American realities.

Their creation was not entirely innocent, guilelessly offered merely to entertain, but was meant to send audiences away believing, as they say, "there was something to it," so that the weekend entertainment would offer weekday lessons. In effect, the films were triply fictitious: (1) they created American stories, just innocent fictions; (2) but the stories created fictitious symbols of America, claiming to point to an America that, in fact, did not exist; (3) finally, the stories helped to create a fictitious America—that is, one that began as a fiction and ended by becoming a fact. The famous last line of *The Man Who Shot Liberty Valance* says it all: "When the legend becomes fact, print the legend." Although Gabler does not discuss this three-step process, his accounts of the studio system can be mined to illustrate it.

At their studio, the Warner brothers, Jack and Harry, built a composite, fictional persona for characters played by Jimmy Cagney, Humphrey Bogart, Edward G. Robinson, Bette Davis, Paul Muni, John Garfield, Joan Crawford, and Joan Blondell. This was a person who had been wronged and was rootless, displaced, angry, sometimes crude, often small in stature, and inclined to solve problems by lashing out. The Warner Brothers' movies offered, first, a highly intriguing fiction about characters struggling through depression, in both its senses. These were people who created a place for themselves, even a personal identity, by taking up the cudgels. But these characters were so extremely drawn that they seemed fictitious in the second sense, in that they claimed to describe ordinary Americans but actually did not. Eventually, however, these stories became fictitious in the third sense, because they helped actually to create an America that was, at first, so different it hardly resembled earlier Americas. As powerful stories sometimes do, these stories slightly changed Americans, making them more inclined to interpret their own attitudes as angry and strident, as the Warner brothers said they should.

Like the Warner brothers, Harry Cohn projected his own experience onto his Columbia Pictures movies, but in a less astringent manner. Cohn worked with director Frank Capra more than anyone else, and their typical movies were about middle-class underdogs fighting corruption, indifference, pretension, and duplicity at the top. Surely, he tapped into the American underdog mentality already manifest in blues musicians and the frontier fighters of athletic fields. His characters ranged from naïfs like Jimmy Stewart and Gary Cooper to the cagier, more sophisticated Ronald Colman, Jean Arthur, Barbara Stanwyck, and Cary Grant. One way or another, they usually adopted a humble scheme whereby to achieve a more advantageous outcome. Cohn's fictions also were triply fictitious: first, they told a story; second, that story was fictional in the sense that its account of America did not square with the actual America; but, third, the story lured others into creating a fictional America, one that began in fiction but ended in fact. As Gabler said, the fiction was put into practice by the millions of Americans who "evidently shared the same thrill of revision."[7]

Much the same was transpiring at Adolph Zuker's Paramount Pictures and Louis Mayer's Metro-Goldwyn-Mayer. They offered fictions that were less desperate, but fictions, nevertheless. At Paramount, Marlene Dietrich and Mae West had an edge, and Gary Cooper and Cary Grant were often ironic, but they all had a moral agenda so ideal that it was itself a fiction. Mae West, for example, was not a floozy but a crusader against phoniness and an advocate for honesty. M-G-M's Greta Garbo, Norma Shearer, Jean Harlow, Myrna Loy, Robert Taylor, William Powell, Walter Pidgeon, Melvyn Douglass, and even Mickey Rooney defined a new stylishness in a country lacking ancient styles. However, when it came to his image of America, Mayer knew, says Gabler, "that he was confecting, not reflecting"[8]—but, it might be added, he must also have known he was actually "effecting" (creating a new America).

The miracle accomplished by the studio heads was that they presented their unreality so realistically that that unreality gradually became reality. For many Americans, the fictions of the movies were so successful, so completely internalized and lived by, that the fictions underwent a metamorphosis: rather than remaining fictions designed only to appear to be facts, they actually became facts. Americans came to have faith in what the movies fantasized and to act on that faith, so that, to paraphrase philosopher William James, their faith in the movie's "fact" was able to "help create the fact."[9]

The Jazz Singer

Jews were ideally equipped to make this creative connection between fantasy and fact in America. Because they were an extraordinarily displaced subculture, their fantasies were germane in extraordinary ways. They were no alien cabal (as the anti-Semites tried to make them), no internal enemy attempting to corner America's most powerful cultural industry. Rather, the Jews were to the twentieth century what the Puritans had been to the seventeenth century. Both had been marginalized in the Old World of Europe through religious persecution or economic deprivation; both came to the New World to create a place of their own. The Jews were to the twentieth century what the "founding fathers" were to the eighteenth century, constructing a world in which they, rather than those who sought to control them, would have a significant place. They were to twentieth-century America what African Americans, women, and a new wave of immigrants were to the nineteenth-century America, improvising their humanity in a world that categorized them as inferior.

The similar cultural displacement of both Jews and African Americans, and their reaction to it, was evident in the parallels between the Jews' creation of fact out of fiction through movies and the blacks' improvisation through jazz. But the Jewish studio heads were Jews *in extremis*. The anti-Semitism normally accorded Jews in America and the hostility accorded Eastern Europeans of any ethnicity, taken together, heavily reduced their odds of joining American culture. Out of their extreme displacement came a desperation and a creativity that typically surpassed that of the Gentiles and of the western European immigrants. At times, they produced an America that was more American than that produced by ostensibly "ordinary Americans." Like the blacks, the Jews better understood America as a nation divorced from Old World standards, and they were better equipped to modify the weak American standards that existed and to put forth new ones. Call this the irony of un-Americanism: the less one fits even the fragile American consensus, the more displaced one is, and the more displaced one is, the more American one becomes.

The parallel between the Jewish and the African American experience in America is illustrated by the first Hollywood feature film to use spoken dialogue as part of its dramatic action.[10] The 1927 movie *The Jazz Singer* played on the similarities between the American Jew and the American black as its plot wove around blackface vaudeville and jazz, played and sung by the Jewish protagonist. Taken from a story and a play written by a Jew about Jewish life, it was produced by the Jewish Warner brothers and starred Al Jolson, also Jewish. The film was maudlin, even by standards of the 1920s; the "jazz" in "jazz singer" was used loosely; and the blacks in the movie were presented from a Caucasian rather than a black perspective.[11] Nevertheless, the important symbols of *The Jazz Singer* depend on parallels between the plights of Jews and blacks in America.

In the story, a cantor wants his son to follow him, thus to extend the family line of cantors. However, the son, Jakie, decides to become a blackface jazz singer instead. After years of struggle, he finally gets his show business break as the blackface singer in a Broadway production. But the very night of the opening is Yom Kippur, and across town his father lies gravely ill. Jakie's mother pleads with him to sing this one time in the synagogue so that his father might die in peace. But Jakie knows that this would deprive the show of its star and could ruin the show's opening. In the film version, departing from both the original play and the original film script, Jakie avoids this central and difficult choice. The movie has Jakie sing the *Kol Nidre* on Yom Kippur, rush to the Broadway show just in time and, in the closing scene, receive a thunderous ovation from an adoring Broadway audience.

Although the movie's deviation from the play made it saccharine, it completed the Americanization of the story. Samson Raphaelson, the author of the short story and the play on which the film was based, claimed his drama was a tragedy. He asserted that "the singer of jazz is what Matthew Arnold said of the Jew, 'lost between two worlds, one dead, the other powerless to be born'"; and, in those terms, he both explained that tragedy and drew the parallel between Jew and African American.[12] While the movie failed as drama, partly because it missed that tragedy, it did not fail as a commentary on history when it argued that the Old World heritage, strictly followed, would not work for Jews like Jakie. In the words of Jakie's mother, the *Kol Nidre* of Yom Kippur might be in Jakie's head, but "it is not in his heart. He is of America."[13] Jakie, though admitting that the old blood "sort of calls you," finds through jazz a new way to affirm his identity as an American.[14]

The explicit and implicit similarities between the struggles of the Jew and of the black in America were not lost in *The Jazz Singer*, nor were they accidental. Because the film presupposed the anguish in the blues of the African Americans, its use of jazz to underscore the anguish of Jewish religious music came naturally. Just as Jakie, in the role of a black, would sing with "a tear in it" or with "the cry in the voice," Jackie's cantor father would instruct a student training to be a cantor to "sing it with a sigh."[15]

The similarities are further reinforced by the religious roots of both Jewish music and black music. In *The Jazz Singer*, Jakie finally understands that his ostensibly black jazz singing is religious, that it is, in fact, his version of the cantor's singing. He tells his father, "You taught me to sing—and you told me that music was the voice of God—and it is just as honorable to sing in the theatre as in the synagogue."[16] Melding jazz and the songs of the cantor, the movie's second-to-last title (in this still mostly-titled film) claims that in hearing Jakie sing at Yom Kippur we are hearing "the stage's greatest blackface comedian singing to his God."[17] Raphaelson put it this way:

> In seeking a symbol of the vital chaos of America's soul, I find no more adequate one than jazz. Here you have the rhythm of frenzy, staggering against a symphonic background—a background composed of lewdness, heart's

delight, soul-racked madness, monumental boldness, exquisite humility, but principally prayer.

I hear jazz, and I am given a vision of cathedrals and temples collapsing and, silhouetted against the setting sun, a solitary figure, a lost soul, dancing grotesquely on the ruins. . . . Thus do I see the jazz singer.

Jazz is prayer. It is too passionate to be anything else. It is a prayer distorted, sick, unconscious of its destination.[18]

In short, as he attempts to probe "America's soul"—which I am calling America's spiritual culture—one of the creators of this early, prominent film turns to jazz because of its religious quality. In the process, *The Jazz Singer* vindicated America's desire to abandon old traditions, to adopt new ways and, in the process, to create a distinctive American culture. Nevertheless, the fantasy of this film and its contribution to culture, like the improvisation of most jazz, seems finally to be empowered by its religious sources.

Gabler himself argues that the Jewishness of the studio heads was crucial to their success, and that "Judaism somehow fructifies show business." But his unintended emphasis lies in the "somehow." He claims that, when it comes to making movies, their Judaism provides one of the Jews' advantages over the Gentiles, and argues that *The Jazz Singer* "defines this advantage as something like soul."[19] But, again, his unintended emphasis lies with the indefinite term, "something." The movies were American, but how they got to be religious remains, somehow, something like a puzzle— one that can be better understood only after examining broader evidence of how the movies were American and how they helped create a new America.

The Movies and Displacement

Rather than project just any dreams onto any screen, the movies projected American dreams onto a very real and only gradually changing American cultural landscape. The movies worked with, among other things, the narrative of the American as displaced person. Having abandoned rich cultural traditions when they emigrated to America and finding a vague cultural tradition in America, Americans tended to be people without a clear cultural location, so they needed to carve out a place for themselves. This fantastic process was extended into the new cinematic art form, but its method was as old as America.

When Americans saw the movies' definitions of themselves as displaced persons, they internalized them, acted on them, and passed them on to others, thereby altering the American story. They usually did not model themselves on the external lives of the movies' characters, but they adopted many of their attitudes. They did not expect literally to become debonair socialites, criminals, cowboys, or small-town heroes, let alone blackface vaudevillians, but they did imbibe the approach to life made famous by the boilerplate characters created by the studios, as I have described them above. As Gabler said, the movies gave "a spell, a landscape of the mind, a constellation of values, attitudes, and images, a history and a mythology that is part of our culture and consciousness."[20]

In the movies' first several decades, the most prominent displaced persons were what Robert Warshow called "men with guns" (a phrase later made into the title of John Sayles's 1998 film).[21] During the Great Depression, the Westerns' version of overcoming the other through acts of violence was gradually replaced by the gangster movies' version, where cops killed gangsters. With an appalling regularity, the standard displaced Americans tended to define themselves through attacking what today we would call "the other." The point was that Americans confronted a cultural and, sometimes, natural wilderness; in order to define themselves, they had to conquer that wilderness, represented in the movies by "bad guys." While they were usually other Americans, the bad guys were sometimes not American. To take one example, in a book titled *Reel Bad Arabs*, Jack Shaheen demonstrates that in the over nine hundred Hollywood films in which Arabs appear, the vast majority are distorted, treated as "brutal, heartless, uncivilized religious fanatics and money-mad cultural 'others' bent on terrorizing civilized Westerners, especially Christians and Jews."[22] From 1896 until today, he asserts, filmmakers have collectively indicted Arabs as Public Enemy #1—ironically, much as the Nazi filmmakers once indicted Jews.

By juxtaposing movie protagonists with evolving embodiments of the other, which he calls "the savage," American studies scholar Richard Slotkin indirectly describes the evolution of the typical American from the 1930s to the early 1990s. If the protagonist must attain a cultural identity through conquering the American cultural void represented by the savage, then the changing image of the American is correlative to the changing image of the savage. Slotkin argues that, in the Westerns from 1915 to 1930, the savage others who were to be overcome were "figures reminiscent of the dangerous classes and human 'scum' of the metropolis: card-sharks, brothel-keepers, and racketeers, many of them half-breeds or 'Mexicans.'"[23] In "Victorian Empire" films like *The Charge of the Light Brigade*, the savage was a non-Caucasian in a strange country. Later, "B" Westerns found savages in everything from Indian warriors to Nazis in a zeppelin over Texas. In an evolution of the image, the savage was even to be absorbed into the character of the protagonist. Sometimes the gangster or the Western hero became ambivalent, neither totally heroic (a displaced person struggling to support the emerging culture) nor totally savage (a very displaced person antagonistic to the emerging culture)—for example, Henry Fonda's Frank James and Tyrone Power's Jesse James. In such instances, the challenge of displacement became also an internal challenge. In ensuing decades, the motif of the savage was extended through World War II movies, Cold War movies, space movies, and urban vigilante movies. Opposition to the savage gave the American the opportunity for "regeneration through violence," where protagonists were redeemed by attaining identity through violently overcoming the savage beyond—or, perhaps, within—themselves. Arguing that the motif is not original to the movies, Slotkin traces it back to the Puritans, who applied it to the Indians, and to the frontiersmen who applied it to Indians and wild animals.

In his 1996 *Lone Star*, John Sayles undertakes a close study of the evolution of displaced persons, analyzing how the very displaced, but no longer savage, others must reinterpret their displacement. In the broadest terms, *Lone Star* is about unexpected complications in the lives of African Americans, Hispanic Americans, and white Americans who live together in a Texas town on the border with Mexico. All are displaced persons seeking a viable place in a violent little desert town; even the whites feel like displaced persons as they face losing their leadership to the growing community of Hispanics. The issue of the movie is how the children of the generation that lived through the civil rights era of the 1960s and 1970s must move beyond their parents' interpretation of displacement. A black father, who has adroitly fought white racism and provided for blacks a local base of social support, must stand by as his son insists on a very different image of how blacks must learn to survive. The son, the commander of a local military base, replaces the tender-hearted compassion of his father's generation with a more conservative, tough-minded, no-exceptions-allowed, earn-your-own-way realism. A young white sheriff, a lonely advocate of racial justice, must drastically revise his "othering" of the town's aging white mayor, recognizing that he was not a racist but was, in fact, the secret slayer of the young sheriff's predecessor, who had harassed and murdered Hispanics. At the movie's end, the young white sheriff and his Hispanic lover learn that his father and her mother, though known for their racial antagonisms, were in fact lovers, making the sheriff and his lover half-brother and half-sister. Ironically, from this tragic history of hatred and violence, thickened by a new generation's unexpected difficulties, new understanding and appreciation arise. In the larger frame of the American narrative, the movie describes a phase of the ongoing negotiation with displacement, where, devoid of a stable tradition, each race must make a new place for itself in what feels like a wilderness.

Conventions and the Creation of Fact

The movies, like other art forms, participate in a critical process that continually converts fiction into fact. Working out of John Dewey's aesthetic, I demarcate three stages in the conversion of fiction into fact and I identify each stage by reference to a cultural figure: the creator, the curator, and the critic. First, when a community confronts a problem that threatens its meaning, a creative artist arises to put forth a new fiction by improvising on or reconstructing the community's traditional identity. Second, if that fiction is widely entertained, curators arise. They set the artist's proposal into the community's tradition, and show how it leads to a minor revision of that tradition. Third, critics arise to defend or attack the creator's fiction and the curator's reinterpretation of tradition by testing how they cope with their community's problem. If their tests prove negative, they implicitly call for a new creator, one who will offer a fiction better able to confront the community's problem.

To illustrate, I turn again to *Lone Star*. John Sayles was the creator; he attempted to show the inadequacy of received thinking about race and to reconstruct the simplicities of the past, arguing that sometimes compassion is inadequate, sometimes reputed villains are not actual villains, and sometimes communities have been complicated by secrets. *Lone Star* proposes a new, more complex version of traditional cultural practices, giving its audience a new appreciation of the ambiguities and difficulties of life in a multicultural society. Curators must explain how the film's images of race in a post–civil-rights era reinterpreted civil rights and pre–civil-rights images of race. The critics' task is to ask whether Sayles's attempt to walk the fine line between old and too-simple solutions and new and postliberal reactions was successful. Was the film's criticism of the black father's compassion too strong, its sympathy for the virtuous cop in a racist society unrealistic, and its implicit advocacy of racial intermarriage, perhaps even incest, likely to undermine treasured ethnic identities?

In a generalized form, this three-step process was implicit in John

Dewey's *Art as Experience*. For Dewey, the figures I am calling the creator, the curator, and the critic identify and cope with social problems. The creators put forth their symbolic reconstruction of an aspect of American tradition and do so not only to please an audience, but to resolve a social predicament. The curators of the reconstruction explain how it has re-interpreted traditional American attitudes; they make explicit its moral, emotional, and spiritual implications, and show how it slightly alters the society's assumptions. The critic evaluates the film's symbols and theories pragmatically, ostensibly for their success or failure in resolving emerging social predicaments. In Dewey's world, each of the three figures works practically to solve a society's problem and must eventually submit to a pragmatic test of truth.

This process can also be religiously effective. Sometimes the creator, the curator, and the critic address a community's spiritual tradition, its sense of the whole, and its vision of what is ultimately real. In reconstructing a spiritual tradition, the creator exercises religious imagination, senses the whole in a new way, and describes it symbolically—even if without claim-ing such grand objectives. In Dewey's terms, the creator proposes "a sym-bol of the mysterious totality of being the imagination calls the universe" and does this with the hope that, as "the unity of ideal ends," it will arouse people "to desire and actions."[24] The curators' efforts at preservation are essentially, even if usually unintentionally, theological, as they interpret the broader implications of the symbol and introduce it into a community's thought about ideal ends. The critic takes on the role of the religious critic, testing the symbol and the theory for their success in transforming a com-munity religiously. When they are religious, the symbol, the preservation, and the criticism all contribute to altering the traditional meaning of the whole, so that that meaning can comprehend a new predicament.

The Western movie, for example, sought to address the psychological and, sometimes, the religious needs of a society of displaced persons, still marked by their ancestors' frontier experience. To the extent that it worked religiously, the Western told its story in ways that shed new light on the ultimate Good that stood behind the particular goods or evils of cowboy justice, style, and craft. But then, as critics uncovered the simple-minded clichés of the Western and its occasional racism, its original forms with-ered and improvisations on the tradition of the Westerns appeared, such as Clint Eastwood's 1992 *The Unforgiven*.

This movie followed a repentant ex-gunslinger who is inexorably driven to take up again a now-hated but apparently necessary gunslinger violence. Eastwood's movie was religiously significant when its plot and style symbolized a new universe, in which moral ambiguities remain unresolved and their irresolution is part of the American spiritual predicament. *The Unforgiven* moved clearly beyond the 1953 ex-gunslinger story *Shane*, starring Alan Ladd, which eventually finds the call of the clichés irresistible. The audience left *The Unforgiven* not just with a different kind of Western hero, but with hints of more complex spiritual forces operating in, with, and under American culture. Its symbolic representation of these forces worked religiously to the extent that it altered slightly the moviegoers' sense of the whole, which, in turn, altered slightly their particular beliefs and attitudes.

In the movies this process is religious when it suggests realities larger than the realities of human activity and fosters reactions that exceed normal human reactions. For many people, Steven Spielberg's 1993 *Schindler's List* accomplished this, showing the magnitude of human evil, the impurity of redemptive good, and the unfathomable depths of both. Oskar Schindler was a Polish industrialist, womanizer, and war profiteer who used desperate Jews from the Krakow Ghetto as cheap labor during the Nazi occupation of Poland. Gradually, without exactly repenting of that unsavory personal history, he developed an appreciation for the predicament of the Jews in his employ and found ways to protect them from the Nazis. Not revealing his new loyalties, he began to deceive his Nazi colleagues, eventually saving twelve hundred Jews from certain death in the Plaszno concentration camp. This movie dealt with ordinary history in such a way that it shed new light on the depths of the good and evil that underlie apparent good and evil. What began as Spielberg's simple reworking of the Holocaust story gave unexpected new life to what by 1993 had been Americans' waning and sometimes overly simple response to the Holocaust. It complicated Americans' understanding of the guilt of the Germans and the ways in which redemptive good is accomplished in ordinary history. It raised religious questions about why and how Schindler's own unpredicted insights occurred. Pragmatically, its symbolism altered slightly Americans' assumptions about the world, their spiritual appraisal of history, and their actions.

The "miracle" whereby a mere fiction becomes or alters a cultural fact has been described by a variety of twentieth-century thinkers, but usually without an appreciation for its religious significance. Among these thinkers, I most appreciate anthropologist Clifford Geertz, historians William H. McNeill and Thomas Haskell, the previously noted literary critic Richard Slotkin, poet William Carlos Williams, sociologists Emile Durkheim and Anthony Giddens, philosopher of science Thomas Kuhn, aesthetician Nelson Goodman, deconstructionist Jacques Derrida, and theologian Mark C. Taylor. They all have contended that cultural themes begin in the imagination and that these themes then take on historical force that is more than imaginary. All, except possibly Taylor, failed to see that this process might access ultimate or divine reality, in that it seems to accomplish what secular historical forces cannot accomplish.[25]

As I have argued, American movies exemplify this fact-making process as it works in secular ways. The movies' improvisations on the myth of America stretched and sometimes burst the old myth's envelope. This occurred whether the myth was that of the American as displaced person, as I have argued, or whether it was some other myth, such as the myth of American uniqueness or the myth of the frontier. The movies' improvisations were sometimes accepted and incorporated into the cultural landscape, which led to new kinds of social behavior. For example, as the movies moved beyond an acceptance of the racist violence in *The Birth of a Nation*, to gangster, outlaw, intergalactic, and urban vigilante forms of violence in the ensuing decades, they altered the myth of America enough to change, however modestly, the meanings, standards, and practice of violence in America. Recognizing the fact-making impact of violence in the movies, many protest violent movies, particularly for their influence on children. Conscious of this interpretation, in the months after the September 11, 2001, attack on the World Trade Center and the Pentagon, leaders of the film industry postponed the release of several violent films.

But the movies also exemplify this practical process as it works in nonsecular ways. The fiction of films can alter religious truths or create new religious truths. For example, violence-laden movies not only tell about bad guys and good guys or fists and guns, but suggest that the world's ultimate reality is more about coercion than persuasion, more about hostile confrontation than about love. If the deepest or most comprehensive meaning of life is properly called "God," then when a movie proposes that violence is endemic to everything about the world, it has commented on God. When a movie makes violence the ultimate truth about the world, it appears to give to human violence a divine sanction. In short, more than morality is at stake in the movies; the realities on which morality is grounded are at stake. Just as the violence in the stories and prophecies of the Hebrew Bible involved the God of the Israelites in violence, violence in the films and other art of Americans involve the Gods or God of the Americans in violence.

Not only peoples' spiritual interpretations but the object of those interpretations is affected. While saying this now seems to give people's religious interpretations unexpected power, I am only applying to religious life and to God the strange power of fictions to alter facts. This is more obvious when God is interpreted as a sacred convention. According to our earlier nomenclature, a convention is a social habit or tradition that takes on a life of its own and begins to interact with society; and a sacred convention is a tradition of ultimate importance to a people, which takes on a life of its own and interacts with a society. If this tradition is called God because it does what Gods do, then God can affect a country's spiritual culture, imparting to it a sense of the whole. I add only that, when movies reinterpret the religious meaning of a community, they may interact with God.

The movies, then, serve not only as entertaining but temporary constructs—screened over a period of 110 minutes and then forgotten as the lights come up—but may be modified by or may slightly modify profoundly important, continuously operating, and shared social conventions, even sacred conventions. These social conventions take hold in the mores and rituals of a society, altering modes of believing and behaving as only a profound social convention can. They function as deep-running social habits, which William James called "the enormous fly-wheel of society, its most precious conservative agent," which "keeps us within the bounds of ordinance."[26]

For example, Arthur Miller's *Death of a Salesman* began as a play, became a movie, was finally produced for television, and in these various forms affected one of America's sacred conventions. Decade after decade, as its title role passed from Frederick March, to Lee J. Cobb, to Dustin Hoffman, and to Brian Dennehy, it described what James called America's "national disease," its "exclusive worship of the bitch-Goddess SUCCESS." Miller, in that play and in others, such as *All My Sons*, gave success what James called its "squalid cash interpretation"[27] and hoped to slow the mercenary flywheel, to diminish its influence over Americans. Decade after decade *Death of a Salesman* spoke in new ways, sometimes because of changes in the American economic and cultural environments. The play became a living institution that, like Jacob Marley's ghost, would rise up and set audiences reeling with unexpected indictments.

This discussion cannot be complete unless it recognizes that the mass audience of moviegoers are the most important critics of the movies. Through attending, not attending, and commenting on the movies, the moviegoing public determines a film's actual life, death, and social impact. The great studio heads were people who felt deprived of a place in American society, as they created living conventions that were to give them a place. But this initiative by itself, without the endorsement of the moviegoers, would have been useless. Out of the studio heads' imagination, a new nation was *introduced*; out of the moviegoers' practice, a new nation was *produced*.

Thus, Americans are not only what John Adams called a "poor, injured, deceived, mocked, and insulted people," but they are a people who learn "to contend, to swim though against the wind and tide as long as [they] can."[28] And the movies, my point is, sometimes helped them contend, even if, very often, at a high moral cost. They responded to the insult of displacement, perhaps altered, however modestly, the Americans' sense of the whole, and thereby contributed, for good or ill, to the religious meaning of their displacement.

The Atheism of the Movies and Its Irony

But as Adams went on to predict, sometimes the process of affecting a society's sacred conventions through the movies leads to the point where "battles and victories and conquests dazzle the majority into adoration of idols. Then come popes and emperors, kingdoms, and hierarchies." The process, in short, can go quite sour. In a country less impressed with popes, emperors, kingdoms and hierarchies, the movies can refer to the great "I," to oneself. Always a potential, in recent years this particular form of idolatry has become acutely manifest.

Neal Gabler attempts to show how this happened. The same Gabler who in *An Empire of Their Own* had celebrated how the movies could serve a social function, particularly for the movie producers, was to write ten years later *Life the Movie*, a lament for the American popular media, principal among which are the movies. Gabler's progression neatly captures how some movies moved from being religiously significant to becoming religiously idolatrous.

In the first book, Gabler demonstrates that the movies proposed a new, often more satisfactory America for the early Jewish producers and for most other Americans. He went on to suggest that that proposal altered American life, so that fiction became fact. Addressing the problem of Americans as displaced people, some movies began to suggest that the ways of living suggested by the various studios would give displaced people a social location, a place in the sun, even a place in the whole of things, or in the firmament of ultimate meaning. All of this gave pragmatic meaning to the movies: they were meaningful because they had social consequences, even religious social consequences.

But by 1998, Gabler was to detect the betrayal of that pragmatic function of the movies. Now he explained not how movies in fact symbolized and augmented reality but, in the words of his subtitle, *How Entertainment Conquered Reality*. It was as if the movies, along with other popular arts, became sheer fantasy, no longer symbolizing anything and becoming simply entertainment. Many films stopped working as metaphors for what American life might mean and become, and they turned escapist, encouraging the viewer not to live better in this world but to enter the unworldly fantasy of the movies. The movies stopped being religious symbols for what beyond themselves is or should be ultimate, and offered simply themselves, as ultimate. They became sheer entertainment without meaning. Or, if the movies had a meaning, it was that the moviegoers should model their own lives on the movies, making their lives equally and similarly entertaining. In a word, when the movies or the moviegoers were made Gods, the movies became atheistic.

Particularly and most obviously, this explains the glut of recent films that offer little more than style unconnected to the life predicaments and practices of actual people. (I think, for example, of *Pretty Woman*, starring Julia Roberts, or of Arnold Schwarzenegger and Sylvester Stallone films.) Their message is to enter the fantasy of the stars and to make one's own life as entertaining as that of the stars. In short, the movies were saying, Make your own life a movie. "Turning life into escapist entertainment," Gabler says, "is a perversely ingenious adaptation to the tumult of modern existence. Why worry about the seemingly intractable problems of society when you can simply declare 'It's morning in America,' as President Reagan did in his 1984 reelection campaign?" Gabler elaborates, explaining how, as president, Reagan would sometimes describe movie incidents as though they had been historical incidents or treat the things that happened to characters he had played in the movies as things that had happened to him.[29] Of course, such reduction of art, particularly of the movies, to entertainment abandons the pragmatic, problem-solving function of art.

Some actors have attempted to convert their own lives into movies, and some moviegoers have followed that pattern. This tendency can be traced back at least to Elizabeth Taylor, Cary Grant, Myrna Loy, and Lana Turner, but it is found also in Hugh Grant, Tom Cruise, Sylvester Stallone, and Julia Roberts. Lana Turner found it irresistible to see one New Year's Eve spent with Tyrone Power as a scene from a movie. Myrna Loy and Cary Grant would complain about how hard it was to be Myrna Loy and Cary Grant in their off-screen lives. Elizabeth Taylor was disgusted by how, in her mind as well as in the mind of the public, the on-screen Elizabeth Taylor often supplanted the off-screen Elizabeth Taylor.[30] The same confusion afflicted the moviegoer. Culture critic Louis Menand argued that "You know how to brood because you have seen *Rebel Without a Cause*. . . . You know how to ruin your life because you have seen *Shampoo*. You know how to win because you have seen *The Verdict*; you know how not to win because you have seen *Top Gun*."[31] In rare instances, this apparently innocent lack of concern for the actual world has become criminal lack of concern. Timothy McVeigh borrowed the video of *Blown Away* shortly before bombing the Alfred P. Murrah Federal Building in Oklahoma City.

Thus, Neal Gabler argues that religion and ideology once provided a "sacred masterplot" for Americans, but that "as both religious and ideological dogma withered under the onslaught of modern life, the burden of drawing the curtain of fantasy fell to popular culture and especially to the movies."[32] While formerly the movies might have been the vehicle for shaping fact to fit the ideals portrayed in fiction, now they unceremoniously abandoned all fact-changing pretense and simply offered fiction. The pragmatic interpretation and reconstruction of society were replaced with utterly nonpragmatic enjoyment.

This has tended to make the movies atheistic. They refer to no Good greater than their own entertainment goods, and they replace symbolic reference with self-reference. Or, to say the same thing, the movies offer their own entertaining fantasy as the ultimate way for people to be. By this means there is introduced an "adoration of idols" like that feared by Adams.

In the early 1930s, English-American philosopher Alfred North Whitehead called attention to such avoidance of pragmatic meaning by noting that, at a certain stage of development, societies arrive at a fork in the road. Take one path, and they will carry on with the pragmatic process of symbolic improvisation, describing a new predicament and imagining a new, pragmatic way to cope with it. Here a society sends its thoughts out ahead of its old ideas so that it "dreams of things to come, and then in due season arouses itself to their realization." Take the other path, and societies will gaze passively at their habits, no longer asking whether or how they pertain to practical problems of present existence. One sign of the latter way appears, Whitehead said, when a society specializes in satire, which constitutes

> the last flicker of originality in a passing epoch as it faces the onroad of staleness and boredom. Freshness has gone: bitterness remains. The prolongation of outworn forms of life means a slow decadence in which there is repetition without any fruit in the reaping of value . . . . [T]he values of life

are slowly ebbing. There remains the show of civilization, without any of its realities.[33]

Whitehead's second, nonpragmatic path recalls Gabler's thesis that the moviegoer has come to care more for the reliving of a movie's entertainment than for the tractability of its argument. When societies follow this path, they memorialize stale abstractions, preferring them to current, concrete events. Although they are disappointed with what has been and with what remains, they abandon efforts to create a new future. The very idea of progress, however modest it might be, is disparaged as a pathetic myth. Practical conversation addressing practical issues seems like childish babble, a nuisance interrupting adult entertainment. Taking this possibility seriously, historian William McNeill pictures a time when "worn-out old myths may then continue to receive lip service, but the spontaneity and force attainable when people truly believe and hope and act in unison will surely seep away."[34]

However, some, like culture critic Susan Sontag, in her famous essay "Against Interpretation," seem to oppose just the pragmatic use of art that Gabler and Whitehead defend. Sontag objects to "interpretation," making it the critic's effort to lift out and explain the ideas implicit in art. It is as though the interpreter were saying: "Look, don't you see that X is really— or, really means—A. That Y is really B? That Z is really C?" The point of the critic is that A, B, and C offer meanings that mean more than the art itself, that at least affect other ideas and at most affect how one should live. Such interpretation sets aside the art itself, in favor of what the art says. This makes interpretation "the revenge of the intellect upon art," "the compliment that mediocrity pays to genius," "the philistine refusal to leave the work of art alone"—in short, the attempt to reduce art to the banal ideas of the cognitive mind. Instead, Sontag says, art should not only ignore interpretation, but make itself so smooth and flawless it will give no handhold to insidious interpreters. "In good films, there is always a directness that entirely frees us from the itch to interpret." A film like *Last Year at Marienbad* should be valued for the "pure, untranslatable, sensuous immediacy of some of its images."

Sontag lifted up a genre of art films and praised them for their pure entertainment. Writing in 1964, Sontag says, "Many old Hollywood films, like those of Cukor, Walsh, Hawks, and countless other directors have this liberating anti-symbolic quality, no less than the best work of the new European directors, like Truffaut's *Shoot the Piano Player* and *Jules and Jim*, Godard's *Breathless* and *Vivre Sa Vie*, Antonioni's *L'Avventura*, and Olmi's *The Fiancés*."[35] It would appear that by rejecting interpretation and affirming entertainment, Sontag was arguing that art, the movies in particular, has no moral, philosophical, or theological meaning, and certainly no pragmatic, problem-solving meaning. On a theological spectrum, it would appear that Sontag has affirmed something equivalent to atheism. If the movies have any use at all, it is the nonpragmatic use of bringing purely aesthetic satisfaction—for its own sake and for nothing else.

I argue, however, that by denying the theoretical, including the theological meaning of the movies, Sontag has, ironically, affirmed the experiential, including the religious meaning of the movies. In the first paragraph of "Against Interpretation," Sontag juxtaposes the *theory* of art, emphasized by interpretation, with the *experience* of art. "The earliest experience of art," she says, "must have been that it was incantatory, magical; art was an instrument of ritual. (Cf. the paintings in the caves at Lascaux, Altamira, Niaux, La Pasiega, etc.)" Interpretation was first practiced by the myth-defenders of classical antiquity, who realized that the rise of science in the classical world undermined the credibility of their myths. To protect their myths, they interpreted the world, offering symbolic meanings so removed from world events that the myths became invulnerable to scientific criticism. Today, she notes, critics use interpretation to cover "their lack of response to what is there on the screen."[36] And the response Sontag most treasures and that they most miss is the ritual experience of art.

Of course, Sontag's sharp rejection of such ancient theological interpretation and its modern successors is, from the point of view of those ancient theologians and their modern successors, an irreverent gesture. However, Sontag's real argument is not irreverent at all. Art that resists interpretation may first secularize art, closing art to theological interpretation and making it appear to be an idol, interested only in its own intrinsic worth. But Sontag's point is that it is the apparent atheism of such art that drives art's observers back to an unencumbered experience of art, allowing them to recover art's incantatory—and, I argue, implicitly religious—power. Interpretation is wrong, then, because it kills, among other things, art's spiritual function. Sontag's irreverence and apparent atheism, it turns out, emphasize art's capacity to instill what, for want of a better word, is religious experience.

Seen in this way, Sontag's ironic twist recalls the strange dictum of Flannery O'Connor:

> What the fiction writer will discover, if he discovers anything at all, is that he himself cannot move or mold reality in the interests of abstract truth. The writer learns, perhaps more quickly than the reader, to be humble in the face of what-is. What-is is all he has to do with; the concrete is his medium; and

he will realize eventually that fiction can transcend its limitations only by staying within them.[37]

In effect, Sontag and O'Connor draw attention to the concrete texture of art and to the entertainment it brings, so that both art and entertainment are undistracted by interpretation and abstract truth. But their point is that such entertainment leads one beyond entertainment to an experience that is religious or implicitly religious. When one stops molding reality through interpretation, when one stops insisting that art offer ostensive and pragmatic moral and religious truth, when one accepts the atheism implicit in that arrest of interpretation, then one is more likely to experience art religiously—and/or, one might add, morally. When one throttles one's own desire to save religion and frees art from theological interpretation, letting art be thoroughly secular, art's religious, incantatory power is more likely to be released.

This is the irony of atheism: the flattening of art into mere secularity, into atheistic shallowness, can open its beholders to a new theism, but one not susceptible to interpretation. This new theism cannot be spoken of, at least not with explicit interpretation, so that its meaning must remain, in that sense, a mystery.

All this complicates Gabler's argument. Gabler is right, when movies such as Ryan O'Neal and Ali McGraw's *Love Story* or James Bond movies become truly entertaining, they do abandon reference to theories, even theories that might work pragmatically to help people overcome the mismatch between their inherited traditions and their current problems. What he fails to note is that some entertaining movies also have the power to open the moviegoer to religious experience. The movies Gabler criticizes lack this power: they lack a surface that is complex and realistic enough to substitute itself for "higher," theoretical meanings and to be in that sense truly entertaining. These popular movies have a surface (plots, characters, etc.) so one-dimensional, infantile, and psychologically undeveloped that they cannot quench the thirst for symbolic and pragmatic meaning, they cannot reduce the world to themselves and, therefore, they cannot be truly entertaining. The movies Sontag lifts up, to which I refer earlier, possess a surface that is complex and realistic enough to truly entertain and then, ironically, to open the moviegoer to incantatory, or religious, experience.

A Flannery O'Connor story, for example, is complex and realistic enough to reduce the world to itself and to become truly entertaining. O'Connor's stories are fantastic (strangely bucolic, grotesque, uncommonly violent), and yet their characters and problems are big and real enough to engage her readers' actual desires and interests. Her stories are set mostly in the poor, rural, mid-century South, and their characters are self-deluded, vicious, cruel, and sometimes murderous in ways so extreme that they are unrelated to the outward lives of most readers; but this all makes them entertaining. However, it is the psychological tension of the stories' characters and the real complexity of the stories' specific issues that make them truly entertaining, able to so captivate the desires and interests of readers that their yearning to interpret is overcome. However, it is just by reducing her stories to their concrete representation that her stories transcend those limitations, opening the readers to the mysteries expressed in the Bible and the church of the Catholic faith. The stories become religiously alive or, as Sontag says, incantatory.

This ironic, self-transcending movement is implicit in several recent American movies. Their practical surface is often fantastic, so that it is easy for the audience to treat them as entertainment. But these movies honor their characters' interior reality. The fantasy surface discourages grand interpretation of the action and encourages the audience simply to sit back and enjoy the movie. At the same time, the stories are complex and psychologically realistic enough to reduce the world to themselves. In other words, their fantastic surface is smooth enough to discourage interpretation *of* themselves, but at the same time true enough to human desires and interests to replace the symbolic and pragmatic meanings *with* themselves. The ironic outcome is that by reducing the world to their secular representations, they open the moviegoer to religious mystery. Although a movie need not be literally fantastic to have this ironic effect, I submit three recent movies that are.

First, *The Truman Show*, a 1998 movie directed by Paul Weir and starring Jim Carrey and Laura Linney, tells the story of Truman Burbank, whose entire life, unknown to him, is televised and whose family, friends, and neighbors are just television actors. He has lived his life within a giant television set, which is the coastal town of Seahaven, a true-to-life place except that it has five thousand hidden cameras. The continuous coverage of Truman is followed by Americans as a twenty-four-hour-a-day television drama that has gone on for thirty years, from Truman's infancy to his present state as a thirty-year-old, married, middle-class man. He is unaware of this and has believed he was conducting an ordinary, private life, but to Americans obsessed by the all-day television coverage, his life is a television fantasy. The movie is easily entertaining because it is fantastic, but it is an evocative and captivating fantasy because it honors the audience's real, inward experience of life as media-dominated, a put-up job, a sham (and a shame). It therefore has the power to reduce the world to itself. The movie climaxes when Truman discovers his life has only entertainment value, and he escapes the set. In the closing shot Truman stares into the camera, suddenly a strangely enlightened man who has recognized that his life has been without meaning. That is, finding his life so limited, he has transcended his limitations, but he leaves this transcendent experience unstated, as though it were a mystery. The audience, also, can undergo for an instant that same ironic transformation.

Something of the same point is made by an independent film, *Judy Berlin*, made in 2000, directed by Eric Mendelsohn and starring Edie Falco. Set in a suburban village on Long Island, it opens by following Judy Berlin, a single woman in her late twenties who is preparing to leave later that day for Hollywood to pursue a career as a movie actress. She is advised, correctly, by friend David Gold that her aspirations are unrealistic, pure fantasy. She seems not to dispute his interpretation, and yet, while indulging her fantasy, she alone, in this despairing suburb, has acquired the energy and hope to build a future. The audience is entertained by this character and by the strange and drifting inhabitants of this village, who, on that same day, witness a total, never-ending eclipse of the sun, which reverberates to the eclipse of their life meaning. Despite the fantasy, the audience feels as utterly real the village's bleakness and the power of Judy's groundless, uninterpreted optimism. Ironically, by entering that strange yet mundane world, the audience can transcend that world to experience the defiant and spiritually important hope that Berlin embodies.

The Purple Rose of Cairo, made in 1985, directed by Woody Allen and starring Mia Farrow, is built around the experiences of Celia, a meek Depression-era woman married to a cold, philandering husband. She escapes her dreary life by habituating the local movie theater, daily entering its fantasy world. One day the romantic lead of a particular movie, *The Purple Rose of Cairo*, having seen Celia in the audience so many times, walks out of the screen and declares his love for her. The movie then revolves around whether Celia's newly extended fantasy life will lead to a revitalized real life. But the movie ends with her rejection of her new lover, his return to the screen, and her reversion to a life of movie attendance and mere movie fantasy. The audience finds Celia's depression quite believable and accepts Celia's descent into fantasy. Celia does not undergo, as Truman did, an ironic transcendence of limits, but the audience can do just that, through recognizing the mistake of Celia's inability to transcend hers.

Gabler's progress from *Empire of Their Own* to *Life the Movie* is itself a commentary on my points about pragmatic meaning and the ironic development. Gabler is right in believing that the great studio heads had once addressed "the awful truths of the twentieth century" and that for immigrants they had "been a veritable primer of acculturation."[38] They were deprived of tradition through emigration and had inherited a country with a weak tradition. Largely to counter that loss, they imagined an America that could locate and ground them as a people. Their movies tended to say, Put yourself in the place of these characters and you too can find a meaning in America. As it turned out, their fantasies created new American facts. The traditional movies offered a workable vision, addressed a culturally vacuous American continent, and sent their audience out with a new purpose. Against the background of *An Empire of Their Own*, Gabler is understandably disappointed by recent movies that are not similarly effective and that dissolve into mere entertainment.

I am arguing, however, that some entertaining movies should not be dismissed as trivial. Some entertaining movies speak so directly to the audience's interior world that their fantasy is able to reduce the world to themselves and, thus, to be atheistic in the sense that the movies are satisfying and sufficient unto themselves. But, ironically, by limiting the world to themselves, these movies can transcend themselves. Like the movies of the earlier producers, these new movies address Americans as displaced people in search of a spiritually sufficient world, but these new movies use irony rather than interpretation to accomplish their ends. Because their entertainment is not subject to metaphoric or symbolic interpretation, their meaning, if they have meaning, must be incantatory and, often, religious rather than theological. Their workings are mysterious, and so is the transcendence they offer.

However, this may be an instance of the movies following life, rather than life following the movies. The entertaining movies' ironic process and their mystery are not far removed from the ironic process and the mystery present in the history of the Jews confronting the desert and their own Diaspora and the early Christians confronting the cross. According to the scholars, the Jewish leaders experienced the breakdown of their interpretation of Israel and then looked backwards and told their patriarchal stories of how out of the emptiness of the sterile desert, ironically, their ancestors discovered a fecund faith. Centuries later, other Jewish leaders knew Israel had experienced the breakdown of the prophetic interpretation of Israel and how its positive meaning had sunk into the sands of Western history. Ironically, it was amid that despair that the synagogue was established and that the Jewish religion arose out of the limitations of the Diaspora. Equally, the early Christians interpreted their story eschatologically, making it the story of the end of time. But when the eschatological leader who embodied their hopes died, their interpretation was invalidated. He was reduced to a corpse, and his corpse was reduced to an empty tomb, offering a signal instance of how an interpretation can be replaced by the starkest conceivable reduction this world can offer. Ironically, the account says, it was only out of that nothingness that the Christians and others were able to experience the mystery of Pentecost.

Conclusion

The Irony of Atheism

The miracle is the only thing that happens, but to you it will not be
  apparent,
Until all events have been studied and nothing happens that you
  cannot explain; . . . .
—W. H. Auden, For the Time Being*

W. H. AUDEN IS RUMINATING OVER WHAT I HAVE CALLED THE
irony of atheism: only after you have decided that everything can be
explained will you find the inexplicable. Elsewhere in *For the Time Being*,
he declares that it is only after you have concluded that the world is a desert
that you will find a garden, and only after you have "consented to die" that
you will find life.

These lines occur in Auden's oratorio for Christmas—a season that cel-
ebrates the irony that, for certain Jews, hope could not return until their
grand expectations for a kingdom had been reduced to a dirty manger,
where, as poet Conrad Hilberry puts it, "A definite baby / squalls into life,
skids out between the legs / of a definite woman bedded in straw on the
longest / night of the year."[1] Those Jews had earlier believed, said St. Paul,
that if they fulfilled God's laws, they would surely be saved. But the Jews
who ultimately became Christians were driven to conclude that this was
fallacious. They would not, in fact, fulfill the laws, for not one of them
would ever be righteous, "no, not one; no one understands, no one seeks
for God" (Romans 3:10-11). Out of the recognition that their explanations
were useless and that they were doomed in what might as well be a godless
universe, salvation simply came . . . unsolicited, unexpected, as an entirely
unearned gift.

Many Americans today regard religion as a relic, an obsolete adaptation

---

*From *W. H. Auden: The Collected Poems,* by W. H. Auden, copyright © 1976 by
Edward Mendelson, William Meredith, and Monroe K. Spears, Executors of the Estate of
W. H. Auden. Used by permission of Random House, Inc.

to the terrifying environments of an earlier day. For them, religion is society's appendix, a residual from a time before the human animal stood tall and climbed out of the savannas of ignorance. British novelist and biographer A. N. Wilson acknowledges that "there will be new generations of conservatives—Catholics, Protestants, and Jews—who think, Enough is enough, let's dig in our heels and go back to the old days." But Wilson says that mature individuals will follow the example of nineteenth-century English novelist and translator George Eliot, who translated David Friedrich Strauss's *Life of Jesus*, a learned analysis that makes Jesus no more than a secular product of his secular historical circumstances. When Eliot reached Strauss's passage describing the now-meaningless crucifixion, "she sobbed as she wrote it and stared for comfort at a sculptured relief of the crucifixion by the Scandinavian sculptor Thorvaldsen." But Wilson goes on to say that Eliot recognized that the consolations of religion "once lost, could never be recovered."[2]

While it is certainly true that faith may be "lost," it may also be "recovered." In fact, it is sometimes precisely through that loss that a new belief can arise. I have suggested that this movement from atheism to a new faith can be seen in three distinct faces of America—jazz, football, and the movies. Each of these activities can lead to an atheistic stance through which Americans can be opened to a spiritual culture and the mystery underlying it.

Jazz presupposes a world that lures us to improvise, but improvisation can seem to be an utterly human procedure, making God unnecessary and offering no true consolation for the blues on which jazz is built. Football presupposes an ambiguous God, itself capable of violence, but this theological interpretation seems reducible to a secular concept of the ambiguity of history, again making God unnecessary. Movies presuppose a way of conjuring up, among other things, a God who could help a displaced people create a place, but when the movies become merely secular entertainment, God is eliminated. Only when such atheisms are recognized and accepted, I have argued, does the mystery behind improvisation, violence, and fantasy, ironically, become evident.

However, this ironic inversion is not working well in America today. Jazz, football, and movies can, in principle, open Americans to mystery, but, my earlier claims notwithstanding, the ironic movement from secular activity to religious mystery seems rare, so that today it is seldom experienced. For most Americans, these popular arts seem to remain incorrigibly opaque, reducible to the mundane historical forces that produced them. They may lead to atheism, but that atheism is seldom followed by a new apprehension of mystery. Perhaps the reason why the irony of atheism works for only a few Americans is that most Americans, whether friends or enemies of religion, have located God outside all history, making it impossible for them to perceive God through the experience of secular history.

In response, and consistent with much recent thought about the social construction of reality, I have described God as a sacred convention experienced *within* history. As a sacred convention, God lives and acts as a spirit lives and acts, often intervening in human history. But there comes a time when even the sacred convention appears to be no more than an aspect of secular history, no longer exhibiting the independent life it once seemed to have. It is then that an awareness of mystery can arise, paradoxically, out of the loss of belief.

This ironic progress applies to the American predicament. Having eventually lost the sacred conventions of their motherland, the American immigrants slowly developed sacred conventions of their own and used them to develop their own spiritual culture. With the accumulation of experience, many began to see their sacred conventions as useless secular fictions that could never become independent facts, so that the gyroscope in this foundering boatload of displaced people began to run down. But this was not necessarily the end of their spiritual culture for, ironically, out of the secularization of their sacred conventions, a sense of mystery sometimes arose.

Such is the course of events in the American spiritual culture as it is described by Thornton Wilder in *The Skin of Our Teeth*. The play carries the audience through the negations and the nonsense of the world to an inexplicable and mysterious hope, which seems to arise from the irony that, just when all is lost, all might be found.

The play is set on the eastern seaboard in 1942 and is built around the Antrobus family, a "typical American family" whom the play's "announcer" congratulates for its "enterprise." Mr. Antrobus has invented the wheel and the lever, is just finishing the creation of the alphabet, is a pillar of the church, and is rummaging through the world's classic literature to salvage its best wisdom. But there is trouble in this Long Island village: a new ice age is setting in. In August, a wall of ice is approaching the city, the sun itself is growing cold, the dogs are sticking to the sidewalk, roads are crowded with fleeing people, and the end of the world seems near. Ground down by eschatological calamity and the force of evil embodied in his son, Henry, Antrobus finally tells his wife, "I've lost it. I've lost it. . . . The most important thing of all: The desire to begin again, to start building."

And yet, inexplicably, out of the depths of his despair Antrobus declares,

"All I ask is the chance to build new worlds and God has always given us that." His friends remind him that once "the Earth was waste and void; And the darkness was upon the face of the deep. And the Lord said let there be light and there was light." They suggest that, unaccountably, God is still operative within history, fostering the creation of "new worlds" to confront new circumstances.

In the last speech of the play, Sabina, the Antrobus's outspoken maid, comes forward and speaks over the footlights directly to the audience, "This is where you came in. We have to go on for ages and ages yet.

"You go home.

"The end of this play isn't written yet."[3]

Nor has the end been written of the ironic play of the American spiritual culture.

Notes

Acknowledgments

1. *Conversations with Flannery O'Connor*, ed. Rosemary M. Magee (Jackson and London: University Press of Mississippi, 1987), 60.

Introduction

1. Allen C. Guelzo, *Abraham Lincoln: Redeemer President* (Grand Rapids: Eerdmans, 1999), 225–26. Guelzo quotes Douglas.

2. Legal scholar Harry Jaffa has argued that those who are "legal positivists" would support any law "incorporated in a constitution by a people," and would disregard any justifications for the law based on anything beyond the preferences of the people. Among these positivists, he includes Robert Bork and Supreme Court justices William H. Rehnquist and Antonin Scalia. Jaffa argues that constitutional law should be based ultimately, as the Declaration says, on "the laws of nature and of nature's God," even though this exposes him to the charge that his approach is "theological." I would argue that Bork's, Rehnquist's, and Scalia's "legal positivism" would force them to defend slavery if it had been incorporated in the Constitution by the American people; and Jaffa argues that it is so incorporated. See Harry V. Jaffa, *Storm Over the Constitution* (Lanham, Md., Boulder, Colo., New York, and Oxford: Lexington Books, 1999), 22–24, 115–26, 134–35.

3. *Thomas Jefferson: Notes on the State of Virginia*, ed. William Peden (New York: W. W. Norton, 1982), 143; Abraham Lincoln, "The Second Inaugural"; Richard Nixon, "Dealing with Gorbachev," *New York Times Magazine*, March 13, 1988, 79.

Introduction to Part 1: The Spiritual Culture

1. Richard A. Posner, *Public Intellectuals: A Study of Decline* (Cambridge, Mass.: Harvard University Press, 2002), 376. Posner's claim arises from intimate acquaintance with impeachment; he has written *An Affair of State: The Investigation, Impeachment, and Trial of President Clinton* (Cambridge, Mass.: Harvard University Press, 1999).

2. Julian Huxley, *Religion without Revelation* (New York: Harper & Brothers, 1957), 92.

3. For Dewey's use of "sense of the whole," see *Art as Experience* (New York: Capricorn Books, 1958), 194. See also John Dewey, *A Common Faith* (New Haven:

Yale University Press, 1952). Public philosopher John Roth interprets American popular culture in light of the public's sense of the whole. As few philosophers would dare to, he applies this subtle category to popular music, sports, politics, news events, and public opinion. See John K. Roth, *Private Needs, Public Selves: Talk about Religion in America* (Urbana: University of Illinois Press, 1997).

4. The Gallup Organization, "America Remains Predominantly Christian, Poll Analyses," April 21, 2000 (http://www.gallup.com/poll/releases/pr000421. asp); 85% say they are Christian; 6% say they have no religious affiliation, and 4% cannot name a specific religion with which they are affiliated. In a poll taken in 1995-96, Wade Clark Roof finds 84% Christian and 3% Jewish (see Wade Clark Roof, *Spiritual Marketplace: Baby Boomers and the Remaking of American Religion* [Princeton, N.J.: Princeton University Press, 1999], 320). In October 2001, the American Religious Identification Survey, 2001, reported finding that 74.5% are Christian, 14.1% adhere to no religion, 1.3% are Jewish and 0.5% are Muslim. (CUNY Graduate Center News, http://www.gc. cuny.edu/press_information/current_releases/october_2001_aris.htm).

5. Robert William Fogel, *The Fourth Great Awakening and the Future of Egalitarianism* (Chicago: University of Chicago Press, 2000); Eldon Eisenach, *The Next Religious Establishment: National Identity and Political Theology in Post-Protestant America* (Lanham, Md.: Rowman & Littlefield, 2000), 29.

6. Sidney E. Mead, *The Nation with the Soul of a Church* (New York: Harper & Row, 1975), 5, 60.

7. Ibid., 4. Mead quotes Paul Tillich, *The Theology of Culture* (New York: Oxford University Press, 1959), 42.

8. Ibid., 73.

9. Robert N. Bellah, "American Civil Religion in the 1970s," *Anglican Theological Review*, Supplementary Series, vols. 1-2 (1973): 9.

10. Robert N. Bellah, "Civil Religion in America," in *Beyond Belief* (New York: Harper & Row, 1970), 179.

11. Robert Bellah, *Broken Covenant: American Civil Religion in Time of Trial*, 2d ed. (Chicago: University of Chicago Press, 1992), xi.

12. See, e.g., *Varieties of Civil Religion*, ed. Robert N. Bellah and Phillip E. Hammond (San Francisco: Harper & Row, 1980). For an early representation of civil religion, see T. S. Eliot, *Christianity and Culture* (New York: Harcourt, Brace & World, 1949).

13. John Dewey, *The Public and Its Problems* (Athens, Oh.: Swallow Press of Ohio University Press, 1927); and Walter Lippmann, *Essays in the Public Philosophy* (Boston: Little, Brown, 1955). See also John Dewey, "Creative Democracy—The Task Before Us," in *John Dewey, The Later Works*, ed. Jo Ann Boydston, 17 vols. (Carbondale: Southern Illinois University Press, 1986), vol. 14.

14 This happens even in ostensibly theological publications; see, e.g., Richard J. Bernstein, "Creative Democracy—The Task Still Before Us"; and Matthew Bag-

ger, "Public Religion," both in *American Journal of Theology and Philosophy* (September 2000).

15. Victor Anderson, *Pragmatic Theology: Negotiating the Intersections of an American Philosophy of Religion and Public Theology* (Albany: State University of New York Press, 1998); Linell E. Cady, *Religion, Theology and American Public Life* (Albany: State University of New York Press, 1993).

16. "Complete liberty of contradicting and disproving our opinion is the very condition which justifies us in assuming its truth for purposes of action; and on no other terms can a being with human faculties have any rational assurance of being right" (John Stuart Mill, *On Liberty* [Chicago: Henry Regnery, 1955], 28; see also 68–69, 75–76).

17. Robert Bellah, Richard Madsen, William M. Sullivan, Ann Swidler, Steven M. Tipton, *Habits of the Heart: Individualism and Commitment in American Life* (New York: Harper & Row, 1985); Christopher Lasch, *The Revolt of the Elites and the Betrayal of Democracy* (New York: W. W. Norton, 1995); idem, *The Culture of Narcissism: American Life in an Age of Diminishing Expectations* (New York: W. W. Norton, 1991); Martin Seymour Lipset, *American Exceptionalism: A Double-Edged Sword* (New York: W. W. Norton, 1996); Michael J. Sandel, *Democracy's Discontent: America in Search of a Public Philosophy* (Cambridge, Mass.: Belknap Press of Harvard University Press, 1996); Robert Reich, *The Work of Nations: Preparing Ourselves for 21st Century Capitalism* (New York: Vintage Books, 1992); Francis Fukuyama, *The Great Disruption: Human Nature and the Reconstitution of Social Order* (New York: Free Press, 1999); Richard Rorty, *Achieving Our Country: Leftist Thought in Twentieth-Century America* (Cambridge, Mass.: Harvard University Press, 1998); Jean Bethke Elshtain, *Democracy on Trial* (New York: Basic Books, 1995).

18. David A. Hollinger, *In the American Province: Studies in the History and Historiography of Ideas* (Bloomington: Indiana University Press, 1985), 162.

19. Alfred Kazin, *God and the American Writer* (New York: Alfred A. Knopf, 1997), 259.

20. Perry Miller, *Jonathan Edwards* (Amherst: University of Massachusetts Press, 1981), 271.

21. Andrew Delbanco, *The Real American Dream: A Meditation on Hope* (Cambridge, Mass.: Harvard University Press, 1999), 96–97, 51, 84, 11; Richard Rorty, "I Hear America Sighing," *New York Times Book Review*, November 7, 1999, 16.

22. Delbanco, *Real American Dream*, 11; Richard Rorty, "I Hear America Sighing," 16.

23. Charles Taylor, "Transformations in Religious Experience," *Harvard Divinity Bulletin* 28 (1999): 18, 20. See idem, *The Varieties of Religion Today* (Cambridge, Mass.: Harvard University Press, 2002).

24. George M. Marsden, *Fundamentalism and American Culture: The Shaping*

of *Twentieth-Century Evangelicalism: 1870–1925* (New York: Oxford University Press, 1980), 224.

Chapter 1: Skepticism

1. George Brown Tindall and David E. Shi, *America: A Narrative History* (New York: W. W. Norton, 1996), 1484.

2. Noted by David M. Kennedy, in a speech before the Commonwealth Club of California in the summer of 1988.

3. James Buchanan, "Saving the Soul of Classical Liberalism," *Wall Street Journal*, January 1, 2000, 29R.

4. Bill Clinton, "Excerpts from Clinton's Speech to Black Ministers," *New York Times*, November 14, 1993, 13Y (quotation marks around "Some of this...human nature" not in original). See also "Administration Tackles 'Great Crisis of the Spirit' in America," *Los Angeles Times*, December 22, 1993, 5A.

5. "Hilary Clinton's Politics of Meaning Speech," *Tikkun* 8 (May/June 1993): 7–9.

6. Richard Nixon, *Beyond Peace* (New York: Random House, 1994), 178, 246, 251.

7. As quoted in Bellah, "Civil Religion in the 1970s," 11.

8. Zbigniew Brzezinski, *Out of Control: Global Turmoil on the Eve of the Twenty-First Century* (New York: Charles Scribner's Sons, 1993), 68–69.

9. David Gress, *From Plato to NATO: The Idea of the West and Its Opponents* (New York: Free Press, 1998), 24; see also 7–14, 23, 504.

10. Samuel P. Huntington, *The Clash of Civilizations and the Remaking of World Order* (New York: Simon & Schuster, 1996), 42.

11. Samuel P. Huntington, "The Clash of Civilizations?" *Foreign Affairs* 72 (summer 1993): 49.

12. *Religion, The Missing Dimension of Statecraft*, ed. Douglas Johnston and Cynthia Sampson (New York: Oxford University Press, 1994), 8; see also 3–5, 12–16.

13. Tim McDaniel, *The Agony of the Russian Idea* (Princeton, N.J.: Princeton University Press, 1996).

14. Ibid., 15, 162. The article appears in *Moskovskie novosti*, February 21, 1993. My analysis here has been much influenced by McDaniel.

15. Jack Matlock Jr., review of *Russia Under Western Eyes*, by Martin Malia, *New York Times Book Review*, April 11, 1999, 11.

16. Alison Smale, "Russia's Leaders Are Different: It's the People Who Are the Same," *New York Times*, January 6, 2002, WK7.

17. Daniel Treisman, "Blaming Russia First: Three Books Examine Russia's Woes," *Foreign Affairs* 76 (November/December 2000): 155.

18. If this particular cultural explanation is true of Russia, which still has a dis-

tinct, though weak, culture and national identity, it might be doubly true of Belarus, which seems never truly to have had either. Conquered by numerous countries, laid waste in two wars, it proceeded in the 1990s to turn itself into a latter-day Communist state. Lacking a truly indigenous culture, its people could well be dubbed, says Matthew Brzezinski, "Homo Sovieticus" (Matthew Brzezinski, "Back in the U.S.S.R.," *New York Times Magazine,* December 17, 2000, 67).

19. Robert A. Segal, "Reductionism in the Study of Religion," in *Religion and Reductionism: Essays on Eliade, Segal, and the Challenge of the Social Sciences for the Study of Religion,* ed. Thomas A. Idinopulos and Edward A. Yonan (New York: E. J. Brill, 1994); Robert A. Segal, *Religion and the Social Sciences: Essays on the Confrontation* (Atlanta: Scholars Press, 1989); idem, *Explaining and Interpreting Religion: Essays on the Issue* (New York: Peter Lang, 1992); and Stewart Elliott Guthrie, *Faces in the Clouds: A New Theory of Religion* (New York: Oxford University Press, 1993). See also *The Insider/Outsider Problem in the Study of Religion: A Reader,* ed. Russell T. McCutcheon (New York: Cassell, 1999).

20. See Bryan S. Turner, *Religion and Social Theory,* 2d ed. (London: Sage Publications, 1991), 11, 242.

21. Tony Edwards, "Religion, Explanation, and the *Askesis* of Inquiry," in *The Insider/Outsider Problem,* ed. McCutcheon, 202–5; and Daniel Pals, "Reductionism and Belief: An Appraisal of Recent Attacks on the Doctrine of Irreducible Religion," in ibid., 189–91.

22. See, e.g., Ian Barbour, *Religion and Science: Historical and Contemporary Issues* (San Francisco: HarperSanFrancisco, 1997), 233–35.

23. This view of quantum theory was advanced as early as 1925 (see Alfred North Whitehead, *Science and the Modern World* [New York: Free Press, 1953], 53 [originally published, 1925]). For a general discussion of these developments, see William Dean, *The Religious Critic in American Culture* (Albany: State University of New York Press, 1994), chap. 7.

24. See A. Aspect, J. Dalibard, and G. Rober, *Physical Review Letters* 39 (December 1982): 1804; Arthur L. Robinson, "Demonstrating Single Photon Interference," *Science* 7 (February 1986): 671–72; P. C. W. Davies, *The Ghost in the Atom: A Discussion of the Mysteries of Quantum Physics* (New York: Cambridge University Press, 1986), 17, 19; Menas Kafatos and Robert Nadeau, *The Conscious Universe: Part and Whole in Modern Physical Theory* (New York: Springer-Verlag, 1990).

25. Elaborating the "uncertainty principle" of quantum physics, physicist John Wheeler and others have argued that the observer contributes to what the world becomes. Wheeler argues that quantum physics presents a "participatory universe" because all observers participate in the creation of the present world. See, e.g., John Wheeler, "Beyond the Black Hole"; and Freeman Dyson, "Comment on the Topic, 'Beyond the Black Hole,'" in *Some Strangeness in the Proportion: A Centennial Symposium to Celebrate the Achievements of Albert Einstein,* ed. Harry Woolf (Reading, Mass.: Addison-Wesley, 1980), 341–86.

26. David Ray Griffin, "Religious Experience, Naturalism, and the Social Scientific Study of Religion," *Journal of the American Academy of Religion* 68 (March 2000): 101.

27. See Erich Przywara, *An Augustine Synthesis* (London: Sheed & Ward, 1945), 53–63.

28. George W. Hunt, S.J., *John Updike and the Three Great Secret Things: Sex, Religion, and Art* (Grand Rapids: Eerdmans, 1980), 16. For Updike's extended comparison of Karl Barth and Paul Tillich, see "To the Tram Halt Together," in *Hugging the Shore: Essays and Criticism* (New York: Vintage Books, 1984), 825–36.

29. Frances Fukuyama, *The Great Disruption: Human Nature and the Reconstruction of Social Order* (New York: Free Press, 1999), 279, 20, 278, 281.

30. Ibid., 278, 279.

31. To deny the universal meanings of God-language is not necessarily to deny divinity, nor is it to make knowledge of God utterly subjective, in the sense that it is determined by the wishes of the believer. In fact, I argue that language about God is powerful. For a splendid defense of the idea that relativity does not imply neutrality, see Thomas L. Haskell, *Objectivity Is Not Neutrality: Explanatory Schemes in History* (Baltimore: Johns Hopkins University Press, 1998), especially chap. 6.

Chapter 2: Displaced People

1. These men being in this order: John Adams, John Quincy Adams, Peter Chardon Brooks, Charles Francis Adams; Brooks Adams, Charles Francis Adams, Jr.; Edward Everett, and Nathaniel Frothingham.

2. Henry Adams, *The Education of Henry Adams: An Autobiography* (Boston: Houghton Mifflin, 1961), 238, 4.

3. Quoted in Ernest Samuels, *Henry Adams* (Cambridge, Mass.: Harvard University Press, 1995), 341.

4. Adams, *Education*, 239

5. Ibid., 383.

6. Alice Walker, *Possessing the Secret of Joy* (New York: Pocket Books, 1992), 212–13.

7. John Higham, *Send These to Me: Jews and Other Immigrants in Urban America* (Baltimore and London: Johns Hopkins University Press, 1984), 4, 248.

8. John Higham, "The Cult of the 'American Consensus,'" *Commentary* 28 (February 1959): 93–100.

9. Nicholas Lemann, "The New American Consensus," *New York Times Magazine*, November 1, 1998, 72. The "cult of dissensus" is my phrase, not Higham's.

10. Eldon J. Eisenach, *The Next Religious Establishment: National Identity and Political Theology in Post-Protestant America* (Lanham, Md.: Rowman & Littlefield, 2000), x.

11. Ronald Takaki, *A Different Mirror: A History of Multicultural America* (Boston: Little, Brown, 1993), 6–7, 17.

12. Michael Walzer, *On Toleration* (New Haven: Yale University Press, 1997), 111–12.

13. Richard Rorty, *Achieving Our Country* (Cambridge, Mass.: Harvard University Press, 1998), 97.

14. See, e.g., Robert N. Bellah, *The Broken Covenant: American Civil Religion in Time of Trial* (Chicago: University of Chicago Press, 1992); Christopher Lasch, *The Revolt of the Elites and the Betrayal of Democracy* (New York: W. W. Norton, 1995); Martin Seymour Lipset, *American Exceptionalism: A Double-Edged Sword* (New York: W. W. Norton, 1996); and Alan Wolfe, *Marginalized in the Middle* (Chicago: University of Chicago Press, 1996).

15. Constance Rourke, *The Roots of American Culture and Other Essays,* ed. Van Wyck Brooks (New York: Harcourt, Brace, 1994), 49–50.

16. John Bodnar, "Immigration," *The Reader's Companion to American History,* ed. Eric Foner and John A. Garraty (Boston: Houghton Mifflin, 1991), 536–37.

17. Peter Brimlow, *Alien Nation: Common Sense about America's Immigration Disaster* (New York: Random House, 1995), 77.

18. J. Hector St. John de Crèvecoeur, *Letters from an American Farmer* (New York: E. P. Dutton, 1957), 39.

19. William Carlos Williams, *In the American Grain: Essays by William Carlos Williams* (New York: New Directions, 1956), foreword; idem, *Paterson* (New York: New Directions, 1963).

20. In Louis Menand, *The Metaphysical Club* (New York: Farrar, Straus & Giroux, 2001), 400.

21. Theologian George Lindbeck argues that acceptance of the story of Jesus defines what a Christian is, whereas the various and diverse Christian denominations discuss the historical ways in which that definition is or is not pragmatically true in history. While I do not claim that Lindbeck's distinction is equivalent to my own, both approaches share a "cultural-linguistic" approach, as they define "American" and "Christian" by reference to a story. I differ from Lindbeck in that I am primarily interested in the historicity, as opposed to the formal character, of the story. See George Lindbeck, *The Nature of Doctrine: Religion and Theology in a Postliberal Age* (Philadelphia: Westminster Press, 1984), especially chap. 2.

22. With historian Alan Taylor, I know that nothing could be "more quaint than to seek [the roots of American identity] in colonial New England." And like American literature scholar Andrew Delbanco, I know that "anyone who has been even half-awake in the last twenty years or so knows it is no longer safe to assume, as Toqueville did, that there is 'not an opinion, not a custom, not a law' that the New England origin of American civilization does not explain" (Andrew Delbanco, *The Real American Dream: A Meditation on Hope* [Cambridge, Mass.: Harvard University Press, 1999], 15). Nevertheless, the fact remains that there are initial clues to the American story within the Puritan mind.

23. Charles Long, *Significations: Signs, Symbols, and Images in the Interpretation of Religion* (Aurora: Davies Group, 1999), 151, 157.

24. Page Smith, *John Adams*, 2 vols. (Westport, Conn.: Greenwood Press, 1962), 1:263.

25. Dominique Moïsi, "The Real Crisis Over the Atlantic," *Foreign Affairs* 80 (July/August 2001): 152.

26. W. H. Auden, "Introduction," in *The Faber Book of Modern American Verse*, ed. W. H. Auden (London: Faber & Faber, n.d.), 18.

27. Perry Miller, *Errand into the Wilderness* (Cambridge, Mass.: Harvard University Press, 1981), 15.

28. Albert Murray, *Stomping the Blues* (New York: Da Capo Press, 1976), 251, 254.

29. William James, *Pragmatism* (Cambridge, Mass.: Harvard University Press, 1975), 125.

30. George M. Marsden, *Fundamentalism and American Culture: The Shaping of Twentieth-Century Evangelicalism, 1870-1925* (Oxford: Oxford University Press, 1980), 226.

31. Cornel West, *Race Matters: Philosophy and Race in America* (New York: Routledge, 1993), xiii.

32. Ward Churchill, *Since Predator Came: Notes from the Struggle for American Indian Liberation* (Littleton, Colo.: Aigis Publications, 1995), 167–68, chap. 4.

33. Paul Tillich, *The Courage to Be* (New Haven: Yale University Press, 1952), 107–8.

34. Michael J. Sandel, *Democracy's Discontent: America in Search of a Public Philosophy* (Cambridge, Mass.: Belknap Press of Harvard University Press, 1996).

35. Todd Gitlin, *Twilight of American Dreams: Why America Is Wracked by Culture Wars* (New York: Metropolitan Books, 1995).

36. Samuel Huntington, "The Erosion of American National Interests," *Foreign Affairs* 76 (September/October 1997): 28–49.

37. Giles Gunn, referring to the American spiritual culture, argues that the "sacralization of the symbolic meaning of America itself may, for better or worse, be the one constant in our spiritual history as a nation." These symbolic meanings, he says, were the product of a people working out its own salvation "in fear and trembling, in outrage and dismay, in wonder and hope, or in madness and despair" (Preface in *New World Metaphysics: Readings on the Religious Meaning of the American Experience*, ed. Giles Gunn [New York: Oxford University Press, 1981], xi). See also Giles Gunn, *Thinking Across the American Grain: Ideology, Intellect, and the New Pragmatism* (Chicago: University of Chicago Press, 1992).

38. His talk was given at a faculty retreat of the Divinity School of the University of Chicago and is now dated by its neglect of multicultural awareness and by its facile comparisons between America and Europe. Perhaps aware of this, Haroutunian said he spoke "with the purpose of provoking a discussion" (Joseph

Haroutunian, "Theology and American Experience," *Criterion* [Divinity School, The University of Chicago] 3 [winter 1964]: 3–11; reprinted in *Dialog* 4 [1965]: 171–79). Haroutunian's comment on his purposes are published only in the *Criterion* version, p. 3; all other page citations are from *Dialogue*. In each version, his remarks are followed by "A Post-Retreat Comment to Professor Haroutunian," by Bernard Meland. Among other things, Meland points out the problems I note just above. For similar comments, see Long, *Significations*, 146–49.

39. Haroutunian names Jonathan Edwards, N. W. Taylor, W. E. Channing, Horace Bushnell, William Newton Clark, Walter Rauschenbusch, A. C. McGiffert, D. C. Macintosh, Shailer Mathews, H. N. Wieman, R. L. Calhoun, Reinhold Niebuhr, H. Richard Niebuhr, and Charles Hartshorne.

40. Haroutunian, "Theology and American Experience," 175–76.

41. As quoted in Herbert W. Schneider, *A History of American Philosophy* (New York: Columbia University Press, 1963), 219. Both McCosh and Haroutunian stress American emphasis on practicality; Haroutunian argues that this calls for a pragmatic outlook.

42. See Daniel Day Williams, "Tradition and Experience in American Theology," in *The Shaping of American Religion*, ed. James Ward Smith and A. Leland Jackson (Princeton, N.J.: Princeton University Press, 1961), 467.

Chapter 3: Pragmatism

1. Andrew Delbanco, *The Real American Dream: A Meditation on Hope* (Cambridge, Mass.: Harvard University Press, 1999), 35.

2. See, e.g., Lawrence E. Toombs, "The Psalms," in *The Interpreter's One-Volume Commentary on the Bible*, ed. Charles M. Laymon (Nashville: Abingdon Press, 1971), 253–55.

3. Referring to several Old Testament accounts of creation, Gerhard von Rad speaks of "the theological derivation of Jahweh's power over history from his authority as Creator. . . ." Later, he says, "only by referring history to the creation of the world could the saving action within Israel be brought into its appropriate theological frame of reference, because creation is part of Israel's etiology" (*Old Testament Theology*, 2 vols. [New York: Harper & Brothers, 1962], 1:138, 2:342).

4. Mordecai M. Kaplan and Arthur A. Cohen, *If Not Now, When?* (New York: Schocken Books, 1973), 22.

5. G. Ernest Wright, *God Who Acts: Biblical Theology as Recital* (London: SCM Press, Ltd., 1960), 12. For more recent discussion of the historicity of God in the Hebrew Bible, see Richard D. Nelson, *The Historical Books* (Nashville: Abingdon Press, 1998).

6. Jack Miles, *God: A Biography* (New York: Alfred A. Knopf, 1995), 99.

7. In the twentieth century, such threats to faith were implicit in the incon-

gruous suffering of Jews in the Nazi death camps. See Richard L. Rubenstein, *After Auschwitz: Radical Theology and Contemporary Judaism* (Indianapolis: Bobbs-Merrill, 1966), especially chap. 2.

8. William James, *The Varieties of Religious Experience* (Cambridge, Mass.: Harvard University Press, 1985), 25.

9. James, *Varieties of Religious Experience,* 25 (italics in *Varieties*).

10. H. W. Brands, *The First American: The Life and Times of Benjamin Franklin* (New York: Doubleday, 2000), 634, 142–43, 153.

11. Perry Miller, *The New England Mind: From Colony to Province* (Cambridge, Mass.: Harvard University Press, 1981), 27–28, 37.

12. Miller, *New England Mind,* 23.

13. Catherine L. Albanese, *Nature Religion in America: From the Algonkian Indians to the New Age* (Chicago: University of Chicago Press, 1999), 9.

14. Bruce Kuklick, *Churchmen and Philosophers: From Jonathan Edwards to John Dewey* (New Haven: Yale University Press, 1985), 222, 9.

15. R. H. Tawney, *Religion and the Rise of Capitalism: A Historical Study* (New York: Harcourt, Brace, 1952), 109.

16. Kuklick, *Churchmen and Philosophers,* xx, 256, xv-xvi. Like Jonathan Edwards, Dewey found God in nature, although, unlike Edwards's God, Dewey's God was not supernatural.

17. Dewey describes this as "some complex of conditions that have operated to effect an adjustment in life, an orientation, that brings with it a sense of peace" (Dewey, *A Common Faith* [New Haven: Yale University Press, 1952], 13). More conscious than his Calvinist predecessors that everything changes, Dewey objected to orthodox Christians who perpetuated earlier but now obsolete views of the universe, particularly when those views falsely and dangerously promised supernatural assistance in today's naturalistic world.

18. Dewey, *Common Faith,* 42.

19. Ibid., 85.

20. Ibid.

21. James had several arguments for the existence of God, all of which have God affecting history. First, God "is not merely ideal, for it produces effects in this world. . . . But that which produces effects within another reality must be termed a reality itself. . . ." In short, "God is real since he produces real effects" (James, *Varieties,* 406–7). Second, if you are forced to choose between two vitally important options, but lack normal evidence, then it is legitimate for you to act from faith in God, if that brings desirable consequences that do not conflict with other beliefs (William James, "The Will to Believe," in *The Will to Believe and Other Popular Essays* [Cambridge, Mass.: Harvard University Press, 1979]). Third, you are entitled to believe in God if you sense "that we inhabit an invisible spiritual environment from which help comes, our soul being mysteriously one with a larger soul whose instruments we are" (William James, *A Pluralistic Universe* [Cambridge, Mass.: Harvard University Press, 1977], 139). The last possibility—that

God works mysteriously within history itself—is of the sort made plausible by James's "radical empiricism." In all these arguments, James refers to pragmatic tests of choices by individuals rather than by societies.

22. Peirce seeks, even in his quest for God, "real generals," and he objects to James's belief in the mutability of truth and the capacity of the will to alter truth (*Collected Papers of Charles Sanders Peirce*, ed. Charles Hartshorne and Paul Weiss, 6 vols. [Cambridge, Mass.: Harvard University Press, 1963], 6:332). Peirce's pragmatic approach to the reality of God relies on a two-step argument. First, we have the mental capacity to examine ordinary facts and to intuit, fallibly but uncannily, the general ideas those facts suggest (he calls this "retroduction"), even though they are not in the facts; this capacity drives us to the simple, unsophisticated conclusion that the facts and these general ideas must resonate with each other because they are both ordered by a God. Second, Peirce tests this conclusion pragmatically by examining how our belief that the world has been divinely ordered alters our conduct (Peirce, *Collected Papers*, 6:311–47).

23. See especially Shirley Jackson Case, *The Christian Philosophy of History* (Chicago: University of Chicago Press, 1941); Shailer Mathews, *The Atonement and the Social Process* (New York: Macmillan, 1930); idem, *The Growth of the Idea of God* (New York: Macmillan, 1931); and Gerald Birney Smith, *Social Idealism and the Changing Theology* (New York: Macmillan, 1912). See also, *The Chicago School of Theology—Pioneers in Religious Thought*, ed. W. Creighton Peden and Jerome A. Stone, 2 vols. (Lewiston: Edwin Mellen Press, 1996); William J. Hynes, *Shirley Jackson Case and the Chicago School* (Chico, Calif.: Scholars Press, 1981); Charles Harvey Arnold, *Near the Edge of the Battle: A Short History of the Divinity School and "The Chicago School of Theology," 1866–1966* (Chicago: Divinity School Association, University of Chicago, 1966); as well as William Dean, *History Making History* (Albany: State University of New York Press, 1988), chap. 3; idem, "Empiricism and God," in *Empirical Theology: A Handbook*, ed. Randolph Crump Miller (Birmingham, Ala.: Religious Education Press, 1992).

24. Thomas L. Haskell, "The Curious Persistence of Rights Talk in the 'Age of Interpretation,'" *Journal of American History* 74, no. 3 (December 1987): 1001 (italics in original).

25. Emile Durkheim, *The Elementary Forms of Religious Life*, trans. Karen E. Fields (New York: Free Press, 1995), chap. 5; Shailer Mathews, *Idea of God*.

26. Dewey, *Common Faith*, 42, 87.

27. See my discussion of new evidence working against neo-Darwinian determinism, where I propose that nonhuman living things have limited freedom. Particularly, I cite evidence for "directed mutations" in bacteria (William Dean, *The Religious Critic in American Culture* [Albany: State University of New York Press, 1994], 122–25).

28. See Dean, *Religious Critic*, 110-25.

29. Making just this point, Alfred North Whitehead referred to "the fallacy of misplaced concreteness," whereby we treat an abstraction as a reality and then

locate that "reality" at a point in space and time, forgetting that a thing is real wherever in the world it has effects (Alfred North Whitehead, *Science and the Modern World* [New York: Free Press, 1967], 51, 58).

30. Adopting a legal analogy to understand the workings of religion is not new. For example, in 1930 theologian Shailer Mathews said that Christian doctrines "do not resemble philosophy so much as statutory law and especially the common law of England and the Constitution of the United States. In order to understand a doctrine," Mathews said, "one must know not only the time and place of its formulation, but also the social and religious tensions which gave rise to it" (Shailer Mathews, *Atonement and the Social Process*, 11).

31. Oliver Wendell Holmes, *The Common Law*, ed. Mark DeWolfe Howe (Boston: Little, Brown, 1963), 8.

32. Ibid., 5.

33. At the end of the twentieth century, postmodern legal scholars argued that laws are changing constructs, always redesigned to adapt to changing cultural and social circumstances. They seem hard-pressed adequately to explain how the law sustains an identity through time and how it occasionally transcends both present and past influence. See Gary Minda, "Postmodernism," in *The Spirit of American Law*, ed. George S. Grossman (Boulder, Colo.: Westview, 2000), 525–34.

34. See Laurence H. Tribe and Michael C. Dorf, *On Reading the Constitution* (Cambridge, Mass.: Harvard University Press, 1991), 14, 15, 18. The authors take the last quotation from Thomas Grey, "The Constitution as Scripture," *Stanford Law Review* 37 (November 1984): 1.

35. Robert A. Goldwin and Robert A. Light, "Preface," in *The Spirit of the Constitution: Five Conversations* (Washington, D.C.: AEI Press, 1990), vii; see also 82. I am indebted to lawyer Anne Kleinkopf for her criticism as I wrote this section.

36. For my earlier and more metaphysical comments on the sense of history, see William Dean, *American Religious Empiricism* (Albany: State University of New York Press, 1986).

37. Luther's position is complicated here. He struggles to vindicate God's goodness, arguing that by "the light of glory," presumably after death, as opposed to the "light of nature" and the "light of grace" in this life, humans will understand that God's "justice is most righteous and evident." Now, however, it is apparent that God "saves so few and damns so many" and that "He makes us perforce proper subjects of damnation. . . ." God appears so wrathful and unrighteous that it requires "the highest degree of faith" to believe in God's goodness. Thus, reasoning from history, Luther opposes Erasmus, who believes that God always does what is pleasing to humans and never what is displeasing to humans. Clearly, Luther says, Erasmus makes God stand or fall by the moral will of people, whereas, in fact the opposite is true: "all things stand or fall by the will and authority of God, and . . . all the earth keeps silent before the face of the Lord (cf. Hab. 2:20)." Thus, when it comes to morality, Luther is more inclined to let God be God, even if that means God appears to be at times immoral (see Martin Luther, *Bondage of*

the Will, trans. J. I. Packer and O. R. Johnston [London: James Clarke, 1957], 317, 101, 98.)

38. For such reasoning, see James, *Pluralistic Universe,* 144.

39. To quote William James: "Take, for example, any one of us in this room with the ideals which he cherishes, and is willing to live and work for. Every such ideal realized will be one moment in the world's salvation. But these particular ideals are not bare abstract possibilities. They are grounded, they are *live* possibilities, for we are their live champions and pledges, and if the complementary conditions come and add themselves, our ideals will become actual things. What now are the complementary conditions? They are first such a mixture of things as will in the fullness of time give us a chance, a gap that we can spring into, and, finally, *our act*" (William James, *Pragmatism* [Cambridge, Mass.: Harvard University Press, 1975], 137–38). See also idem, *Will to Believe,* 55.

40. James, *Will to Believe,* 55; idem, *Pragmatism,* 137–38.

41. James, "The Will to Believe," in *Will to Believe,* 52. By that, he was not promoting wishful thinking, as some critics have argued. For a discussion of this charge, which James called "the usual slander," see Nancy Frankenberry, "Pragmatism, Truth, and the Disenchantment of Subjectivity," in *Language, Truth, and Religious Belief: Studies in Twentieth-Century Theory and Method in Religion,* ed. Nancy Frankenberry and Hans Penner (Atlanta: Scholars Press, 1999), especially 511–13.

42. James, *Will to Believe,* 29, 28; see also idem, *Pragmatism,* 137–38.

43. "Seem" is an advisable qualification because complete dependence on, or determination by, the historical past is a Newtonian way of describing complex events rather than quantum physics' way of describing such events (most clearly, at the atomic level).

44. Sacvan Bercovitch, *The Rites of Assent* (New York: Routledge, 1993), 29.

45. Reinhold Niebuhr, *Moral Man and Immoral Society* (New York: Charles Scribner's Sons, 1932), 81.

Chapter 4: Mystery

1. William James, *Pragmatism* (Cambridge, Mass.: Harvard University Press, 1975), 143.

2. William James, *A Pluralistic Universe* (Cambridge, Mass.: Harvard University Press, 1977), 137–38.

3. Erich Przywara, *An Augustine Synthesis* (London: Sheed & Ward, 1945), 53–63.

4. Paradoxically, this approach enabled Barth to agree with Ludwig Feuerbach, who a century earlier had argued that statements of the Christian faith were little more than the projection of human ideals. Barth, however, seemed unaware that he was doing roughly what he accused the liberals of doing, only adopting the pre-

vailing world view of the sixteenth-century Reformers rather than that of nineteenth-century cultural and scientific thinkers. See Karl Barth, *Humanity of God* (Richmond: John Knox Press, 1960), 23, 26; see also Ludwig Feuerbach, *The Essence of Christianity,* trans. George Eliot (New York: Harper, 1957).

5. Gary Dorrien, *The Making of American Liberal Theology: Imagining Progressive Religion, 1805–1900* (Louisville: Westminster John Knox Press, 2001), 399.

6. As quoted in William R. Hutchison, "Introduction," *American Protestant Thought in the Liberal Era,* ed. William R. Hutchison (Lanham, Md.: University Press of America, 1968), 12.

7. Reinhold Niebuhr, *The Nature and Destiny of Man: A Christian Interpretation,* 2 vols. (New York: Charles Scribner's Sons, 1949), 1:4, 14–15.

8. Jean-Pierre Torrell, O.P., *Saint Thomas Aquinas: The Person and His Work,* trans. Robert Royal (Washington, D.C.: Catholic University of America Press, 1996), 1:289.

9. Here I deviate from Paul Tillich, who defined "theism" as faith in a God-being but then went on to refer to faith in "the God above the God of theism." But in common parlance Tillich was certainly no atheist. Therefore, I am allowing "the new theism" to include the beliefs of those who hold for something like what Tillich called the God above the God of theism (Paul Tillich, *The Courage to Be* [New Haven: Yale University Press, 1952], 184, 186). In the last analysis, even Tillich did not reject a *theism* of mystery, for, although he rejected what he called a "theological theism," he continued to write theology (*theos*-ology) and to call himself a theologian (one who thinks about *theos*).

10. Jonathan Edwards, *The Nature of True Virtue* (Ann Arbor: University of Michigan Press, 1984), 24; idem, "A Divine and Supernatural Light," in *Jonathan Edwards: Basic Writings,* ed. Ola Elizabeth Winslow (New York: New American Library, 1878), 129.

11. Charles Sanders Peirce, "How to Make Our Ideas Clear," in *Collected Papers of Charles Sanders Peirce,* ed. Charles Hartshorne and Paul Weiss, 6 vols. (Cambridge, Mass.: Belknap Press, 1978), vol. 5, paragraphs 317, 257–58.

12. Peirce, *Papers,* vol. 6, paragraphs 495–96, 340–41.

13. Charles Sanders Peirce, "My Belief in God," in *Papers,* vol. 6, paragraphs 340–47. To my knowledge, Peirce does not explain how instinct differs from "qualities of feeling," about which his pragmatism has "nothing to do" (*Papers,* vol. 6, paragraph 318).

14. James, *Pluralistic Universe,* 138–41.

15. John Dewey also made the move from conventionalism to mystery, but for him it was more subtle (see chap. 5).

16. See G. W. F. Hegel, *Science of Logic,* trans. W. H. Johnston and L. G. Struthers (New York: Macmillan, 1951), 94ff.

17. Paul Tillich, *Dynamics of Faith* (New York: Harper & Row, 1957), 64.

18. Tillich, *Courage to Be,* 190. Here Tillich reserves the word "theism" for reference to a God being.

19. Max Weber, *From Max Weber* (New York: Oxford University Press, 1958), 139, 152.

20. Peter L. Berger, *The Sacred Canopy: Elements of a Sociological Theory of Religion* (Garden City, N.Y.: Anchor Books, 1969), 100. Berger began with what he called "methodological atheism," which concludes that the truly scientific historian will see society empirically and know that all its norms are illusions, mere human constructions projected on an empty sky but (mis)taken for realities in their own right, and then worshiped. It is this "methodological atheism" that issues in "the great paradox" that the illusions come to be signals of transcendence.

21. Søren Kierkegaard, *Concluding Unscientific Postscript*, trans. David F. Swenson and Walter Lowrie (Princeton, N.J.: Princeton University Press, 1941), 188.

22. Flannery O'Connor, *Mystery and Manners*, ed. Sally and Robert Fitzgerald (New York: Farrar, Straus & Giroux, 1975), 184, 175, 153, 145–46, 171.

23. Accordingly, theologian George Lindbeck argues that propositional and metaphysical explanations of religious stories should be abandoned. He suggests that faith's story can become more than a story, with "its own domain of meaning and that the task of interpretation is to extend this over the whole of reality" (George Lindbeck, *The Nature of Theology: Religion and Theology in a Postliberal Age* [Philadelphia: Westminster Press, 1984], 117–18). Here Lindbeck follows Hans Frei, who said, "It is not going too far to say that the story is the meaning or, alternatively, that the meaning emerges from the story form, rather than being merely illustrated by it, as would be the case in allegory and in a different way, in myth" (Hans W. Frei, *The Eclipse of Biblical Narrative: A Study in Eighteenth and Nineteenth Century Hermeneutics* [New Haven: Yale University Press, 1974], 280). Frei recommended that the Bible be understood as one might understand an eighteenth-century English realistic novel, where "inside the territory of fiction, everything was depicted realistically or in history-like fashion" (p. 146; see also p. 149). The story's religious meaning is accepted only after the arguments designed to explain its meaning are abandoned, leaving one with a temporary atheism. Then, ironically, the story's religious truth can become apparent.

24. O'Connor, *Mystery and Manners*, 153.

25. Jerome A. Stone uses transcendence in this way in *The Minimalist Vision of Transcendence: A Naturalistic Philosophy of Religion* (Albany: State University of New York Press, 1992).

26. Flannery O'Connor, *Collected Works* (New York: Library of America, 1988), 976–77.

27. Critic Robert R. Spivey argues that O'Connor believed that a symbol was a sacrament with "the power to relate the individual to divine grace" (Robert R. Spivey, *Flannery O'Connor: The Woman, the Thinker, the Visionary* [Macon, Ga.: Mercer University Press, 1997], 93).

28. T. S. Eliot, "East Coker," in *The Complete Poems and Plays 1909–1950* (New York: Harcourt, Brace, 1980), 127.

29. See Reinhold Niebuhr, *The Nature and Destiny of Man*, 2 vols. (New York: Charles Scribner's Sons, 1964), 1:141, 145. Niebuhr says, "It is, in fact, impossible to interpret history at all without a principle of interpretation which history as such does not yield." He makes it clear in other passages that this principle can come only from what is "eternal." By his own accounting, this would seem to introduce a Hellenistic eternal form to explain a biblical response, even though the eternal is foreign to the prophetic literature on which Niebuhr so heavily relies. However, Niebuhr does not allow the principle of the interpretation of history to contradict history: ". . . the religious faith through which God is apprehended cannot be in contradiction to reason in the sense that the ultimate principle of meaning cannot be in contradiction to the subordinate principle of meaning which is found in rational coherence. . . ." (p. 165).

30. Freeman Dyson, *Disturbing the Universe* (New York: Harper & Row, 1979), 250–51.

31. Freeman J. Dyson, *Infinite in All Directions* (New York: Harper & Row, 1988), 296–97.

32. Weinberg's comment comes in an interview with Margaret Wertheim, in "Lonely Planet," *Science and Spirit* 10 (May/June 1999): 20. I am not claiming that religion and science are unconnected and independent. Admittedly, religious meaning is independent of science in the sense that it is, to some extent, about existential (lived) meaning, rather than the order of things. For this reason, religious meaning cannot be placed beside science, as though science and religion were similar enterprises simply working at different levels. Nevertheless, science and religion are connected and mutually dependent in the sense that they make demands on each other. If the sciences reduce all existential meaning to order, they effectively destroy religion; if religion reduces all order to existential meaning, it effectively destroys the sciences. Further, religion and science should be in dialogue, for (at least Western) religion presupposes natural order and science presupposes that at least scientific work is existentially meaningful (how else could scientists ask government to support science?). Religion's history must depend on social continuities that only an orderly physical universe can provide. Science's very real purposes would be eliminated in a world that was mere physical process, devoid of meaning. Ian Barbour discusses "dialogue" as one mode of relation between religion and science in *Religion in an Age of Science* (New York: Harper & Row, 1990), chap. 1.

33. O'Connor, *Mystery and Manners*, 153. While O'Connor seems to imply that naturalism leads to mystery when she says that mystery does not "begin except at a depth where these things [natural motivations] have been exhausted," she refers to an *occasion* for mystery's introduction, not to a *logical justification* for its introduction, which would make mystery not a mystery after all.

34. James, *Pluralistic Universe*, 138. Nevertheless, James argues that God is not discontinuous with all natural experience, for God is "a reality continuous with our tenderer parts," "a *more*" (p. 139).

35. William James, "A Pluralistic Mystic," in *Essays in Philosophy* (Cambridge, Mass.: Harvard University Press, 1978), xxxiv, 189–90 (italics in original).

36. William James, *The Varieties of Religious Experience: A Study in Human Nature* (Cambridge: Harvard University Press, 1985), 36-37.

37. Alfred North Whitehead, *Science and the Modern World* (New York: Free Press, 1967), 41.

38. Ibid., 192.

39. For Dewey's aesthetic interpretation, see John Dewey, *Art as Experience* (New York: Capricorn Books, 1958); for Dewey's theistic interpretation, see John Dewey, *A Common Faith* (New Haven: Yale University Press, 1952).

40. See Henry Nelson Wieman, *The Source of Human Good* (Carbondale: Southern Illinois University Press, 1964); and idem, *Religious Experience and Scientific Method* (Carbondale: Southern Illinois University Press, 1971). See also Meland's comments on appreciative awareness in Bernard Eugene Meland, *Faith and Culture* (New York: Oxford University Press, 1953), chap. 7. For an introduction to radical empiricism, particularly in religion, see William Dean, *American Religious Empiricism* (Albany: State University of New York Press, 1986), especially chap. 1, and idem, *History Making History* (Albany: State University of New York Press, 1988), chaps. 4 and 5; and Stone, *Minimalist Vision of Transcendence*.

41. See, e.g., William Carlos Williams, who pursued his own naturalistic American way to non-sensuous perception. This movement beyond sensuous perception did not cause poet and physician Williams to deny the medical science he practiced, but it did allow him to hear "the roar of the present" and "to see whatever was before one's eyes without aforethought or afterthought but with great intensity of perception" (William Carlos Williams, *Paterson* [New York: New Directions, 1963], 144). He attempted to subordinate his poetic line to a rhythm dictated by breathing, which might be found in what preceded words and was only copied by words. See also Paul Mariani, *A New World Naked* (New York: McGraw-Hill, 1981), 151, 107. Williams finished reading Alfred North Whitehead's *Science and the Modern World* while crossing the Atlantic in 1927 and could not have missed Whitehead's treatment of the English poets as radical empiricists in chap. 5 (see Margaret Glynne Lloyd, *William Carlos Williams's Paterson: A Critical Reappraisal* [Rutherford, Madison, and Teaneck, N.J.: Farleigh Dickenson University Press, 1980], 191).

42. Whitehead, *Science and the Modern World*, 59.

43. Their interest in the perception of mystery or sacred history is criticized even by theologians. For example, Gordon Kaufman appears to reduce radical empiricism to a virtual naïve realism, unqualified by relativity and attempting to capture raw truth. See Kaufman's criticisms of religious experience and radical empiricism in, respectively, *An Essay on Theological Method*, rev. ed. (Missoula, Mont.: Scholars Press, 1979), 5–7; and "Empirical Realism in Theology: An Examination of Some Themes in Meland and Loomer," in *New Essays in Religious Naturalism*, ed. W. Creighton Peden and Larry E. Axel (Macon, Ga.: Mercer University

Press, 1993). In the latter, he seems to overlook the recognition by both Meland and Loomer that all empirical knowledge is perspectival, interpretive and, therefore, incapable of directly knowing what is mysterious.

44. Dewey, *Common Faith*, 42, 85.

45. See Valerie Saiving, "The Human Situation: A Feminine View," in *Womanspirit Rising: A Feminist Reader,* ed. Carol P. Christ and Judith Plaskow (New York: Harper & Row, 1979), 25–42; and Judith Plaskow, *Sex, Sin and Grace: Women's Experience and the Theologies of Reinhold Niebuhr and Paul Tillich* (Lanham, Md.: University Press of America, 1980).

46. Quoted in Anthony Thistleton, *The Two Horizons* (Grand Rapids: Eerdmans, 1980), 216.

47. Rudolf Bultmann, "On the Problem of Demythologizing," in *New Testament and Mythology,* trans. and ed. Schubert Ogden (Philadelphia: Fortress Press, 1989), 118.

48. "Our radical attempt to demythologize the New Testament is in fact a perfect parallel to St. Paul's and Luther's doctrine of justification by faith alone apart from the works of the Law" (quoted in Thistleton, *Two Horizons*, 213).

49. Eliot, *Complete Poems and Plays,* 126–27, 129.

50. Alfred North Whitehead, *Religion in the Making* (New York: Fordham University Press, 1996), 71.

51. O'Connor, *Mystery and Manners,* 184.

52. Spivey, *Flannery O'Connor,* 63

53. "The type of mind that can understand good fiction is not necessarily the educated mind, but it is at all times the kind of mind that is willing to have its sense of mystery deepened by contact with reality, and its sense of reality deepened by contact with mystery" (O'Connor, *Mystery and Manners,* 79).

54. An idea or an event taken seriously enough will legitimately and literally negate itself and evoke its opposite, but this opposite will be enriched by what has been negated. In short, if logic is considered in the moment (synchronically), these ironies are self-contradictory; but if logic is considered through time (diachronically) these ironies are not self-contradictory. For example, in the dialectic movement as conceived by the philosopher G. W. F. Hegel, there is a "passing over of thoughts or concepts into their opposites and the achievement of a higher unity" (Roland Hall, "Dialectic," in *The Encyclopedia of Philosophy*, ed. Paul Edwards, 8 vols. [New York: Macmillan, and Free Press, 1967], 2:388).

55. Taking a basically Hegelian stance, Altizer argued that God died in secular history (was emptied into secular history as the incarnation) and yet through that act gave secular history new meaning. The acceptance of the thoroughly historical incarnation as all that is left of God, says Altizer, is a form of Christian atheism. But functionally and historically, Altizer's Jesus accomplishes in secular history what God once was thought to accomplish. See Thomas J. J. Altizer, *The Gospel of Christian Atheism* (Philadelphia: Westminster Press, 1966).

Introduction to Part 2: America the Visible

1. Reinhold Niebuhr, *The Nature and Destiny of Man,* 2 vols. (New York: Charles Scribner's Sons, 1964), 1:viii.

2. Catherine L. Albanese, *Sons of the Fathers: The Civil Religion of the American Revolution* (Philadelphia: Temple University Press, 1976), 7.

3. Flannery O'Connor, *Mystery and Manners: Occasional Prose,* ed. Sally and Robert Fitzgerald (New York: Farrar, Straus & Giroux, 1975), 157.

4. William James, *The Varieties of Religious Experience* (Cambridge, Mass.: Harvard University Press, 1985), 36.

5. In Terry Teachout, review of Arlene Croce, *Writing in the Dark: Dancing in The New Yorker, New York Times Book Review,* November 19, 2000, 10.

Chapter 5: Jazz

1. *Jazz,* executive producer, Ken Burns, 10 Parts, all aired on Public Broadcasting System in January 2001 (The Jazz Film Project, Inc.: Florentine Films, 2001), part 4.

2. Lewis Porter, *Jazz: A Century of Change: Readings and New Essays* (New York: Schirmer Books, 1997), 25.

3. Lewis A. Erneberg, *Swingin' the Dream: Big Band Jazz and the Rebirth of American Culture* (Chicago: University of Chicago Press, 1998), 8–9.

4. Albert Murray makes the controversial argument that jazz is an "extension, elaboration, and refinement of blues-break riffing and improvisation" (*Stomping the Blues* [New York: Da Capo Press, 1976], 63).

5. Gilbert Chase, *America's Music: From the Pilgrims to the Present,* 2d ed., rev. (New York: McGraw-Hill, 1966), 73.

6. Eileen Southern, *The Music of Black Americans: A History,* 2d ed. (New York: W. W. Norton, 1971), 10–14.

7. Ibid., 10, 16.

8. Ibid., 200.

9. Ted Gioia, *The History of Jazz* (New York: Oxford University Press, 1997), 7.

10. *The Collected Essays of Ralph Ellison,* ed. John F. Callahan (New York: Modern Library, 1995), 574–75 (italics in original).

11. As quoted in James H. Cone, *The Spiritual and the Blues: An Interpretation* (Maryknoll, N.Y.: Orbis Books, 1992), 105.

12. Albert Murray, *The Blue Devils of Nada: A Contemporary American Approach to Aesthetic Statement* (New York: Vintage International, 1997), 14–15.

13. Ellison, *Collected Essays,* 575 (italics in original). Albert Murray claims that singer Paul Robeson left the concert stage partly because he was never allowed to

move beyond the role of tragic hero—such as Othello in Shakespeare's *Othello*—
to play the affirmative role of the epic hero (Albert Murray, *The Omni-Americans:
Some Alternatives to the Folklore of White Supremacy* [New York: De Capo Press,
1970], 28).

14. Ellison, *Collected Essays,* 575 (italics in original).

15. Ibid., 582.

16. Vincent Harding, "Is America in Any Sense Chosen? A Black Response,"
Review of Politics 38 (July 1976): 415–17.

17. Vincent Harding, "Healing at the Razor's Edge: Reflections on a History of
Multicultural America," *Journal of American History* 81 (September 1994): 579,
581. Harding acknowledges that such a master narrative would likely be immediately challenged by "a generation now in waiting." See also Vincent Harding, "Out
of the Cauldron of Struggle," *Soundings: An Interdisciplinary Journal* 61 (fall 1978):
350, where he calls for "a common vision of the public good."

18. Ellison, *Collected Essays,* 583.

19. Cornel West, *Race Matters* (Boston: Beacon Press, 1993), 7.

20. Murray, *Omni-Americans,* 21, 22 (italics in original).

21. For a development of this point, see Constance Rourke, *The Roots of American Culture and Other Essays,* ed. Van Wyck Brooks (New York: Harcourt, Brace,
1942), 284.

22. As quoted in Murray, *Omni-Americans,* 16.

23. The authors of these books are William (Least Heat Moon) Trogdon, John
Steinbeck, Robert Pirsig, and Jack Kerouack. See Rowland A. Sherrill, *Road-Book
America: Contemporary Culture and the New Picaresque* (Urbana and Chicago:
University of Illinois Press, 2000).

24. Much the same can be said for American improvisational theater, whose
actors usually use old lines and routines but subject them to spontaneous reinterpretation.

25. Gover Sales, *Jazz: America's Classical Music* (New York: Da Capo Press,
1976), 18.

26. See, e.g., Eddie S. Glaude, Jr., *Exodus! Religion, Race, and Nation in Early
Nineteenth-Century Black America* (Chicago: University of Chicago Press, 2000).

27. Cone, *Spirituals and Blues,* 106.

28. In Western religious thought, history is a complex term, referring both to
an object of study and to a process of studying that object; to a sequence of events
or to a study of a sequence of events; to a past actual object studied by a historian
or to a later literary object produced by a historian. For example, a book on Rome
can be a *historical* study of *historical* events, where "historical" (and, by implication, "history") has two meanings—the literature produced and the thing studied.
It is important to add that if the historical study is improvisational, it can alter the
present course of history by giving it ideas it would not have received from past
history. In this case, it can be said, "history makes history."

29. I do not use these terms quite as Matthew Arnold used "Hebraism" and

"Hellenism" in *Culture and Anarchy*, ed. Samuel Lipman (New Haven: Yale University Press, 1004). Arnold used them to distinguish between the different weight Hebraists and Hellenists gave practice and knowledge (p. 86). "The uppermost idea with Hellenism is to see things as they really are; the uppermost idea with Hebraism is conduct and obedience" (p. 88). I, on the other hand, believe both Hebraists and Hellenists use "history" to refer both to conduct and to how things really are (but each group gives to the latter a different meaning).

30. Specifically, the conquest story was an etiological saga constructed by the Deuteronomic editors.

31. Manfred Weippert, *The Settlement of the Israelite Tribes in Palestine: A Critical Survey of Recent Scholarly Debate*, trans. James D. Martin (Naperville, Ill.: Alec R. Allenson, 1967), 38.

32. I would suggest that the exodus narrative, showing the success of people displaced in Egypt, must have been attractive to people already actually displaced in Palestine.

33. A picture of the gradual settlement was developed by Albrecht Alt, extended by Martin Noth, and is neatly summarized and augmented in Manfred Weippert, who generally supports their conclusions (Weippert, *Settlement of the Israelite Tribes in Palestine*). This entire picture has been criticized by W. F. Albright and G. E. Wright, who argue that archaeological evidence corroborates a story of the conquest like that described in Joshua and Judges, and by George Mendenhall, who argues that the so-called conquest was really a peasant's revolt within Palestine. For the academic landscape preceding recent thinking about the settlement, see Martin Noth, *The History of Israel* (New York: Harper & Brothers, 1958), part 1.

34. Weippert, *Settlement*, 102–6.

35. Martin Noth, "The Laws in the Pentateuch: Their Assumptions and Meaning," in Martin Noth, *The Laws in the Pentateuch and Other Studies* (Philadelphia: Fortress Press, 1966), 104. It is not an exaggeration to say that the settlers and their God conspired to construct the law and that, later, the exercise of the laws went on to reconstruct the Israelites as well as the God originally constructed by the law.

36. Bruce C. Birch, Walter Brueggemann, Terence E. Fretheim, and David L. Petersen, *A Theological Introduction to the Old Testament* (Nashville: Abingdon Press, 1999), 131.

37. Gerhard von Rad, *Old Testament Theology*, 2 vols. (New York: Harper & Brothers, 1962), 1:v, vi, 119.

38. Douglas Knight, "Revelation Through Tradition," in *Tradition and Theology in the Old Testament*, ed. Douglas A. Knight (Philadelphia: Fortress Press, 1977), 169. I would add that it would be impossible to measure improvement, so long as there is no single, fixed standard that applied to both new and past situations.

39. Weippert, *Settlement*, 102.

40. Thus, says Arnaldo Momigliano, "The significance which the Jews came to

attach to the Torah killed their interest in general historiography" (*The Classical Foundations of Modern Historiography* [Berkeley: University of California Press, 1990] 23).

41. *The Histories of Herodotus*, trans. Harry Carter, 2 vols. (New York: Heritage Press, 1958), 1:1.

42. Thucydides, "History of the Pelopennesian War," trans. Richard Crawley, in *The Greek Historians*, ed. M. I. Finley (New York: Viking Press, 1959), 230.

43. Momigliano, *Classical Foundations*, 20.

44. Eusebius was a disciple of Origen and accepted Stoic and Neoplatonic traditions of thought, while Augustine was a reformed Neoplatonist.

45. Eusebius, *The Ecclesiastical History and The Martyrs of Palestine*, trans. Hugh Jackson Lawlor and John Ernest Leonard Oulton, 2 vols. (London: SPCK, 1954), 1:3–4.

46. Ibid., 1:3, 4, 9, 37.

47. Saint Augustine, *On Christian Doctrine*, trans. D. W. Robertson, Jr. (New York: Liberal Arts Press, 1958), book 2, sections 28, 63.

48. This is clearest in Augustine's debate with Pelagius in "On Nature and Grace," in *St. Augustine: Four Anti-Pelagian Writings*, trans. John A. Mourant and William J. Collinge (Washington, D.C.: Catholic University of America Press, 1992) and in Luther's debate with Erasmus in *The Bondage of the Will*, trans. Henry Cole (Grand Rapids: Baker Book House, 1979).

49. Thomas Aquinas, *Summa Contra Gentiles*, trans. Anton C. Pegis, 6 books (Notre Dame, Ind.: University of Notre Dame Press, 1975), 1:86–104.

50. However, Tillich followed the romantic and idealistic traditions of modern Europe, particularly F. W. Schelling's nineteenth-century idealism, rather than Augustine's fifth-century Platonism. In his theory of history, Tillich did not deviate significantly from Friedrich Schleiermacher (1768–1834), also a philosophical idealist. Tillich's modern idealism led him to an imitation theory of history, closer to the classical Greeks than to the biblical Hebrews.

51. Paul Tillich, *Dynamics of Faith* (New York: Harper & Brothers, 1957), 86.

52. Paul Tillich, *Systematic Theology*, 3 vols. (Chicago: University of Chicago Press, 1951), 1:120.

53. For example, American theologians Reinhold Niebuhr, Langdon Gilkey, and Roger Shinn and German theologian Wolfhart Pannenberg. See my discussion of "old historicists" in *History Making History: The New Historicism in American Religious Thought* (Albany: State University of New York Press, 1988), 1–4; and "The Challenge of the New Historicism," *Journal of Religion* 66 (July 1986): 261–81.

54. See especially Georg Wilhelm Friedrich Hegel, "Introduction: Reason in History," in *Lectures on the Philosophy of World History*, trans. H. B. Nisbet (New York: Cambridge University Press, 1975).

55. Troeltsch referred to the "historico-critical" theories of Schleiermacher and Hegel as the only serious acknowledgments of the importance of historicity

in religion, but then claimed they identified Christianity with the Absolute in history—an identification that for all intents and purposes absolutized one religion and freed it from dependence on its particular historical circumstances. See Ernst Troeltsch, *The Absoluteness of Christianity and the History of Religions*, trans. David Reid (Richmond: John Knox Press, 1971), 45, 71–72.

56. Ernst Troeltsch, *Christian Thought: Its History and Application*, ed. Baron F. Von Hügel (New York: Meridian Books, 1957), 43, 44.

57. Carl Becker, *Every Man His Own Historian* (New York: Appleton-Century-Crofts, 1935). Troeltsch's recognition of the problems with historicism and his trust in faith's access to the Absolute were to reappear in the historical relativism of American theologians H. Richard Niebuhr and Gordon Kaufman, both of whom acknowledged dependence on Troeltsch.

58. Troeltsch, *Christian Thought*, 61.

59. Shailer Mathews, "Theology as Group Belief," in *Contemporary American Theology: Theological Autobiographies*, ed. Virgilius Ferm, 2d series (Freeport, N.Y.: Books for Libraries Press, 1969), 180.

60. Shirley Jackson Case, "Whither Historicism," in *The Process of Religion: Essays in Honor of Dean Shailer Mathews*, ed. M. H. Krumbine (New York: Macmillan, 1933), 65–66.

61. Ironically, those neo-Reformation critics seem to have been animated by an even stronger form of optimism. They affirmed that humans, out of an unimaginably vast universe, had been singled out for attention and rescue by the creator of that universe.

62. Jacques Derrida, *Of Grammatology*, trans. Gayatri Chakravorty Spivak (Baltimore: Johns Hopkins University Press, 1978); and Richard Rorty, *Contingency, Irony, and Solidarity* (Cambridge: Cambridge University Press, 1989).

63. For a valuable summary of these historicists, see Sheila Davaney, *Pragmatic Historicism* (Albany: State University of New York Press, 2000). See also Delwin Brown, *The Boundaries of Our Habitation* (Albany: State University of New York Press, 1994); William Dean, *History Making History: The New Historicism in American Religious Thought* (Albany: State University of New York Press, 1988). (The foregoing were the three Iliff new historicists.) Gordon Kaufman's most influential historicist book is *An Essay on Theological Method*, rev. ed. (Missoula, Mont.: Scholars Press, 1979.

64. E.g., James H. Cone, *God of the Oppressed* (Maryknoll, N.Y.: Orbis Books, 1975); Mary Daly, *Beyond God the Father: Toward a Philosophy of Women's Liberation* (Boston: Beacon Press, 1973); and Cornel West, *Prophesy Deliverance: An Afro-American Revolutionary Christianity* (Philadelphia: Westminster Press, 1982).

65. Cone, *Spirituals and Blues*, 111, 6.

66. "AAJ Giants of Jazz: John Coltrane," in *All About Jazz! The Web's Ultimate Guide to Jazz*, at www.allaboutjazz.com/coltrane/quotes.htm.

67. *The Metaphysics*, in *Aristotle*, trans. and ed. Philip Wheelwright (New York: Odyssey Press, 1951), 78–79.

68. Alfred North Whitehead, *Adventures of Ideas* (New York: Free Press, 1967), 262; idem, *Science and the Modern World* (New York: Free Press, 1953), 2; William James, *Essays in Radical Empiricism* (Cambridge, Mass.: Harvard University Press, 1976), 13; John Dewey, *Art as Experience* (New York: Capricorn Books, 1958), 35–37 (italics in original). See also William Dean, *American Religious Empiricism* (Albany: State University of New York Press, 1986), chap. 4.

69. John Dewey, *A Common Faith* (New Haven: Yale University Press, 1952), 60, 59, 85, 87. Although Whitehead said that "religion is what the individual does with his own solitariness," he also acknowledged that great individuals are products of great societies, which would suggest that solitary experience was partly a product of community experience (see Alfred North Whitehead, *Religion in the Making* (New York: Fordham University Press, 1996), 16; idem, *Science and the Modern World*, 205.

Chapter 6: Football

1. David Riesman and Reuel Denny, "Football in America: A Study in Culture Diffusion," in *Sport, Culture, and Society: A Reader on the Sociology of Sport,* ed. John W. Loy, Jr,. and Gerald S. Kenyon (London: Macmillan, 1969), 315.

2. Richard Slotkin, *Regeneration Through Violence: The Mythology of the American Frontier, 1600-1860* (New York: Harper Perennial, 1996), 4.

3. Larry Weisman, "Why the NFL Rules," *USA Today,* December 22, 2000, 1A.

4. Michael McCarthy, "The Changing Face of Super Sunday Marketers," *USA Today*, January 25, 2001, 1B.

5. The full text is, "THIS STONE COMMEMORATES THE EXPLOIT OF WILLIAM WEBB ELLIS WHO WITH A FINE DISREGARD FOR THE RULES OF FOOTBALL, AS PLAYED IN HIS TIME, FIRST TOOK THE BALL IN HIS ARMS AND RAN WITH IT, THUS ORIGINATING THE DISTINCTIVE FEATURE OF THE RUGBY GAME A. D. 1823" (Riesman and Denny, "Football in America," 308).

6. Allison Danzig, *The History of American Football: Its Great Teams, Players, and Coaches* (Englewood Cliffs, N.J.: Prentice-Hall, 1956), 4.

7. Riesman and Denny, "Football in America," 310.

8. Edward R. Bushness, as quoted in Danzig, *History of American Football*, 25.

9. Danzig, *History of American Football*, 29.

10. Jeff Benedict and Don Yaeger, *Pros and Cons: The Criminals Who Play in the NFL* (New York: Warner Books, 1998), x, 6.

11. Taken from "Morning Edition," National Public Radio, December 2, 1998.

12. All data are from *USA Today* as it appeared on www.footballguys.com/ salaries.cfm. The web site notes that the method used for calculating salaries

"might not reflect the actual amount paid that year. Example: while a player generally receives all of his signing bonus in the first year of a multiyear contract, the team, for salary cap purposes, accounts for that bonus in equal portions over the life of the deal. A player who received a $5 million signing bonus on a 5-year contract in 1999 would be represented here with $1 million in bonus." In 2000 NFL minimum salaries ranged from $193,000 for zero credited seasons to $413,000 for four credited seasons (www.buffalobillsinsider.com/NFLMinimumSalaries. html).

13. Richard Slotkin, *Gunfighter Nation: The Myth of the Frontier in Twentieth-Century America* (Norman: University of Oklahoma Press, 1992), 12–13; idem, *Regeneration Through Violence*; idem, *That Fatal Environment: The Myth of the Frontier in the Age of Industrialization, 1800–1890* (New York: Atheneum, 1985).

14. Slotkin, *Regeneration Through Violence*, 556, 8 (italics in original).

15. Alfred North Whitehead, *Science and the Modern World* (New York: Free Press, 1953), 206.

16. David Herbert Donald, *Lincoln* (New York: Simon & Schuster, 1995), 188.

17. As quoted from a letter to Thurlow Weed, in William J. Wolf, *The Religion of Abraham Lincoln* (New York: Seabury Press, 1963), 187. For a more complete account of Lincoln's comments to Weed, as well as a fully theological interpretation of the Second Inaugural, see Ronald C. White Jr., *Lincoln's Greatest Speech: The Second Inaugural* (New York: Simon & Schuster, 2002), 197–98, 202. Because White's book was published after the completion of the present volume, I could not include it in my discussion.

18. Donald, *Lincoln*, 188.

19. Gary Wills, *Nixon Agonistes: The Crisis of the Self-Made Man* (New York: New American Library, 1971), 39.

20. Tom Wicker, *One of Us: Richard Nixon and the American Dream* (New York: Random House, 1991), 686-87.

21. Robert Kaplan, "The New Evils of the Twenty-first Century," a speech delivered at the fifty-second Annual Conference on World Affairs, University of Colorado in Boulder, April 10–14, 2000.

22. Henry Kissinger, *Years of Renewal* (New York: Simon & Schuster, 1999), 55.

23. Wicker, *One of Us*, 686.

24. Richard Nixon, "Dealing with Gorbachev," *New York Times Magazine*, March 13, 1988, 79.

25. Henry Kissinger, *Diplomacy* (New York: Simon & Schuster, 1994), 709, 705.

26. See Reinhold Niebuhr, *The Nature and Destiny of Man*, 2 vols. (New York: Charles Scribner's Sons, 1949), 2:264. Of course, most secular thinkers, possibly including Kissinger, would rather have taken Niebuhr without his theology. ("Many of Niebuhr's liberal friends liked the somber tones and tempered hopes, but wondered with Harvard historian Arthur Schlesinger, Jr., if the part about God and sin was really necessary" [Richard Wightman Fox, *Reinhold Niebuhr: A Biography* (San Francisco: Harper & Row, 1987), 225]). Kissinger attributes the balance-of-power doctrine to European Enlightenment realism and rationalism,

not primarily to American, let alone biblical, sources. Ironically, Kissinger embeds optimistic Wilsonian idealism in Puritan concepts of America as a beacon to the world or as a crusader to set the world straight, omitting the Puritans' deep sense of human sin and divine retribution. However, Kissinger also roots realism in the very American example of Theodore Roosevelt, with his big-stick imagery of violent American power and his implicit balance-of-power thinking. See Kissinger, *Diplomacy*, chaps. 1 and 2.

27. Wicker, *One of Us*, 14. Wicker quotes from Ken Clawson, "A Loyalist's Memoir," *Washington Post*, August 9, 1979, Outlook Section.

28. Richard Nixon, *Six Crises* (New York: Simon & Schuster, 1990), 402; idem, *RN: The Memoirs of Richard Nixon* (New York: Simon & Schuster, 1990), 19–20.

29. "Over 620,000 Americans died in the conflict, 50 percent more than in World War II" (George Brown Tindall and David E. Shi, *America: A Narrative History*, 4th ed. (New York: W. W. Norton, 1996), 697, 701.

30. Richard Nixon, *Beyond Peace* (New York: Random House, 1994), 174.

31. Donald W. Calhoun, *Sport, Culture, and Personality* (Champaign, IL: Human Kinetics Publishers, 1987), 207.

32. Joyce Carol Oates, *On Boxing* (Garden City, N.Y.: Dolphin/Doubleday, 1987), 104–5 (ellipses in original).

33. Flannery O'Connor, "*Mystery and Manners: Occasional Prose*, ed. Sally and Robert Fitzgerald (New York: Farrar, Straus & Giroux, 1975), 209.

34. For an account of most of the instances that follow, see James L. Crenshaw, *A Whirlpool of Torment: Israelite Traditions of God as an Oppressive Presence* (Philadelphia: Fortress Press, 1984).

35. Biblical citations and some inferences are taken from Terence E. Fretheim, "The Repentance of God: A Key to Evaluating Old Testament God-Talk," *Horizons in Biblical Theology* 10 (1988): 47–70. Fretheim argues, however, that God, while caught in the dynamics of ambiguous history, does not sin.

36. Judith Plaskow, *Standing Again at Sinai: Judaism from a Feminist Perspective* (San Francisco: Harper & Row, 1990), 132; see also eadem, "Facing the Ambiguity of God," *Tikkun: A Bimonthly Jewish Critique of Politics, Culture and Society* 6 (September/October): 70, 96.

37. Jack Miles, *God: A Biography* (New York: Alfred A. Knopf, 1995), 106 (italics in original); see also 81, 104.

38. Niebuhr, *Nature and Destiny*, 1:181.

39. Gary Comstock, *Gay Theology without Apology* (Cleveland: Pilgrim Press, 1993), 38–45.

40. Delores S. Williams, *Sisters in the Wilderness: The Challenge of Womanist God-Talk* (Maryknoll, N.Y.: Orbis Books, 1993), especially Introduction and chap. 1.

41. Robert Allen Warrior, "Canaanites, Cowboys, and Indians," *Christianity and Crisis* 41 (September 11, 1989): 261–65.

42. Paul Tillich, *The Dynamics of Faith* (New York: Harper & Row, 1957), 13–

15; Paul Tillich, *Systematic Theology*, 3 vols. (Chicago: University of Chicago Press, 1951), 1:216–17. See also Paul Tillich, "The Demonic: A Study in the Interpretation of History," trans. Garrett Paul, in *Paul Tillich on Creativity*, ed. Jacquelyn K. Kegley (Lanham, Md.: University Press of America, 1989), 66.

43. Wilhelm and Marion Pauck, *Paul Tillich: His Life and Thought* (New York: Harper & Row, 1976), 130.

44. Just as Tillich's critique of the unalloyed justice of God applies to many of today's prophets, his critique of the unalloyed creativity of God applies to many of today's process theologians, such as Henry Nelson Wieman and David Griffin. Wieman saw God as the creative good working in the world and found human evil only where people depart from that creativity and worship "created goods." See Henry Nelson Wieman, *The Source of Human Good* (Atlanta: Scholars Press, 1995), especially chap. 4. For a more elaborate defense of the unambiguously moral creativity of God, see David Griffin, *God, Power, and Evil: A Process Theodicy* (Philadelphia: Westminster Press, 1976). Both Wieman and Griffin, however, made efforts to argue that God could never be captured by cognitive language, so that, at least, God could not be identified with the *concepts* of creativity and goodness.

45. Bernard Loomer, *The Size of God: The Theology of Bernard Loomer in Context*, ed. William Dean and Larry E. Axel (Macon, Ga.: Mercer University Press, 1987), 48–49, 41 (italics added). With this, Loomer intended to refute Henry Nelson Wieman's concept of an unambiguously good and creative God and to allow for the ambiguity of God. Loomer first accepted ambiguity as a metaphysical principle and then applied it to God (ibid., 51, 45).

46. Edward N. Luttwak, "Give War a Chance," *Foreign Affairs* 78 (July/August 1999): 44.

47. Loomer, *Size of God*, 41, 26, 42, 38.

48. Tillich, *Dynamics of Faith*, 15.

49. Paul Tillich, *The Courage to Be* (New Haven: Yale University Press, 1952), 184, 186.

50. Rudolph Otto, *The Idea of the Holy: An Inquiry into the Non-rational Factor in the Idea of the Divine and Its Relation to the Rational*, trans. John W. Harvey (New York: Oxford University Press, 1958), 7, 16.

51. David Drew, liner of the compact disk of Henryk Górecki, *Third Symphony* (New York: Electra Entertainment, 1992).

52. Flannery O'Connor, *Collected Works* (New York: Library of America, 1988), 808.

53. Flannery O'Connor, "The Fiction Writer and His Country," in *Collected Works*, 805; see also 1183.

54. Richard Gilman, "On Flannery O'Connor," in *Conversations with Flannery O'Connor*, ed. Rosemary M. Magee (Jackson and London: University Press of Mississippi, 1987), 54.

55. "I suppose the reasons for the use of so much violence in modern fiction will differ with each writer who uses it, but in my own stories I have found that violence is strangely capable of returning my characters to reality and preparing them to accept their moment of grace. Their heads are so hard that almost nothing else will do the work. This idea, that reality is something to which we must be returned at considerable cost, is one which is seldom understood by the casual reader, but it is one which is implicit in the Christian view of the world" (Flannery O'Connor, "On Her Own Work," in *Mystery and Manners*, 112).

56. Betsy Fancher, "My Flannery O'Connor," in *Conversations*, 112. O'Connor describes the American "freak" as "a figure of our essential displacement" (see *Mystery and Manners*, 45).

Chapter 7: The Movies

1. With the advent of digital films, this particular set of machine-based illusions of the movies will be augmented, if not replaced, with another set of machine-based illusions.

2. See Stephen Powers, David J. Rothman, and Stanley Rothman, "The Poverty of Film Theory," in *Hollywood's America: Social and Political Themes in Motion Pictures* (Boulder, Colo.: Westview Press, 1996), 217–47.

3. This is the thesis of Neal Gabler, *Life the Movie: How Entertainment Conquered Reality* (New York: Alfred A. Knopf, 1998).

4. Neal Gabler, *Empire of Their Own: How the Jews Invented Hollywood* (New York: Doubleday, 1988), 2.

5. Ibid., 1, 4 (italics in original).

6. Ibid., 6–7. Gabler cites Isaiah Berlin, who argued that it is just those most outside a society who will most admire (or hate) that society. The Jews, said Berlin, were "the most discriminated-against minority in history." Accordingly, Benjamin Disraeli's "entire life was a sustained attempt to live a fiction, and to cast its spell over the minds of others" (Isaiah Berlin, *Against the Current: Essays in the History of Ideas* [New York: Viking Press, 1979], 257, 275).

7. Gabler, *Empire of Their Own*, 201.

8. Ibid., 201, 216.

9. William James, "The Will to Believe," in *The Will to Believe and Other Essays, Popular Philosophy and Human Immortality: Two Supposed Objections to the Doctrine* (New York: Dover Publications, 1956), 52.

10. Robert L. Carringer, *The Jazz Singer* (Madison, Wis.: University of Wisconsin Press, 1979), 28.

11. The author of the short story and the play on which the movie is based, Samson Raphaelson, said, "I had a simple, corny, innocent, well-felt little melodrama, and they made an ill-felt, silly, maudlin, badly timed thing of it" (as quoted in Carringer, *Jazz Singer*, 20). The word "jazz," used in the title and represented by the movie's music, is used loosely, as in F. Scott Fitzgerald's "The Jazz Age" or as in

the black patois—the latter referring to "bands which by their rhythm produced excitement" (*New York Times*, June 30, 1921). It is not used in the technical sense, to refer to music belonging to a precise genealogy beginning in New Orleans. Nevertheless, in the movie "jazz" does refer to music with an African American origin. Finally, whatever the white standpoint of the movie's picture of blacks, it was never intentionally derogatory. Harry Warner believed the movie was sympathetic to blacks and that it could have been made "for the sake of racial tolerance, if nothing else" (Gabler, *Empire of Their Own*, 140).

12. Carringer, *Jazz Singer*, 23. Jakie's girlfriend claims that Jakie's singing is "different," though presumably different from blackface style rather than from black music.

13. Ibid., 59. This and the quotations that follow are taken from the film script of Alfred A. Cohn, and may depart slightly from the movie's actual language.

14. Ibid., 119.

15. Ibid., 76, 122, 77.

16. Ibid., 99.

17. Ibid., 133.

18. Ibid., 23. See also Carringer's endorsement of that parallel on p. 23.

19. Gabler, *Empire of Their Own*, 144.

20. Ibid., 432.

21. Robert Warshow argues that "The two most successful creatures of American movies are the gangster and the Westerner: men with guns" (*The Immediate Experience: Movies, Comics, Theatre & Other Aspects of Popular Culture*" [New York: Atheneum, 1974], 135).

22. Jack G. Shaheen, *Reel Bad Arabs* (New York: Olive Branch Press, 2001), 1–2.

23. Richard Slotkin, *Gunfighter Nation: The Myth of the Frontier in Twentieth-Century America* (Norman: University of Oklahoma Press, 1998), 245.

24. John Dewey, *A Common Faith* (New Haven: Yale University Press, 1952), 85, 42.

25. Clifford Geertz, *The Interpretation of Cultures* (New York: Basic Books, 1973), chap. 4, 87–125; William H. McNeill, *Mythistory and Other Essays* (Chicago: University of Chicago Press, 1986), chaps. 1 and 2; Thomas L. Haskell, *Objectivity Is Not Neutrality* (Baltimore: Johns Hopkins University Press, 1998), especially "The Curious Persistence of Rights Talk in the 'Age of Interpretation'"; Slotkin, *Regeneration Through Violence: The Mythology of the American Frontier, 1600–1860* (New York: Harper Perennial, 1996), "Introduction"; idem, *That Fatal Environment: The Myth of the Frontier in the Age of Industrialization, 1800–1890* (New York: Atheneum, 1985), chap. 2, "Introduction"; idem, *Gunfighter Nation*, especially 663–66; William Carlos Williams, *In the American Grain* (New York: New Directions, 1956); idem, *Paterson* (New York: New Directions, 1963); Emile Durkheim, *The Elementary Forms of Religious Life*, trans. Karen E. Fields (New York: Free Press, 1995), especially 8–18, 107–216; Anthony Giddens, *The Constitution of Society* (Berkeley and Los Angeles: University of California Press, 1984);

Thomas Kuhn, *The Structure of Scientific Revolutions* (Chicago: University of Chicago Press, 1974); Nelson Goodman, *Ways of Worldmaking* (Indianapolis: Hackett, 1978); Jacques Derrida, "Structure, Sign, and Play in the Discourse of the Human Sciences," in *Writing and Difference*, trans. Alan Bass (Chicago: University of Chicago Press, 1978); Mark C. Taylor, *Erring: A Postmodern A/theology* (Chicago: University of Chicago Press, 1984).

26. William James, *The Principles of Psychology* (Cambridge, Mass.: Harvard University Press, 1981), 125.

27. William James in a letter to H. G. Wells, September 11, 1906, in *The Letters of William James*, ed. Henry James, 2 vols. (Boston: Atlantic Monthly Press, 1920), 2:260.

28. John Adams in a letter to Benjamin Rush dated October 22, 1812 (quoted in Page Smith, *John Adams*, 2 vols. [Westport, Conn.: Greenwood Press, 1963], 2:1080).

29. Gabler, *Life the Movie*, 6–7, 111.

30. Ibid., 218–19, 164–73.

31. Ibid., 196.

32. Ibid., 238.

33. Alfred North Whitehead, *Adventures of Ideas* (New York: Free Press, 1967), 277–79.

34. McNeill, *Mythistory and Other Essays*, 26.

35. Susan Sontag, "Against Interpretation," in *Against Interpretation and Other Essays* (New York: Delta, n.d.), 7, 9, 8, 11, 9.

36. Ibid., 3, 6, 10.

37. Flannery O'Connor, "The Church and the Fiction Writer," in *Flannery O'Connor: Collected Works* (New York: Library of America, 1988), 808.

38. Gabler, *Life the Movie*, 238.

Conclusion

1. Conrad Hilberry, "Wise Man," in *Sorting the Smoke: New and Selected Poems by Conrad Hilberry* (Iowa City: University of Iowa Press, 1990), 74. Permission to quote was granted by the poet.

2. "An Interview with A. N. Wilson," *Science and Spirit* 11 (March/April 2000): 44.

3. Thornton Wilder, "The Skin of Our Teeth," in *American Literature: The Makers and the Making*, ed. Cleanth Brooks, R. W. B. Lewis, Robert Penn Warren, 2 vols. (New York: St. Martin's Press, 1973), 2350–52.

Index